# KILL THE PRINCESS

*Why Women Still Aren't Free
from the Quest for a Fairytale Life*

**Stephanie Vermeulen**

SEAL

*Kill the Princess*
Why Women Still Aren't Free from the Quest for a Fairytale Life

Copyright © 2007 Stephanie Vermeulen

Published by Seal Press
A Member of the Perseus Books Group
1400 65th Street, Suite 250, Emeryville, CA 94608

ISBN-10: 1-58005-223-1
ISBN-13: 978-1-58005-223-8

9 8 7 6 5 4 3 2 1

CIP data is available.
Cover design by Susan Koski Zucker
Interior design by Kate Basart/UnionPageworks
Printed in the United States of America
Distributed by Publishers Group West

*Names, places, and identifying details in this book have been changed or obscured by the author to protect the privacy of individuals.*

for Irene Vermeulen
thanks, Mum, for being the inspiration
that put me on this path.

# Contents

INTRODUCTION:

# To Sleeping Beauty: A Wake-up Call

There's no question that women have challenged the rules and made headway. Many have used their access to more money, information, and time to gain power, progressing us to the point that we are now living in a woman's world. Financially, women control the earth's biggest single economy,[1] and socially we live in matriarchal societies.[2] Females are gaining ground politically and are no longer blindly accepting that men have a right to govern our spiritual lives. We have limitless career choices, the right to make our own decisions, and conveniences to free us from drudgery. We are more independent and more sexually liberated, and can choose to be married or stay single, have children, or remain childfree.

Yet if what we're doing is going all out to satisfy our independent needs, but at the same time we're still upholding traditions that undermine those very needs, then so what if it's a woman's world?

Are we happier or more fulfilled than generations of women before us? If not we must ask ourselves why we continue to allow social expectations to dwarf the power of our female potential. Could we still be waiting, like the proverbial Sleeping Beauty, to be awakened? But, by whom?

Is it that our version of "progress" necessitates constant patching up of the social facade so that we can keep on pandering to the needs of men? If so, we're paying a great price for whatever we've gained.

Many women make this contradictory choice then complain to each other about how exhausted they are and how bad, rotten, and insensitive men have become. Then, instead of confronting the situation, they adopt a girlie smile and pretend to carry on happily.

+ + +

For many the answer is simple. Ideas about equality or liberation are easy to ignore if you believe that you've never really been abused. But if you have ever been exhausted for any length of time, accepted lower pay or a position that's inferior, been ashamed of your body, felt guilty about the effect of your career on your children, or had to fight for childcare, then the system is abusing you. The same applies if you are the passive recipient of lewd remarks, believe being "nice" is virtuous, struggle to assert yourself or to say no, suppress your anger, get no time alone, or use quick-fix slimming products or antiwrinkle cream. In different forms these all are signs of a traditional system that violates women's power by making us relinquish vital parts of ourselves.

### SELF-SACRIFICE—THE FINAL FRONTIER

How do we make lasting progress if, after 150 years of feminist influence, we are still sacrificing ourselves and vacillating between tradition and liberation? I believe the only way is for us to deal with the core emotional issue that makes women vulnerable to the manipulation of others, especially men. This means we have to address our own conditioned faith in self-sacrifice as the noblest life principle for women.

The habit of self-sacrifice is so entrenched that women are almost totally unconscious of it, to the point that many will defend it as intrinsic to the female gender. But self-sacrifice does not exist naturally in the makeup of women; it is behavior that has been programmed by cultural myths and religious beliefs that span many generations. Its primary aim is to make women serve the needs of men.

In the women's debate, the significance of dealing with self-sacrifice is far from new. More than 150 years ago pioneers in the suffrage movement, like Elizabeth Cady Stanton, pointed out that the inability to remove self-sacrifice from the female agenda would impede women's progress.[3] More than a century later, the fact that we're still struggling with the conflicting ideas of tradition and liberation proves true the prophetic nature of her sentiments.

Self-sacrifice is one of two pillars upholding the falsehood of male superiority; the other is the male ego, which only survives because it is fed by the complementary notion of self-sacrifice in women. Through our silent compliance we unwittingly support violence, warfare, environmental destruction, and our own demise.

If we remove this central obstacle to women's freedom, the current social structure, built to feed and venerate the male ego, will come tumbling down.

It is, however, important to make the distinction between self-sacrificing behavior and a woman's inclination to give of herself. Women are extraordinary in their capacity to support others, but when this is motivated by self-sacrifice, it conceals a hidden trade-off: "If I give to you, you'd better care for me." This manipulative behavior is absorbed from many previous generations; it is not a course of action that young girls consciously embark upon.

Giving, on the other hand, is a conscious decision that a woman makes because it suits her and because she has sufficient inner resources to choose to nourish the people she cares about. But if she's exhausted, it is only the pay-off that comes with self-sacrifice that keeps her giving beyond her limits. When the pay-off is not forthcoming, the disappointment she feels is often expressed as an unhealthy resentment. This is how the conditioned notion of self-sacrifice lets women down. Giving up the self-sacrificing habit does not imply that a woman becomes mean-spirited or hard-nosed; it is rather a matter of consciously discerning when to give and to whom.

## WHERE DID IT ALL BEGIN?

Our self-sacrificing habit starts with being socialized to living with low self-esteem. It extends to self-denial, in which we suppress our own needs or comply with idealized stereotypes. It may also take the form of self-defeating behaviors such as allowing ourselves to be manipulated by disapproval and guilt. Together, self-sacrifice and socialization become self-regulating, and instead of experiencing freedom, many women just seem to have busier lives.

No matter how liberated you consider yourself to be, think about how much time you have for yourself. To what extent do your own needs get priority? What portion of the family budget is invested in your well-being? And how much recognition, praise, or gratitude do you demand for what you do?

For most women the answer is probably "very little." To the exhausted, even the questions themselves may appear ludicrous.

While many of today's women may well have access to more money, information, luxury, and time, we're battling to take advantage of these benefits because our amplified exhaustion is self-sacrifice in action. Although we're probably leading lives very different from those of our mothers, it seems that thus far, liberation has simply forced us to take on more responsibilities.

On top of caring for children and working in the home, most women have a career. And we've also taken on the third full-time job of maintaining our image. Our underlying emotional habits have prevented us from exchanging an unsatisfactory role for a more fulfilling one. While decades of feminism may have persuaded our intellects to think differently, our traditional hearts keep forcing us to add more to the load. Feelings are slow to catch up with the pace of our thinking, and it is our conditioned hearts that make us sacrifice so much for the financial independence we've gained. This conflict between our emotions and our intellect is the reason why the progress we've made has often been at great cost to ourselves.

So much so that the Superwoman of the 1980s has been replaced by today's Super Mom, who not only manages the home and raises the children but also brings home the bacon . . . and if that's not enough, she works hard at trying to look like a waifish supermodel in the process.

Talk to any woman today and one factor appears to be consistent: Women are too busy to be concerned about equality issues and feminism. Our key anxieties are about work and family security, with the result that many women have little time to be concerned about global issues and no energy to respond if they are.

This is one of the reasons that interest in women's liberation is waning. The other is that many women appear to be satisfied with the gains that have already been made.[4] But settling for a job half-done puts women in a particularly invidious position. If our current lot is as good as it's going to get, equality issues can only slide backward from now on.

Women who claim to be satisfied with their present equality status fail to realize that male puppeteers are still upholding women's self-sacrificing behavior so as to maintain their power base. But only if we collude against ourselves by submitting to their demands do we choose the role of victim, and leave the world for men to run. Once we understand that both external forces and our own compliance with them have created our conflicts, we can stop responding unconsciously and work at regaining our freedom. This requires replacing self-sacrifice with a healthy dose of self-development.

## CHANGING OUR WAYS

We need to shift more than our thinking and take the next step, which requires changing the way we behave. This will make our lives far less frustrating than continuing to blame men, or anyone else for that matter. The problem with blame is that it is based on the assumption that we can change others, in this case men. When we stop living under this illusion, we make our own conflicts simpler to address.

Men aren't going to shift simply because we want them to; after all, they created traditional structures to suit themselves. For most men, an increase in women's status is seen to hold no benefit.

Instead of continuing to prop up the illusion of male control, we need to actively address the systems men have created. The only area where males can consistently outdo females is in the domain of physical strength. So it makes sense that aggression and brute force are the means men have used to gain superiority and keep control. Aggression works because it breeds fear, which inevitably makes people back off. For generations, aggression, or the threat of aggression, has been used to oppress women and silence our voices.

Destruction is the means that men use to maintain their superiority, according to Mary Daly, the great feminist philosopher.[5] Throughout hundreds of generations, males have been conditioned to unconsciously respond to the threats they face by destroying the enemy, perceived or real.

Mostly, men are not aware of their own destructive reflexes, but a few examples suffice: In the home many men use physical or emotional violence to assert their position as head of the household; in business the system is geared toward annihilating competition; when it comes to the uncontrollable environment, the only means men have of dominating it is to destroy its natural systems; and the raison d'être of any army is obliteration. The male response to the first wave of feminism was initially to kill, maim, or incarcerate the early suffragists, and when that didn't work men attempted to tear down women's liberation through ridicule.

Physically, men have been responsible for millions of women's deaths, but their most potent missiles are aimed at the minds and spirits of the female collective. One such weapon, described by Daly, is the manipulative mechanism known as "reversal."

## "REVERSAL"—A MANIPULATIVE TOOL

Centuries ago reversal meant taking what was sacred in a woman and demonizing it, or turning powerful female attributes such as our potent sexuality into a source of great shame. One of the most coercive methods that men used in biblical times was to appoint the Almighty as their spokesman. This is how the Jewish, Christian, and Islamic views of women metamorphosed into God's judgment, providing myths such as females being the source of all evil and the first woman being created from Adam.

Cultural myths gradually stifled the collective female spirit, and women internalized the false identity of being "weaker vessels" needing to be controlled by men.

What's important though is that men didn't simply persuade

women to believe this. Over time they destroyed the archetypal female spirit by manipulating, bullying, torturing, beating, murdering, and raping, until women complied with the dictates of male superiority. For women this meant giving up their individuality and forgoing their desires in order to serve the needs of men. Thus was born the notion of self-sacrifice, the most powerful means of forcing women to destroy their authentic self. Those who resisted were erased . . . burned at the stake for their "heresy."

The sentiments contained in the 2004 Vatican document intended to explain the role of women in society are disturbingly familiar. "A woman is defined by her 'capacity for other,' which is her ability to persevere in adversity and to sacrifice for others."[6]

## STATS THAT HOWL

When it comes to the reality of a female's lot in this woman's world, the Feminist Majority Foundation provides some startling statistics:[7]

- The selling of girls and women into prostitution claims the lives of millions, earning human traffickers $7 billion annually.
- Approximately 130 million women are victims of female genital mutilation, and 2 million girls in more than twenty-eight countries still suffer this practice annually, despite bans in many countries.
- About 700,000 women are raped annually in the United States.
- More than 50 percent of the people murdered in India in 1995 were wives murdered by their husbands.

To this, the National Organization for Women (NOW) adds the following statistics:[8]

- Of the 854 million illiterate adults in the world, 540 million are female.
- Women make up 70 percent of the 1.3 billion people who live on less than $1 a day.

The Fourth World Conference on Women hosted in Beijing in

1995 noted the "feminization of poverty";[9] with insufficient legal, social, and economic support, countless women are turning to petty crime and prostitution to scrape together a living. When it comes to women's health, breast and uterine cancer are escalating at an alarming rate,[10] close to 600,000 young women globally die in pregnancy-related complications, far more women than men are treated for depression,[11] contraception is still not safe for the female body, and combination hormone replacement therapy doubles the risk of breast cancer.[12] A UNICEF study conducted in preparation for Beijing + 5 (hosted in New York in 2000) projected that 20–50 percent of the world's female population would become victims of domestic violence.[13] This translates into millions of women and girls being raped, abused, and murdered—mostly by the people closest to them. The same study reported that such violence cuts across culture, class, education, income, ethnicity, and age in every country.

It also adds that an estimated 60 million women are missing from population statistics globally: "They are victims of their own families, killed deliberately or through neglect, simply because they are female."

While millions of men who abuse women remain free to walk the streets, scores of females spend their lives in jail for killing their violent partner despite overwhelming evidence that their action was in response to years of physical and sexual abuse. In many countries evidence of the abuse women experience from their partners cannot be entered into the courtroom.

The NOW website stated, "Piece by piece, Bush (George W.) is tearing down the progress women and other disenfranchised groups have made over the last thirty-five years, ensuring that rich white males and giant corporations will rule the U.S. for generations to come. . . . This reversal of women's rights is happening both in the U.S. and abroad."[14]

Like many women, you may become immobilized by statistics such as these and conclude that there's nothing you can do. But in sitting back we collude with abusive behavior and give men permission to use our gender as the sacrificial lamb of global society.

If each of us becomes more conscious of the spiritual poverty created by this false identity and learns to speak out (loudly) about the issues affecting our own lives, the critical mass of demanding women will have a profound impact upon the world.

## EMPOWERMENT, NOT EXPLOITATION

If we're to take advantage of this new woman's world, we need to wake up, smell the gunpowder, and take a stand. This requires unleashing our female power, which is more likely to be wielded through persuasive diplomacy than through missiles or misleading political agendas.

When it comes to the battle of the sexes, women's priorities are completely different from those of men. Most women don't want power over men—we just want power over ourselves.

Male power is motivated by actively pursuing personal gain, while female power strives to benefit all. Women are more likely to feed people than to shoot them, and it's more common for us to engage with other women than to abuse them. Power in its healthy form depends not on physical prowess, but on a balance between the male and female aspects within each person, and within society. Women who lean more toward their male energy can be as pathological about power as many men are. While it may be convenient to distance ourselves from these "men in drag" (such as Margaret Thatcher, Indira Gandhi, Madeleine Albright, and Condoleezza Rice), we will never have the freedom to explore the true force of our female power unless we accept our propensity to misuse masculine energy.

Although the force of feminine energy may appear less dramatic, it is no less potent than masculine energy. Nelson Mandela, in the latter part of his life, had more success with persuasive diplomacy than other world leaders had with their bombs and gunboat "humanity."

In recent decades, feminine power has dramatically changed the nature of business. With influences like participative management, Stephen Covey's *The Seven Habits of Highly Effective People*,[15] Peter Senge's *The Fifth Discipline*,[16] and Daniel Goleman's *Emotional Intelligence*,[17] the workplace is starting to become a more humane environment.

It's interesting that the authors of these concepts are men. While both genders have access to feminine power, progress will be accelerated when women learn to balance their masculine energy with the power they were born to.

Consider the fact that important human qualities, like morality and social conscience, have been attributed to women, diminishing the power such traits should wield. Emotions too became a female attribute, which meant that on the feeling/thinking continuum, reason became valued as number one in the hierarchy of human qualities.[18] Of course it was a faculty attributed mainly to men.

Morality has been assigned a female face, so by owning it we equip ourselves with one of the most powerful negotiation tools available. Men may talk about morality, but if women demand that wisdom and ethics form the foundation of decision making, the only people who can argue against these ideas are those willing to reveal their hidden agendas, like personal gain for instance.

It is more urgent now than ever for the wisdom of the feminine conscience to prevail in business, government, academia, politics, and religion. For that matter it is needed within any agency that uses ego power to deprive and manipulate people.

However, many women are reluctant to get involved and unleash the fighting spirit they have suppressed for so long. This pluck is the aspect in women that most threatens men—as a result, it now frightens many women too. But when we suppress this impulse, we can only resort to its most ineffectual form, nagging, and we know this doesn't get us very far!

## IF WOMEN RULED THE WORLD . . .

After the shock waves of 9/11 began to settle, part of the broader debate involved the role of women. Female talk show hosts asked whether these events, and their consequences, would have occurred if women ruled the world. Predictably, female callers believed they would not have happened.

However, it is unlikely that these sentiments can be anything more than wishful thinking with self-sacrifice still topping the agenda. With self-denial preventing us from taking a stand to get even our own demands met, how are we going to take our place as the keepers of world values and principles?

It's of concern that many younger women's thinking seems to be more conservative than ever. Although younger women may be earning reasonably well, they seem hesitant to fight for their rightful place in the world. Sadly, many younger women still hold on to the safety of beliefs that bind women to self-sacrifice and subservience. This regression in upcoming generations is simply testimony to the fact that parents are still pretending that nothing's changed. If our daughters are seeing us as little more than employed (but exhausted) replicas of our mothers, then their "so what's all the fuss about?" attitude is understandable.

It is also pointless for different groups or generations of women to continue squabbling about correct definitions of feminism. If feminism stands for free choice for women—in every area of life—then ideas about women's liberation need to be as diverse as the women it represents.

The fact that women outnumber men in most countries is a critical point in any argument about female power in society.[19] Nowhere in the world do women form a small special-interest group whose concerns can continue to remain stewing on the back burner. But the reality that our issues, challenges, and obstacles are still not prioritized on political agendas shows that true democracy is in many respects a fallacy.

Dr. Martha Burk, chair of the National Council of Women's Organizations, exposes the covert agenda of macho power. In her book *Cult of Power,* she details how a single letter sent in 2002 to the Augusta National Golf Club expressing concern over the club's all-male membership policy led to a firestorm. The boys' club threw all the usual tactics at Burk: They tried lesbian-baiting, man hating, being divisive, and both discrediting or attacking her personally, but when none of these silenced her, the men resorted to the all-too-familiar strategy of aggressive rhetoric and violence. For Burk the closed gates of the Augusta National symbolized all the ways women are barred from the highest echelons of power—in governmental, social, and religious organizations, but, more importantly, in corporate America.[20]

If feminism's first wave was a fight about basic rights, the second wave a fight for personal freedom, then the third means addressing the global systems created originally by men to ignore or dilute the power of the feminine.

So until such time as women represent the majority in all key positions, relaxing our efforts will be nothing less than self-defeating.

Although the task facing women may appear daunting at first, it no longer necessitates having to make a stand by demonstrating in public. What's required is nothing more than for each of us to reclaim our power by changing behaviors that no longer suit the authentic person we consciously want to become.

Isn't it time for Sleeping Beauty to come out of her coma?

# CHAPTER 1.

## The Kiss of Life

The impact of a century and a half of feminism has brought about significant changes in our social structures. We women now have access to opportunities that can be used to leverage considerably more freedom for ourselves.

There are five significant shifts that have caused this major social evolution. One is the "accidental" global switch to a matriarchal society.[1] According to the *New Webster's Dictionary of the English Language,* a matriarchal society is a form of social organization in which the mother is head of the family and in which kinship and descent are reckoned through the female line.[2] Given that the choice of single motherhood is on the increase[3] and that men are absent due to work pressure, divorce, or simply because they are emotionally unavailable, women have had to take control. They raise both boys and girls, often single-handedly, and pass their female legacy on to future generations. However, I prefer the term "virtual matriarchal society" because the self-sacrifice agenda—referred to earlier—prevents so many of us from embracing the power we've gained.

The second transformation is the blurring of male and female roles. During the last fifty years, women's lives have changed so substantially that it's now impossible to say whether the female engineer is any less womanly than the fashion model. As a result, masculinity is also being redefined, and men too have had to alter their thinking. Men's magazines and a growing number of books exploring the male role are talking the language of humanity, not machismo. With popular reading opening the door for men to develop a deeper understanding of the issues that concern women, real power sharing is becoming possible.

The third change, which is dramatically altering the traditional male power base, is in the work context. Full-time office-bound jobs are being replaced by outsourcing, teleworking, contracting, and working from home, which are better suited to women. These options allow far more flexibility in terms of working hours, but, more importantly, success in these informal structures relies more on skills such as persuasive diplomacy. Unlike the characteristically masculine "kick-ass" style of management, diplomacy epitomizes female power.

The fourth shift is the ever-increasing economic clout of women. Tom Peters in his book *Re-imagine!* claims that the amount of money spent by women controlling corporate America's purse strings adds up to more than half of the U.S. gross domestic product, "That is to say: around five trillion dollars."[4] This makes American women the world's largest single economy. According to Faith Popcorn's *EVEolution,* American women head 40 percent of households with assets over $600,000 and 22.7 percent of wives out-earn their husbands. Women also buy or influence the purchase of 80 percent of all consumer goods, they compose 48 percent of stock market investors, and half of all women own mutual funds.[5] This is particularly relevant as global accounting systems only prioritize matters to do with money. With numbers like these, the economic power of women is asserting itself.

The fifth change is the somewhat unexpected consequence of a world awash in pollutants. Derivatives of petrochemical products produce estrogen-mimicking substances in the human body, known as xenoestrogens.[6] These can be found in drinking water, meat hormones, detergents, household cleaners, pesticides, and food wrapped, contained, or cooked in plastic, so it's difficult to avoid them. While the consequences to our health are dire (producing cancers in both genders' reproductive organs), these estrogen-mimics are also causing girls to reach puberty at an earlier age (some around eight or nine years),[7] and some boys' penises are getting smaller, their testicles are not descending, and their sperm counts are declining.[8] Although this is wholly undesirable, it's ironic that the biggest current crisis within the patriarchal system is oil, the very substance causing the hormonal feminization of men.

## A REVOLUTION FROM WITHIN

Although the fifth factor is a tragic consequence of striving for low-cost convenience, these issues nevertheless add up to the feminization of the world. But if women wish to take advantage of the first four shifts, progress will not necessarily depend on females joining mass rallies, or becoming raging women's libbers. All we need do is address the issues that dilute the strength of female power in ourselves.

If most women were to systematically scrap the outdated beliefs and values of our social conditioning, this personal revolution alone would be sufficient to shift the power balance irreversibly.

This revolution from within is the kind of rebellion that male power structures are not equipped to counteract. If we, the majority, make the most of these opportunities, global society will adopt new ways. If we don't, we can expect the brutality of corrupted male power to continue harming women, children, and our world.

Our starting point is to question our own motives, as this will break the nauseating habits of the false identity created by the self-sacrificing agenda.

## MOTHERS AND MARTYRS

The practice of self-sacrifice is maintained by two potent influences that unconsciously control women's thinking: the reality of our rearing and nonstop conditioning by forceful social influences. Both encourage self-defeating behaviors, and as such have succeeded, with our help, in turning us into our own worst enemies.

When it comes to rearing, girls are still raised emotionally to be good wives and mothers. Even though daughters may be playing with toy cars and climbing trees, "girl's blouse" programming still operates unconsciously in all cultures. It turns "maters" into martyrs.

Despite this there are women in powerful positions around the world. They are pioneers who, to get where they are, have had to find ways to remedy their rearing. The good news is, once we unshackle ourselves, any one of us can do the same.

## REMEDYING YOUR REARING

Although we may experience success in our career, self-sacrifice doesn't stay at home when we leave for the office. This is why many women accept lower salaries and inferior positions, while at the same time spending far more than men maintaining their image. In *Women Don't Ask,* authors Linda Babcock and Sara Laschever show that a professional woman with a starting salary of $35,000 will accumulate $2 million less than a man because women shy away from negotiation.[9] Women also don't demand the same level of acknowledgment as men do, they are less outspoken, and often they take up the causes of others instead of fighting battles for themselves. Indeed, whether at work or at home, our conditioning makes us prioritize everyone and everything over our own needs.

With many generations of women having been exposed to the "reversals" referred to earlier, we have been persuaded to loathe ourselves and to despise our bodies. Women's ideas continue to be ridiculed as being "emotional" or are put down to a lack of rational thought. Even after decades of liberation, the generally held stereotype still shows women to be stupid, evil, weak, and frivolous . . . in other words, feeble.

In response many women, especially from the generation of Baby Boomers onward, subconsciously compensate by believing that nothing less than perfection is good enough.

But for today's Super Moms, having perfection as the new female dogma doesn't help—it just adds new pressures to the burden.

## WHERE ARE OUR TRUE COLORS?

How many women do you know who act according to a life prescription similar to the following? After behaving perfectly at the office, they rush to the gym (to work on the imperfections of that body), then touch up their unblemished makeup, go home to their impeccably decorated abode (which they have organized themselves), greet their exemplary children (who are at the right school doing perfectly well, of course), cook a flawless meal, and then listen attentively to their husband's troubles. All this before transforming into the hottest hooker to ensure he doesn't run off with his perfect young secretary. Just managing the perfection of this false identity requires skillful juggling and superhuman energy.

If you think I'm exaggerating, during every seminar I present, I meet versions of these Stepford wives.[10] In the original sci-fi novel, men replaced their women's lib wives with perfectly traditional robotic clones, but in the modern remake of the 1970s movie, the character played by archetypal screen witch Glenn Close is responsible for the cloning. This reversal mirrors real life, in which the only thing that has changed is the extent to which women are being made responsible for their own demise.

Although the material in my seminars challenges every female stereotype, I'm always astounded that conversations during breaks are about quick-fix slimming products, who wore what at the Oscars, nail polish, husbands' bad habits, children's schools, and the "wisdom" expressed in women's magazines. With every aspect of our conditioning constantly being reinforced in our own conversations, what hope do we have of convincing ourselves to show up in the true colors of our female power?

"But what's wrong with all of this?" was a question posed to me by a female radio interviewer. "Someone" she said, "has got to be nice and look after everyone else."

The important question is, Why does it always have to be a woman?

It's worth noting what the *Oxford English Dictionary* says about the origin of the word "nice." It has its history in Middle English and Latin words meaning "stupid" or "ignorant."[11] Being "nice" is not something that comes naturally to women, and as the saying goes, no well-behaved woman has ever made a name for herself in history!

Being "nice" is learned behavior. It ensures that we won't fight for ourselves, and this unnatural habit of avoiding conflict is society's best guarantee that women will keep serving the ends of men, both literally and figuratively!

Emphasizing that a woman is only her body is an essential part of this, and it's no coincidence that the pornography industry has grown dramatically since women became more liberated. Nothing shouts louder about the male ownership of women's sexuality than mainstream pornography. To give you an idea of the extent of this need, in the 1990s pornographic material was estimated to rake in $10 billion annually, and by 2004 it was expected to make more money than the film and music industries combined.[12]

Every step toward liberation is counteracted by this sordid debasement of female power. But, would this still be possible if each of us found our internal Joan of Arc?

Feminism is an obvious target for male attack, since it poses the greatest threat to the self-sacrificing behavior essential to maintaining patriarchal systems. As we've seen, powerful tactics like ridicule have been used against it, with the result that for many women today, feminism is still a dirty word. It has been shrouded in myths and false premises, and is still tarnished with derogatory connotations of bra-burning dykes who despise men.

Linking feminism to lesbianism was a male tactic to manipulate women, but it is not an accurate reflection of what liberation stood for. Men took the biblical "for us or against us" line, and concluded that women fighting for themselves must be anti-male, and therefore lesbian. Fallacious but forceful, it became the signature tune of feminist-bashing. As a result, many independent working women are in denial about both their beliefs and experience. They claim never to have been victims of prejudice and "can't understand what the feminist fuss is about."

## FEMININITY—A FLEETING THING?

However, feminism was never specifically anti-male. It was pro-female and has been defined by authors like Mary Daly as the refusal to be captured again in a stereotypical symbol.[13] Even in the early 1900s, writers such as Dame Rebecca West claimed, "People call me feminist whenever I express sentiments that differentiate me from a doormat or a prostitute." These are hardly unreasonable opinions, yet feminist-bashing continues relentlessly.

From great modern works such as Susan Faludi's *Backlash*,[14] we know that right-wing religious movements have been flooding the global media with misinformation about modern women. The lies have been going on for decades, and the stories are familiar. They range from how female independence damages children to—when that gets a bit tired—how it is detrimental to our own mental health. This conservative crusade toils tirelessly to get us all back to the kitchen sink.

Divorcing the wicked witch of feminism from the princess of femininity has been another of the movement's consistent themes. Here the lines were clearly drawn. Feminism and sensuality were mutually exclusive. In itself the argument is laughable. I have never heard of a single vagina shriveling up because a woman had a career! Yet the threat of losing one's sexual appeal has forced many women to mask their ambition behind the perceived safety of a softer feminine persona.

The *Stepford Wives* idea of replacing real women with traditional cyborgs may be absurd, but reality certainly provides us with a more subtle form of brainwashing. Over the past fifty years, we've seen a flood of all things feminine in the media. This is no coincidence.

The more the feminist movement challenges the notion of what it means to be a woman, the more the media serves up our modern dose of mental programming.

A documentary titled *The Science of Beauty* revealed that every day we are exposed to some 400–600 media images influencing what we should look like.[15] With women's magazines, television, cinema, and billboards emblazoning the theme of the superficial princess everywhere, these messages are invasive and their images powerful.

From the success of propaganda, we know that constant exposure to the same ideas convinces people that the message is true. This is how the modern version of femininity has been driven home. No longer is femininity a mystique that's intrinsic to all women. It now depends entirely on a cunningly manufactured external image. How feminine does the modern version of femininity consider fat, large, plain, or elderly women to be?

Given the images we're bombarded with, we can be forgiven for believing that our femininity is a fleeting thing that we have to keep proving. For, with just one swipe of the cosmetic remover, we risk flushing our femininity down the drain!

## PAYING FOR PERFECTION

This commercial version of femininity is merely a superficial facade that distracts us from what's really important. So powerful has the propaganda been that instead of focusing inward, we cling to solutions that make our external image fit the feminine role. The most alluring of these seem to be those that promise to make us thinner, more beautiful, and more desirable. This is so, even though our intelligence tells us that the promises are an illusion that will always remain just out of reach.

This is precisely what marketers want, because then they can assure us that if we spend just a little more, the elusive magic elixir will be ours for the taking.

For this promise of femininity, we have to pay—and pay handsomely we do. From fashion to cosmetics and perfumes, women, proving their femininity, have supported the growth of huge global industries. In the process we've made many people in the beauty business wealthy, and most of these are men.

This is the monetary cost of self-sacrifice—one of the biggest hidden agendas behind the image business—but more blatant is the reversal of the value that women contribute. Whereas women's wisdom was once revered, the images we see today diminish a female to nothing more than the frivolity of her physical attributes. She has been reduced to a canvas for the cosmetics industry to paint, putty for the surgeons to sculpt, and a coat hanger for the fashion industry to dress.

If you're obsessed with your image, ask yourself this: Is our preoccupation with physical frippery the decoy that distracts us from our social conscience? If the only thing that's really changed is the amount of money, time, and energy we spend patching up the old social facade, then is the price we are paying worth what we've gained?

For most women, sacrificing freedom is the real price we're paying.

This freedom is the most critical of all, for it's the freedom to choose who we'd like to become.

Sure, women today can become engineers, scientists, housewives, or concubines, but this isn't what I mean. This is about not allowing our lives to be dictated to us by others, which is a hard one, because bending to other people's demands is as unconscious as dreaming for most women.

Examples abound. Even while writing this, I was telephoned by a well-known and successful journalist. She wanted a quote for a story she was writing. As we were discussing the merits of anarchy, her cell phone rang. It was her teenage daughter. The conversation went like this: "Yes, hello dear . . . okay. I'll get you. But it will only be a little later, do you mind? . . . [Pause while teenager whines] . . . Oh, all right, I'll come right away. Stephanie, I'll have to call you back in half an hour."

This inability to put ourselves first, even briefly, shows the irony of the women's revolution!

In short, the manipulation of women won't change unless we stop buying into this conspiracy. We can carry on nagging or blaming, but what is much more powerful is for us to unravel the damage done by the self-sacrificing nature of the traditional female role.

Tradition is always difficult to tackle, because it's seen to be sacred. Tradition pretends to define what is right or wrong, but in all societies the reality is relatively simple: Tradition is used as the most powerful excuse to continue unconsciously conserving male power. So how much longer are we women going to humor tradition by forfeiting our health and happiness?

## TACKLING TRADITION

In the interest of future generations, it is necessary to break the tradition of self-sacrificing subservience. For our daughters to experience freedom, we need to make the myths transparent and expose the absurdities. We also need to stop talking and change our own behavior. Discussing choices with our daughters is one thing, but they will inevitably mimic our actions. As long as we behave like suicidal lemmings, so they too will reject vital aspects of themselves.

It is not a woman's responsibility to feed energy (or time, or money, for that matter) to men. It's just part of the myth we've bought into.

In a BBC interview on the television show *Parkinson,* the popular singer Cher (who quips about her body being as genuine as a $19 bill) put the opposite sex into perspective. She said, "Men are just a luxury. They're not a necessity in our lives."

So if the men in your life aren't assets, either physically, emotionally, mentally, or spiritually, what benefit is there in having them around?

Banks of research exist to show that men need marriage more than women do. *Why Men Marry* quotes research concluding that married men achieve more and are emotionally better off.[16] Research at the University of California found that in a group of unmarried men (ages between forty-five and fifty-four), 23 percent died within ten years. Only 11 percent of their married peers met with the same fate in this time frame.[17] Marriage is good for men, which is why male divorcees are much more likely to remarry earlier than their ex-wives do. The reason men need women is for more than their svelte looks or the putty on their faces. They need women to give substance to their lives. Why then have we not insisted that the power base in relationships is the other way around?

Women are emotionally stronger than men are. If we weren't, there would be no need to manipulate, abuse, or fight against us. Instead men would take the lead and women would follow. (And pigs will fly, boys!)

We know that the schoolboy bully is a coward at heart. So if destruction and persecution are the primary weapons of the male arsenal, then the same cowardly tendencies must apply to bullying men.

Understanding and accepting our inborn potency makes women more secure. This means that to be okay we don't have to play a role. No longer need we be the silent handmaiden or the voluptuous whore. Just by unraveling these social roles, we can embrace the opportunity to explore the essence and freedom of our womanhood.

The notion of womanhood is important because it shifts us out of the stereotypes and takes us into the realms of the spiritual and creative. As such it's far more solid than having to choose between our aspirations and our sexuality.

When it comes to our womanhood, ambition (the feminist) and sensuality (our femininity) make comfortable bedfellows. They also happily coexist with the ideologies of the bitch and the princess, the prostitute and the prude.

Getting in touch with our womanhood means exploring the fullness of the diversity inside us. Every woman is born with this richness. It's the wild woman Clarissa Pinkola Estés refers to in *Women Who Run with the Wolves*.[18] What it boils down to is harnessing our personal power.

### ANY REAL WOMEN OUT THERE?

This enormous source of strength is exactly what women have been cajoled into wiping out of their existence. Without it men might find us more acceptable, but it means we can live only superficial lives. I'm reminded of something a powerful female singer told me. Having traveled the world, she said, "I've met many collapsed women and many bitches. But I've yet to meet a real woman."

Sadly the bitches are protecting their vulnerability with a brittle shell, and the collapsed women have imploded. I've met lots of these imploded older women, who know that their biggest problem is that they haven't a clue who they are. Mostly they have lived according to the old rules. Now in their twilight years, and often alone, they're trying to fathom themselves. This is difficult when you've spent fifty or sixty years renouncing your own needs for those of others.

It wasn't always this way. In some African and Native American cultures, older women were revered for carrying the wisdom of the community. Tragically, in our society we call older women things like the "blue-rinse brigade"—and erase them by dismissing their value.

### GUTSY GIRLS GO SOMEWHERE

Nothing will change until we take a stand. Take an outspoken woman such as Oprah Winfrey. Whether she's exposing atrocities, spreading healing messages, or raising money to fund houses for the poor, her lifework is guided by her social conscience.

Likewise each of us is here to do something important. For many it's on a much smaller, but no less important, scale.

But unfortunately, the "bitches" and "collapsed" are more likely to criticize the active and successful. This is a legitimate complaint often lodged against women. It happens when individuals can't tap their own power, and instead lead a critical, negative, reactionary movement. But the real challenge we face is to lead with what is positive and productive.

Like the wise women of old, we need to live more appropriately. Here I'm not referring to our restrictive social rules—we know that living according to these rules makes women feel shallow and exist in a superficial vacuum. It's about living through our spirit, and particularly the strength of our womanhood. This starts with understanding appropriate behavior.

As I show in my book, *EQ: Emotional Intelligence for Everyone,*[19] living appropriately is simple. It means choosing our actions and reactions according to the outcome we want, and this is one of the most effective ways of stripping ourselves of the self-sacrificing habit. We can all be intellectual or silly, wild or serious, polite or vulgar, and while holding on to our own opinions, we can size up the other person and temper our response to get the reaction we want from them. The trick is to use the different aspects of ourselves in the right context.

Women are particularly adept at picking up different social contexts and can respond appropriately without having to compromise their dignity or professional integrity. But, falling back upon the stereotypes of always being nice or always being bitchy are both roads to nowhere. People get to know and anticipate your predictability, so instead of getting the outcome you want, they'll use your one-dimensional responses to manipulate you.

## YOU CAN GET WHAT YOU WANT

I define "success" as you achieving what you want, and as such, it requires dealing with conflict through negotiation. Achievement means being able to get our own way most of the time. So while it's important to remember that petty issues aren't worth wasting our energy, when it comes to fulfilling our lifework, we simply can't afford to take no for an answer.

When I run seminars for men and women, men have no problem

with these sentiments, but many women find this line of thinking hard to swallow. They believe it to be self-centered, which rubs up against their life-operating principle of self-sacrifice. This is why for many women, being labeled "selfish" often hits harder than any four-letter insult. But think about it: The person judging you to be selfish is really saying you are meeting your needs instead of theirs. So who's being selfish after all?

When it comes to making a difference, no one becomes successful without being appropriately selfish. This doesn't mean stabbing others in the back—it's about ensuring that your own needs are met. If not, your supply of energy will run dry. Without the *vooma* of this natural fuel, it will be impossible to fulfill your dreams or lifework.

Every human being needs to be loved, appreciated, and recognized in order to thrive. Social conditioning makes men more likely to demand this, while we women slave away, hoping someone will notice. We're not even very good at acknowledging one another's achievements, for if I've got to get through life unappreciated and unnoticed, I don't have much left to give you, my friend!

When it comes to getting your needs met, think about it as feeding the body. How productive can you be if you haven't eaten for four or five days? Somehow we understand this, but we run into trouble when it comes to our less tangible needs.

While the process of liberation has not been without its problems, it has provided many unexpected gifts. Most of all, our struggles have had the potential to make us stronger. As Eleanor Roosevelt said, "A woman is like a tea bag. You never know how strong she is until she gets into hot water."

In *Unlimited Power,* the author Anthony Robbins claims that one of the key differences between successful people and those who are not is that the successful have the ability to manage frustration.[20] Simply having to deal with men and their egos gives women much experience in this department!

Through adversity we have become more aware of our capabilities. Some women are now great examples of how adversity can make us resourceful, wise, and authentic—and they'll tell you that they started off no different from you or me. So, like them, any one of us can tap the courage, bravery, and strength of our womanhood.

This means swimming upstream, which isn't always easy. However, either we answer to society or we answer to ourselves. Imagine being eighty years old and looking back on a life in which your own passions, desires, and priorities were sacrificed for other people. Millions of older women are living examples of just such a form of slow suicide. Picture what your life will look like in decades to come, and if it gets to feel a little uncomfortable, use this discomfort to mobilize changes right now.

Getting in touch with your real self starts with consciously learning more about who you are. Watch how you respond without negatively judging your reactions. This will teach you much about yourself, your likes, dislikes, and the things you deem important. It will also reveal your conditioning.

No matter how old you are, it's never too late to start living your priorities. Remember that you create your future by the decisions you're making right now.

CHAPTER 2.

# Poor Little Me

**W**hen I was growing up, my mother was determined that I shouldn't follow in her footsteps—she had chosen to be a stay-at-home wife and mother. Surrounded by four demanding children, she'd stand at the stove and say, "Don't do this simply because it's the accepted thing to do. Have a career if you want it, because being a homemaker may not make you happy." I was a stubborn little thing, so I'm grateful that this is one of the few pieces of advice I heeded. But my mother's words were not enough to drown out the world, and like so many other girls I was influenced by the dependent, pretty princess theme, which was, and still is, all around us.

A walk through a toy store is always revealing. Have you ever tried to buy a gift for a little girl that doesn't have something to do with beauty or domesticity? And give some thought to poor Barbie. Even though she's more than forty years old, she hasn't yet landed an executive position. Like so many of the women of our mother's generation, her most ambitious career choice is teaching.

The princess stereotype is deeply ingrained, so don't underestimate the challenge we face in letting go of it. But the fact is, unless we do so, we'll never reach the full maturity of our womanhood.

And what is this very same programming doing to our daughters? Fairytales, television, the behavior of other kids, teachers, grandparents, aunts, and uncles are all involved in influencing their highly impressionable minds. So it's not surprising that women are still telling me that their daughters are naturally attracted to "princess behavior"—they want pretty dresses, fairy costumes, and baby dolls.

But this overemphasis on the superficial princess role is what grooms young girls to grow up poorly equipped for the robust modern world. Instead of learning healthy self-assertion, the whimsical princess model teaches them to sacrifice their inner strength, fighting spirit, ambition, courage, and determination.

## LIKE MOTHER . . .

Your life, like mine, may not look anything like your mother's. But even so, nearly all of us grew up with the very same underlying conditioning that groomed our mothers and our grandmothers for subservience. Today this translates into the emotional mix-up that makes us loathe ourselves, silence our voices, and dismiss our own accomplishments. Contradictory impulses make sure that we stay hyperbusy, lonely, and striving for perfection, while sabotaging our ability to get our own needs met.

These are the burdens of our upbringing, and until we see them for what they are, we won't be able to heal ourselves and tap our personal power. Our first step is to understand exactly what traditional rearing has done to us. For one thing it's taught us that we can never be good enough, so we keep on trying to compensate by "being good" and fitting in perfectly with society.

In *Understanding Women* the insightful psychologists Susie Orbach and Luise Eichenbaum explain that our problems start with being raised to be good wives and mothers—the emphasis here on the word "good."[1] Good wives and mothers are expected to sacrifice their lives for their husbands and children. Their primary job is to manage the feelings of the entire family and be the emotional pillar. So standing on their own feet emotionally is seen as essential to fulfilling this mommy role.

In preparation for this job, young girls are shown the harsh ropes of emotional independence. They grow up being taught to deny their own emotional needs and make no demands. This is how we learn to be "nice" girls or women, which amounts to forgetting who we really are. So from an early age, we start losing touch with our authentic emotional needs, making it impossible for any of us to reach full maturity.

## THE UNSPOKEN MESSAGE

It is difficult for mothers to teach their daughters emotional independence. We are unlikely to sit our developing daughters down and say, "Well, sweetie, this is what life's about: Your accomplishments will seldom be recognized as important, and because of this you'll grow up not believing in yourself. As a result you won't be able to achieve much. What you will be expected to do is look pretty while exhausting yourself supporting other people's dreams. While doing this you'll feel undeserving and unable to get your own needs met. In fact, most people will think that you haven't actually got any needs at all. You can expect to be happiest when you're working as cheap labor in the service of husbands and children. Every now and then you'll be required to make yourself sexually available, as subservience is your lot. If you do go into business, it'll add more to your load, as no one will be prepared to support you. Millions of women have done this before you, so quit complaining and get on with it."

But even if we don't literally deliver this message, one way or another it will get through, and it will prepare our girls for self-sacrifice, which, as we know, is key to maintaining women's oppression. As such this form of conditioning knows no ethnic, class, national, or religious boundaries, nor does it differ with education or income levels. There may be some cultural variations on the theme, but essentially the phenomenon is planetary.

For mothers, passing this conditioning on involves responding differently to the dependency needs of girls and boys. Orbach and Eichenbaum write, "The fact that women are raised to provide nurturance, care, and attention, to have others depend on them emotionally, and that boys are not, acts as a pressure in the mother-daughter relationship."[2]

For boys, the only way they can grow into the socially prescriptive role of appearing to live "independently" is if their dependency needs are met by others: initially by mothers, later on by girlfriends and wives. Boys are encouraged to experience the "feeling" aspect of their lives through females, which too often results in a lifelong emotional dependency upon women. The price that males pay for this is lifelong emotional dependency upon women. Boys are taught to suppress their own feelings, beginning with the squelching of any unhappy emotions by their moms.[3] The findings of a study concluded that mothers interpret a boy baby's natural demonstration of unhappy emotions as their son's being psychologically off balance or unwell.[4]

As sons grow older their mothers go on caretaking their emotional life, so that boys grow into the habit of accepting female support, without learning to give much back.

Sons develop an understanding of who they are by competing with other boys, but daughters learn to define themselves through relationships, where they are expected to be "nice" and give of themselves. The upshot is that girls are taught to be emotionally depended upon, so when it comes to their own feelings, they must learn to be self-reliant.

## THE CONTRADICTIONS OF GIRL GROOMING

For a mother this makes raising girls a highly complex task; while she may be naturally inclined to nourish and protect her little girl, the mother's primary job is to show her daughter the ropes of her role. When the mother's nurturing instinct prevails, she responds from her heart, but when the demands of socialization win, then she'll ignore or misinterpret her daughter's emotional needs. This can only translate into confusing inconsistencies in a mother's response to her daughter. Girls soon learn to make no demands at all, since their needs are so often trivialized or dismissed. And given that emotional expressiveness is considered appropriate for females, mothers are likely to simply gloss over any upsets that girls show, rather than trying to understand their underlying feelings. This type of repeated emotional neglect and denial eventually makes girls insecure and uncertain about themselves. If the emotional neglect is severe, girls may resort to extreme behavior, simply to draw attention to the seriousness of their needs. But no matter how much girls up the ante, their stance is still written off as being "typically female": emotional in childhood and hormonal (or both) later on.[5]

The one emotion that is not socially acceptable in girls is anger, which becomes a punishable offense. What happens to little girls who are upset? They are told to go to their room until they can be "nice" once more. Along with driving a girl's anger underground, traditional socialization also demands that a mother suffocates a daughter's desire to be powerful, autonomous, self-directed, energetic, and productive.[6]

While for past generations this may have been the accepted norm, today it creates ambivalence in mothers who believe girls are capable of more than the traditional wife/mommy role. On the one hand these mothers are still complicit in the suffocation that ensures that their daughters become socially acceptable, but on the other they are acutely aware of the powerlessness that traditional roles create in their girls. This further charges the complex minefield of the mother-daughter relationship.

As girls become teenagers the difficulties with their mothers become even more complicated. The mothers themselves may still be seeking the deep connection they craved, but didn't get, with their own mothers. These needy moms, with their strong desire for attachment, now expect to be on the receiving end of the "giving" behavior they've instilled in their daughters.[7] By now the daughters are acutely attuned to the needs of others, and while they may be aware of this thorny reversal of roles, they are still deeply confused by a mother who is both emotionally needy and dismissive of them. As a result many teenage girls not only reject their mother's values and lifestyle but also their confusing emotional demands. Instead they seek out the comfort and relative ease of their friends, only to discover that these relationships too are fraught with emotional problems.[8]

Eventually most girls resign themselves to the fact that there is no one to take care of their deep emotional needs, and they simply do what society expects of them. Emotionally they learn to stand alone . . . and so the groundwork for the self-sacrifice agenda is done.

An example from a seminar delegate tells a powerful story. Her parents got divorced when she was very young, and her mother raised her. As a child, she and her brother would visit friends in the evening with their mother. Inevitably, on the way home both children would fall asleep in the car. Although the girl was younger, her mother would carry the brother to bed, expecting the sister to waddle in behind. Today this still incenses her.

## MAMA'S BOYS

I've heard many mothers who are raising both genders referring to their sons with a certain joy and pride that is rarely expressed for their daughters.

So prevalent is this boy favoritism that I urge you to think about your own upbringing. How many of your own examples can you identify? Although the events may seem insignificant now, they contain powerful lessons. Events like these, especially when they are repeated, subconsciously teach us that boys are valued and girls are not.

As children we probably had no idea that this same story was playing out in all of our neighbors' homes, so we took our mother's behavior personally. Our young minds told us that Mom was acting this way because there was something wrong with us. *I'm bad, or not good enough,* we thought, *that's why he gets more attention.* Over time, these repetitive negative thoughts settle into our psyches and play out as crippling insecurity.

If you were raised as an only child or had sisters rather than brothers, you may not have experienced this blatant comparison to boys but still will have been emotionally conditioned to be passive and compliant.

The habit of viewing females as subservient is further reinforced by our mothers' behavior. Most of our mothers seemed never to make demands. They didn't even express needs. Some may have tried to voice their wishes by playing the role of victim or martyr, but these too were subservient responses. Even with feminist influences, traditional emotional conditioning is so powerful that most women in our mothers' day were not forthright about what they wanted, and putting themselves first was considered the biggest of sins.

Our mothers' lack of emotional response coupled with their

submissive behavior started us on the path of unconsciously squashing our hopes, dreams, and aspirations. In suppressing our anger we buried our personal power and denied our right to express authentic feelings and get our own needs met. The slow emotional suicide starts with girls systematically obliterating behaviors that are tagged socially unacceptable in favor of those that generate rewards, like pleasing others by giving.

Warping children to develop only one side of their potential leaves both genders off whack. Consequently neither girls nor boys are able to simultaneously experience personal power and express their nurturing impulse.[9] These are not opposing qualities; the potential exists for both attributes to coexist in men and women.

Feminism encourages the expression of the full range of qualities in women, with enormous rewards. Cracking the challenge of allowing both qualities to coexist in us means we no longer struggle with the push-me, pull-you conflicts that originated in the confusing relationship with our moms. As a consequence we can resolve the ambiguities that manifest as dilemmas between the following:

- tradition and liberation
- self-sacrifice and self-development
- financial independence and the need to be taken care of
- personal achievement and not wanting to stand out from the crowd
- getting our own needs met and giving of ourselves

## DOING THE RIGHT THING?

It must be said, however, that mothers can't be blamed for these problems. Given their conditioning, they were only doing what they thought was right. Seldom is a mother's emotional neglect of daughters malicious or vindictive. Most mothers don't spend time concocting ways to punish their daughters! It is purely the way they subconsciously prepare their daughters for the self-sacrificing roles of marriage and motherhood.

For the daughters, though, this emotional neglect doesn't happen without a great deal of pain and plenty of anger. Yet whether we raged against it, wept, sulked, or withdrew, the situation remained. Even if we told ourselves to be better and more cooperative, it didn't seem to improve matters. No matter what we tried, preparation for wifehood and motherhood left us feeling disconnected from vital parts of ourselves and insignificant in the eyes of other people, and these blows to our self-worth hurt badly.

## GROWING A SHELL

To soothe the hurt and fill the vacuum left by the burial of their authentic self, many girls shop around for more acceptable selves. Quite often sitcom characters provide the personas they adopt. But no matter whether these personas are taken from *That's So Raven* or the local prom queen, girls use these false identities to bury their feelings and live inauthentically.

Developing a false identity further anesthetizes our real self, only exacerbating the situation. Inside we may feel needy and dependent, but we dare not show this. Instead we numb our feelings and live the lie. This makes us as emotionally unreachable as our mothers were, which in turn pushes others away, leaving us lonely and with a deep yearning for connection. We ache to connect with our authentic self and hunger for a real sense of bonding with other people.

Many women try to fill this gaping wound with perfectionism, image obsession, or even compulsive shopping. This wounding also creates problems for women in business, which mostly relate to the unrealistically low aspirations many women have. With little faith in our own abilities, it seems just too much of an uphill battle to keep up the fight for what we want, so instead we settle for the paltry crumbs left at the men's table.

For as long as we can keep up the illusion of our confident outer shell, we remain hollow emotionally and unable to heal the wound. The pleas of the needy and undernurtured little girl keep plaguing our adult self. Her cries tell us that we were unloved as a child and are still unlovable now. It's why so many women settle for unsatisfactory relationships. Prince Charming arrives and our neediness overrides our intelligence, blocking our ability to see him for what he really is.

When it comes to the severity of our conditioning, birth order is significant. Usually the oldest daughter, or only daughter, will be far more affected than those who come third or fourth in line.

## SELF-WORTH

Our self-esteem is important because it affects what we contribute to the world. It also significantly affects our pockets. Suze Orman, author of *The Courage to Be Rich,* claims that our self-worth dictates our net worth.[10] Devaluing ourselves means we struggle with the notion of financial independence. Financial support is one of the core dependencies guaranteeing the continuance of self-sacrifice, and this is the reason many women comply with men who provide. Given these pivotal factors, it's obvious why success dodges so many women. After all, we're trained to have no faith in ourselves. This becomes a vicious cycle. We feel bad, so it's difficult to do anything. But when we achieve little, we feel more devalued, making it even harder to break the cycle.

Most adult women I've met complain about having poor self-esteem. They know it holds them back in many situations. Whether it's avoiding inevitable conflict in marriage or not taking a stance at work, shoddy self-esteem will rob you of your potential. If we don't believe in ourselves, it's difficult to convince others to appreciate our abilities. But instead of reclaiming their power, have you noticed how many women use their low self-esteem as an excuse for ongoing dependency? As a handy crutch, they are saying, "My self-worth is shot. I can't achieve. I need looking after." All they're doing is confirming that they are in fact a "real girl" ripe for the prince's picking.

## UNWOMANLY, UNLOVELY, UNLOVED?

Colette Dowling in her book *The Cinderella Complex* writes that "the fear is that if we really stand on our own feet, we'll end up stranded: unwomanly, unlovely, unloved."[11] As Dowling was a magazine journalist (rather than a women's counselor), critics pooh-poohed many of the psychological aspects of her ideas, but the issues she raised about economic independence are still relevant for many women today. For career women, this is one of the push-me, pull-you conflicts referred to earlier. It's between wanting financial independence and also needing to be taken care of.

I know many women who unwillingly support their man, husbands who collapsed when their wife became successful. These women feel uncomfortable about the situation. I also remember a divorcée who vowed never to remarry. Without a man in her life, she turned to the bank to support her. With lesbian couples, when one supports the other, sometimes the provider feels insecure about the process (some even seek out male business partners to fund their ventures).

Think about how the conflicting needs of dependence and independence could be affecting your ability to fulfill your own potential. For women this is a tricky one to resolve. If we break the rules and succeed, we're damned by society. If we don't, we damn ourselves. Again, healthy self-esteem helps resolve this conflict.

People who say they don't care about what other people think amuse me. Our human fear of alienation makes it natural to care what others think, but the trick is to increase the value you place on yourself—then what other people think will affect you much less.

In business, healthy self-belief is the ax necessary for women to smash through the glass ceiling. In its absence, most women hesitate to put themselves forward. They are afraid of being labeled pushy or aggressive, both of which are considered singularly unladylike behaviors. But if you think about it, luncheon is the right place for ladylike behavior, not business.

You can't achieve anything without a healthy dose of self-belief,[12] but success also depends on being in love with your own ideas and having the passion to get others to join you.[13]

## THE NEW "F" WORDS

In the commercial environment we must start identifying some new behaviors. These needn't be based on society's superficial ideas about our femininity, but more on the solid foundation of our womanhood. Imitating men not only puts us at risk of misusing male power but, according to Harriet Rubin, author of *The Princessa,* it's also pointless. "Practicing men's power only makes you more subject to them, because you can never be as good at it as those born to it."[14] Instead of fighting on their turf, she recommends creating a new playing field built from the material women find important, like their individuality, their creativity, and their wisdom.

To do this means dispensing with the old labels. Both the words "feminist" (hard) and "feminine" (soft) are tags of the past—they box us into unhealthy stereotypes.

The harsh judgments about feminism were designed to make us fearful of our potential, while traditional rearing was intended to make us succeed only in the home. Both influences have had a profoundly negative effect upon the way we view ourselves.

When we stop labeling ourselves, we are released to try new things. Instead of being harsh or acquiescent, we're free to experience the real strength and range of our womanhood.

When it comes to tradition, we know that the tough lessons of our poor self-esteem were not without purpose. For how can you be a good wife and mother (in the customary sense) if you selfishly focus on your own needs?

After all, if we put ourselves first, who's going to take care of husbands and children? Of course what we were not told is that grown men can look after themselves.

They are also perfectly capable of raising youngsters.[15] Sadly, today not even career women are convinced of this.

When I run weekend seminars for women, at the end of the day I ask mothers to raise their hand if they have telephoned their husband to check up on the children. More than three-quarters do. This may seem natural, but it will sink you even deeper into the traditional mommy role. After all, how are men ever going to take responsibility unless we leave them to it? Already I can hear the objections. "But he doesn't know what to do!" is a common lament. The question I often ask is, "I wonder why?"

I would find it absurd if daily my husband telephoned to check up on how I was looking after our cat. Imagine the call. "[Sing-song voice] Hi dear, how are things going? [Not listening to the response] Have you fed her yet? [Nagging] Why not? You know she gets grumpy if she's out of her normal routine. [Sigh!] Did you at least remember to put her bed outside in the sun? [Impatient] Now before you do anything else, go and . . . [list of instructions follow]"

Sure this sounds ridiculous. But it's as asinine when we do it to men. It makes them feel inadequate and ineffectual. So it's no wonder they're happier leaving the whole job of children in our so-called more-capable hands. This is how we make a rod for our own backs. Then when we're tired and fed up, we use our irritation to beat up on our men.

## STANDING IN OUR OWN WAY

These peculiar forms of behavior show that the emotional rearing of girls ultimately turns us into our own worst enemies. If you think about your life, how much of your behavior is counterproductive? How many of your foibles give others permission to continue being ineffectual?

We also stand in our own way when we devalue our achievements. As our low self-esteem stubbornly rejects the idea of our own success, we believe that our accomplishments are either flukes or attributable to others. This is known as the Impostor Phenomenon.[16] Research has shown that the feeling of being a fraud is likely to evolve in adults who grew up in families in which support for the individual was lacking, communication and behavior was controlled by rules, and considerable conflict was present. In such an environment, self-worth is built purely upon achievement, with one important rider: What matters most is how others react to your performance.

With your sense of self in the hands of other people, receiving acknowledgment means having to live up to a high-achieving false persona. Already girls are prone to developing a false sense of self because of female conditioning, so it's not surprising we have difficulty celebrating our own achievements.

In school, teachers and parents put down underachievement in boys to a bad break, yet failure in girls is more likely to be attributed to lack of ability.[17]

Additionally, twenty years of research into the "hidden curriculum" of American schools shows that girls receive less praise for the intellectual quality of their ideas and are encouraged to defer to boys. They are also taught to value neatness over innovation and appearance over intelligence, and they are rewarded for being nice and being quiet.[18] Given what a girl really learns in school, when females achieve, it's not surprising that their success is attributed to luck or the abilities of others around them. We often believe this, dealing further blows to our already battered sense of who we are and what we're capable of.

Many women achievers hit this obstacle at more than one time in their life. I have a friend who is a most interesting travel writer. Yet when offered a multimedia opportunity for her wealth of talent, she suddenly experienced a crisis of confidence. "Am I good enough?" she asked. "Maybe someone will call me out," she worried. "I'm not worthy of opportunities as big as this."

All are expressions of the Impostor Phenomenon. They are familiar to many of us. But essentially they relate to what the deprived little girl inside of us thinks we deserve.

Even on the most mundane level, have you ever noticed how women will seldom take the last cookie or piece of pizza from a plate? This has little to do with losing weight and a lot to do with feeling deserving. If we believe we don't even deserve the last cookie, how are we going to feel worthy enough to assert ourselves on global agendas?

The feeling of being unworthy goes right back to our unconscious belief that we have no right to our existence. I've seen so many women act as if they're gate crashing the party of business, politics, religion, and economics. Even in the boardroom, some women can be excessively polite, and they keep apologizing for everything.

It's almost as if being nice, charming, and courteous (and sexy, if we're young enough) is our only guarantee of not being chucked out. So it's no wonder "nice" women are labeled shallow. But what happened to forceful, determined, and persistent? These are essential qualities if we're going to become more confrontational in the corridors of power. What inhibits us is our poor self-esteem.

## CAN WOMEN BE TRUSTED?

The second major consequence of our rearing is the influence it has over our friendships. Emotional deprivation causes the well-documented difficulties in the mother-daughter relationship, and trust becomes a key issue.

Our mothering showed us that women are at best inconsistent, and at worst emotionally absent. When we were needy and our mom responded unpredictably (sometimes nourishing, sometimes needy herself), we learned that we couldn't always trust her to be there for us. Over time we generalized this knowledge to other adult females. One of the great tragedies of this is that we become suspicious of other women's motives. We question whether they are going to encourage or restrain us, nourish or feed off us, please or disappoint, control or connect, support or put us down. These are some of the characteristics that led Orbach and Eichenbaum to liken female friendships to a patchwork quilt where the interplay of materials moves between being "dark and light, patterned and plain, soft and rough" all at the same time.[19]

Understandably this complicates our friendships and is a source of great sadness for many women. Women seek deep connections with each other; firstly to compensate for the lonely relationship they had with their mother, and secondly because the false persona created by female conditioning left them feeling disconnected. Many feel detached from themselves, from other people, the universe, and even from a spiritual source.

When I first became aware of this, I realized that although I have many great friends, we only share with each other up to a point. Our deeply felt vulnerabilities seldom get put on the table.

We tend to disguise these insecurities in talk about stuff that's happening (children, spouses, bosses, time pressure, retail therapy) rather than opening up about deeper personal issues. The same applies to men, but it is we women who pride ourselves on having close relationships.

How well do your girlfriends really know you? They may know a lot about the things that fill your day. But what do they know about your real fears and anxieties? These are the things that make us feel vulnerable, and as we have seen, our conditioning has taught us to hide our neediness in shame.[20] This shame makes it difficult for women to talk about problems and difficulties arising within friendships. Dealing with the issue means having to "fess up" to being needy, and it's why women experiencing conflict will rather bide their time, swallow their feelings, or even withdraw instead of confronting the issue. Also having first learned about women-to-women relationships from our mothers, the mutual dependency we experienced provided no context to discuss the hurt and anger occurring in this relationship. Our need for one another overrode our ability to learn how to deal with healthy conflict.[21] Many of our friendships with other women tread the thin line between suffocation and bonding that characterized our relationship with our mother.

According to Phyllis Chesler in *Woman's Inhumanity to Woman,* female friends are shadow-mothers (or shadow-sisters) and the fierce love one feels in these relationships can be equally matched by hurtful behavior. Women experience this as putting one another down, ganging up against each other, being cold and critical, gossiping, giving one another the silent treatment, and envying. While these destructive behaviors may interplay with times of closeness, the stronger a woman is the harsher the treatment she gets. Chesler says, "If a woman is effective and visible . . . she is expected to be also Santa Claus and Wonder Woman and God combined and *therefore* [her italics] anything can be done to her, because she's so strong and they're so weak." She makes the point that most of us can remember all too well the harm other women have done to us but are in denial when it comes to the hurt we may have doled out to others.[22]

Of course none of this bodes well for lesbian relationships, and the myth that females in same-sex unions are more peaceful, nonviolent, and egalitarian than heterosexual partnerships is shattered by a recent study. No less than 57 percent of lesbian relationships experienced sexual victimization, 45 percent reported physical aggression, and 65 percent experienced psychological abuse in the form of verbal/emotional aggression.[23]

Often the closest we get to trust is attaching to other women who are in the same boat as we are. From these friendships we receive love, care, understanding, support, and compassion, and because more of our emotional needs are met, they are also a catalyst for growth. But this growth can in itself be problematic because change or growth threatens relationships that are formed on the basis of our limitations rather than on genuine intimacy. Many women experience discomfort when their good friends land work promotions, marry, give birth, divorce, go into therapy, or move physically. Change in one person leaves the other feeling deserted. So while these friendships may be rewarding for a time, they trap us into an unspoken bargain: For the relationship to last, both of us must stay the same.[24]

Fairytales not only serve to reinforce the lessons of traditional rearing but also women's mistrust of each other. Pick up any popular tale and you will notice that Mom is not only emotionally absent, but either plays no role at all or dies. The powerful women are wicked witches, bad fairies, and/or cruel stepmothers. All lead to the same conclusion: Adult women can't be trusted.

If these stories were read once or twice, they wouldn't have a profound influence. But they are our ever-repeated bedtime stories. Even worse ... most are now available as full-length movies, which little girls watch over and over again. It's no wonder that even as early as primary school, girls turn on each other and let each other down.

A significant consequence of this lack of trust is the difficulty women have in grouping together as a powerful lobby. Even among themselves women struggle to express an honest opinion. All that happens is we become increasingly suspicious, yet we seldom voice our opinions, whether we agree or disagree.

Chesler claims that in the women's movements not only do females fail to stand together, but they are devious in the ways they compete. They blatantly sabotage leaders and viciously trash each other in the media. She believes that the unexamined mother-daughter relationship is where women are stuck "obstinately marking time" rather than moving toward finding our freedom.[25]

The need to take a stand is urgent, and in women's groups we can no longer afford to satisfy ourselves with breakfast rituals, exclusive women's conferences, and entertaining dinner awards. In Congress, women need to have greater influence in all fields, not just on female issues. Like in the old days, this is akin to females huddling in the kitchen while the men discuss the important matters in the library. Congressional debates about economics, health, taxation, armaments spending, and foreign policy affect all our lives. But things will only shift when we learn to trust and support the Joans of Arc who are fighting for change.

If we can't stand together, it's men's best guarantee that running the world will be left to them. Of course after a lifetime of conditioning, we're not going to trust others overnight. But we can begin by healing our own issues so that we are confident enough to open discussions with our friends. Women are social creatures, and many belong to clubs exchanging and debating anything from books to lingerie and sex toys. Some of these may be ideal forums to start exploring these deeper issues.

## DADDY'S GIRLS

Many girls, finding that they can't deeply trust their own mother, transfer their dependency needs to their father.[26] Not all fathers respond, but those who do turn their daughter into Daddy's girls, and princess behavior is more than likely to be rewarded. When fathers are absent or don't react, girls compensate for being abandoned by both Mom and Dad by fantasizing about being rescued by princes; either way, they learn to see men as their prime avenue for emotional sustenance. Because of this, many women will put themselves at the disposal of men, no matter what the cost.

Given that our world is structured to prioritize males, it should come as no surprise that fathers are the main players in the sex-role stereotyping of children. Few men are pleased by naughty girls who disobey or stand up to them. Looking pretty, being cute, making tea, or serving him a beer are more likely to grab Dad's attention. Such actions show fathers that their daughters are being brought up "correctly."

Children are highly sensitive to their parent's approval, and, for girls, self-sacrificing behavior such as caring for others receives both Mommy's and Daddy's approval. Daughters learn to please by giving, even if it means giving up or giving in. This conditioning is powerful, and it is the reason why a woman's self-value is based on what she gives, while a man's is based on what he gets.

Consistently being rewarded for displays of kindness and consideration encourages women to develop the people-pleasing syndrome, the epitome of self-sacrifice in action.[27]

The relentless need to people-please means that women attempt to respond to too much at once. Since other people's needs drive this syndrome, women battle to prioritize the tasks they deem important. If you have a punctuality problem, is it perhaps because you are unable to put your foot down about taking on too many responsibilities?

The transfer of neediness to Dad cements the trade-off in male-female relationships. Girls give and boys (supposedly) make them feel secure. It's exactly this that convinces us that we're only half a person until we find a man. Again fairytales prepare the ground for this transfer of affection to men. As we know, the princess or the little girl's sole attribute is her beauty, and mostly the message is painfully clear: If being rescued from the evil witch (as in mother) is what you want, brains are unappealing and beauty scores. Recall the young girl, Belle, in *Beauty and the Beast*.[28] She is a bookworm, which offends the handsome hunter, who bellows, "Get your head out of that book and pay attention to more important things—like me!" Talk about saying it like it is!

In a traditional family, fathers are supposed to introduce daughters to the outside world. The father-daughter relationship profoundly influences both the way a girl values herself and the relationship she will have with men later on. Mary Pipher in *Reviving Ophelia* identifies three types of fathers: (1) supportive, (2) distant, and (3) abusive, with distant fathers forming the majority by far. While distant fathers may be well-meaning, the lack of emotional connection with their daughters deepens the wound of loneliness experienced by girls.[29]

In an attempt to make sense of their world, teenage girls can unconsciously blame their own emerging womanliness for Dad's inattention (read: desertion), and this limits their ability to mature sexually.

Although girls hope that the transfer of neediness to Dad will provide them with nurturing, it further complicates matters with Mom. As adult women have the same emotionally deprived little girl inside of them, they don't expect to compete with daughters for their husband's attention. We're not talking about sexual perversion here—simply about who gets Dad's attention.

This competition sets up unnatural jealousies between mothers and daughters, and too often this generalizes to other adult women. Sometimes this is acted out as envy or professional jealousy, or in competing to be the thinnest, or the most beautiful or vivacious.

There's good reason why men are distant from both their daughters and their wives. Husbands who were brought up by stay-at-home mothers find this particularly complicated. They fail to understand that women have needs—after all, their own mothers needed nothing from them. They wonder where you come from with your demanding ways, even if it's for the smallest amount of attention.

From a man's perspective a girl, because she is young and vulnerable, may qualify for some nurturing, but a grown woman must look after herself and also of course her husband, children, and extended family.

## ACTING IT OUT

Television soap operas, like fairytales, reinforce these familiar themes. No matter which soap you watch, the roles are the same. There's always one autocratic, wealthy, and very powerful king supported by a few handsome princes who are learning the chauvinist ropes. Even if the king or princes perform the dastardliest acts, their behavior is never questioned. In some series the men have whored around with all the princesses, but it is the women who are labeled sexually deviant! Go figure!

In soaps, older queens who have lost their looks never get laid, of course. They play the witch/bitch roles and fiercely protect their men (and family values) by manipulating the rather dumb princesses.

If there is more than one hag, they usually fight with each other. When it comes to princesses, it's standard practice to have a blond, a brunet, and a redhead. In this way all Caucasian women viewers can identify with at least one of them. Needless to say the princesses are beautiful.

Modern princesses now have token jobs, but although you may see them in their office, they're never actually working. Mostly they spend their time scheming about how best to manipulate the vagina-struck princes.

What makes these soaps addictive is they show adults playing out childhood fantasies. For women this keeps the promises (or more to the point, the lies) alive. It also allows them to escape from their mundane real-life relationships. Repeated daily for fifty-two weeks every year, and with billions of viewers of all ages, these soaps are part of the invasive programming that keeps women serving the ends of men.

## AFRAID OF OUR POTENTIAL

The myth that security can be found in a man is one of the barriers that blocked the voice of early feminists. The resulting frustration, combined with the fact that women struggle to trust each other, unleashed a new wicked witch: the angry woman. Without reclaiming our right to be angry, many women battle to reconcile their internal princess with Ms. Independence. In *The Fountain of Age* Betty Friedan wrote, "There is a great need to knit together the pieces of our life . . . and then you become a truth-teller."[30] The key section left out of the knitting pattern is the role of female anger, which will be dealt with in depth in the next chapter.

What is seldom recognized is that young girls fantasize about aggression, power, and fame. Prior to teenage years they dream about being the triumphant explorer, the tomb raider, the keeper of secrets, and even the queen; these are not roles in which they are looked after but in which they are in charge of everything.[31]

Even in games involving offices and work, young girls jockey for the position of boss. But instead of society valuing leadership qualities in females, behaviors like cooperation are rewarded, making popularity first prize for young girls. Once the teen years hit, many girls believe that being popular is far more important than being smart and that everything can be traded in for it, especially individuality.

Unlike boys' games in which a clear winner is evident, popularity has no measure, and because of this girls grow up without a context for accepting that females have legitimately won a leadership position through merit.[32] It's why the misguided idea of women sleeping their way to the top still lives on.

This notion of context is central to the conflicts facing many women today. With achievement prized in boys, men have a clear idea of what is expected of them. But with cooperation valued in girls, what measure do women have for success? Do you know of women who believe they are good mothers? And of businesswomen who think their string of achievements is proof enough of their value? At what stage can we say we've given enough? When are women sociable enough, lovable enough, kind or generous enough, thin enough, good-looking enough? This lack of measurable context literally means a woman's work is never done, because as long as there are people making demands, our conditioning forces us to respond.

One of the most common, but unhealthy, expressions of this conflict manifests as a fear of success.

Being fearful of our own success epitomizes our ambivalent feelings about power. We may wish to be powerful, but deep down the idea frightens many women. Drawing upon the male version of power is not only pointless, it also carries the risk of rejection; the reaction to angry feminists proved that "not-so-nice" women are ostracized. So instead of developing our own sense of female power, we tend to reject the notion of being powerful altogether. Too many women resign themselves to experiencing power through men.

In women's lives this manifests as a fear of their own potential. Not only will women's individual achievements change relationships with their female friends, but if they're single, women are scared that success will make them unattractive. If they're attached it may threaten their existing relationship. Although many men say they'd like their women to provide, there are still only a handful of househusbands out there proving it.

Research dealing with intellectually gifted girls is particularly revealing here. It shows that during early teens, bright girls start holding back, and this can continue from fourteen to forty.[33] Sadly, this is the time during which careers are usually cemented. Yet instead of gestating success, these years are often sacrificed for the norm of childbearing.

Some girls I was schooled with probably fell into the "gifted" category. Most have ended up as housewives with mundane part-time jobs (which makes me wonder about "good" schools for girls). Certainly in the 1970s careers were not even mentioned on the academic agenda. What the girls I knew considered important was exposure to boys at the brother school next door, and while the boys were competing for glory, the girls competed for the boys.

Boys' brilliance held the promise of becoming wealthy corporate princes; all their potential wives could hope for was to become a well-educated princess living up to no more than their Cinderella complex. Yet these are girls whose intelligence was staggering. Only one that I know of is a neurosurgeon, and she is matched by a couple of businesswomen. Tragically, less than 10 percent have chosen nontraditional paths. For the rest, good (and expensive) education seems to have only prepared them for marriage and motherhood.

## MARRIAGE AND MOTHERHOOD

For ambitious, gifted women, marriage and motherhood need deep questioning. There is much talk about the widespread pressure of the maternal instinct, but more and more, I'm becoming convinced that this deep yearning does not apply to all women. If it were instinctive, every woman would feel it. From my own life and those of many other childfree women, I know we've never experienced it.

Instead I think it's more apt to talk about the instinct for sex. This is an urge most men and women feel strongly, and until about fifty years ago it would have naturally led to children. A well-known study on marriage conducted in the 1970s opened my eyes to the reality of procreating. It showed that marital satisfaction declines dramatically with the advent of children.[34] Worse still, it doesn't recover until the last child leaves home! Couple this with the inevitable interruption to one's ambition and it is understandable that, for a growing number of women, throwing the baby out with the bathwater becomes the logical option.

The National Center for Health Statistics reports that the number of childfree women grew by 35 percent between 1982 and 1995,[35] and in corporate America the number of women over forty who've chosen not to have children now sits at 42 percent.[36]

To give young women permission to make well-informed choices, we need to teach them about the facts of life, not the fictions; they deserve to be better educated about the reality of marriage and children. Instead of constantly punting the "cute baby" version, we can teach them that it's not always fun and rewarding. We also need to stress that girls' lives are not about living out the daddy's girl role of constantly trying to be the perfect little girl, in the service of men. Often young women meet and marry their husband while still playing this role. We know that relationships are healthier if we begin them on the basis that we intend to continue. It is also helpful to encourage daughters to determine what they want prior to getting married. For without intervention, these young women will also struggle to reach emotional maturity in a union of prince and princess.

In reality, marriage suits men. But what does it do for women? When the handsome prince turns into a monstrous misogynist or an ineffectual wimp, painful disappointment sets in. Marriage is a difficult institution for women to thrive in. When a married friend was asked why she'd remained childfree, she quipped, "I find mating in captivity quite unappealing." Humor aside, most marriages demand a lot from women with very little return.

Although much has recently been written about men's dilemmas, only a few men have really shifted their traditional behaviors. To ease our own difficulty with this, we need to pay attention to how we enable men's testosterone-induced behavior. For instance, one of the big issues women complain about is that men never pick up after themselves. Well, why should they when you're so willingly doing it for them? So when next he asks where his clean shirt can be found, tell him, "It's on the floor where you left it last Friday, sweetie."

If you're currently single, here's a quick tip. The first question you should ask your prospective beau is, *Did your mother work?* If the answer is no, kiss your prince goodbye. A working mother makes a big difference, because her boys learn to look after themselves. As adults they don't expect their wives to act like self-sacrificing doormats who cook, clean, and pick up after them.[37] They also have far greater respect for women, seeing them as interesting company rather than handy slaves or erotic playthings.

To escape these undesirable roles, we must understand that no one can empower us except ourselves. A major reason that we keep up our harmful practice of self-sacrifice is that we are trapped in what psychology calls an "external locus of control."[38] This means that our thoughts and beliefs are guided and formed by what other people want.

Talk to successful women and more often than not they'll put their achievements down to external factors like luck, fate, or even the coincidence of being in the right place. Even when it comes to children who are achieving or happy, mothers will deny their own influence by claiming these children raised themselves or had some special spiritual qualities. Only in the face of failure do women blame themselves, and, because of this, females have difficulty objectively judging the contribution they make.

To internalize this control and heal ourselves, we need to have a better understanding of our emotions. Emotions provide an accurate system of feedback, giving us reliable information we can use to live more consciously. If we're unhappy, something is wrong. The more severe the feeling, the more it drives us to address the issue. This is powerful stuff for women, particularly because our real feelings are divorced from the self-sacrificing thoughts conditioned into our thinking minds.

The richness of our emotions holds the clues for our healing, and only through feelings can we unshackle and empower ourselves. This is sometimes easier said than done. Yet if we don't respond, the severity of our feelings gets more intense. Emotions will never let us off the hook, so by avoiding them or failing to act we make ourselves more miserable.

Depression is a good case in point. Depression is often thought of as the end of the road. It occurs when we've completely given up our personal power. We do this by continually compromising ourselves rather than confronting other people. In a marriage this is what's expected of wives. So it's little wonder that more women than men suffer from depression.

We can largely avoid depression by listening and responding to our feelings. As guidelines for life, feelings are much more powerful than other people's feedback. Feedback from others only tells us how to meet their needs, not our own. But when we learn to respond instinctively to our feelings, we can rely upon our emotions to keep us on track. Deeply connected to our spirit, feelings always tell us what's best for ourselves and our lifework or mission.

Reading feelings as messages helps women move beyond their emotional self. Men often accuse us of being overly emotional and, to our detriment, sometimes we are. As we've never learned the healthy purpose of feelings, we tend to stew in an emotional spot for weeks, months, or even years. In arguments we often become "historical," not hysterical. Usually it starts something like this: "Four years ago on our anniversary you didn't even . . . blah, blah, blah!"

If instead we use emotions as rational feedback rather than weapons, we become healthier. This means developing new habits. Make a point three times a day of asking yourself, *What am I feeling?* Dig deep and respond by changing your choices. Live your new choice and eventually it too will become a habit.

Certainly this won't be comfortable at first, but get used to it, because it's more than worthwhile; it's emotional survival in practice.

To further unshackle ourselves of the constraints of our conditioning, it's important to be vigilant about what we think. Question your beliefs and values constantly. If what you hear in your head doesn't support the kind of life you want, change your thinking. Learn to distinguish between thoughts conditioned into your psyche and thoughts that are your own. With conditioned notions, question how useful these are right now. If they suit, they stay. If not, dispense with them. There's no point in retaining thoughts that no longer fit our current development.

For those who remain a little unsure of this thinking, consider your life in terms of your mother's. If you want to end up like she has, stick to her generation's ideas. However, if going down the same road is not for you, it's time to find out more about yourself. This means breaking traditional rules, making new, more-conscious decisions, and constantly reinventing yourself. It's fun, albeit at times scary. Whichever it is, it sure beats the hell out of unconsciously complying with the self-sacrificing "Little Women" role society would have us fit into.

Instead of "Poor Little Me," make your new motto "No More Ms. Nice Person," and you'll find out just how powerful you can become.

# CHAPTER 3.

# Hell Hath No Fury

The traditional Chinese practice of binding a girl's feet is abhorrent. How men find these deformities arousing is beyond understanding. But the long and excruciating process of foot binding is little different from the anguish all females go through when our psyche gets contorted by a society ignoring our needs. The psychological "binding" of females can distort a girl's psyche for life.

We may have succeeded in burying the pain pretty deep, but it will, without a doubt, have twisted our sense of who we are. It will have left us with unresolved rage, fear, and guilt. Rage is the consequence of living with self-sacrifice, fear is the unhealthy motivator, and guilt is the social gatekeeper locking our psyches into traditional behaviors. These three emotional "peas under our princesses' mattresses" have untold side effects and, if unresolved, are the obstacles that keep us from taking our rightful place in the world.

## RAGE: THE CONSEQUENCE OF SELF-SACRIFICE

Before addressing self-esteem issues, we must first untangle our fury. All human beings have needs, and when these are systematically disregarded, rage is the result. As we've seen, the dismissal of female needs is consistent throughout a young girl's social conditioning. In addition to ignoring female needs, society also sanctions the abuse and humiliation of women. Sexual abuse, violence, unequal pay, harassment, and emotional disregard harm all women.

Rage is the most powerful feeling we know, which also makes it the most difficult to control. But it is a vital part of our survival instinct, mobilizing us to fight any threat.[1] Considering that female socialization is the biggest onslaught against our real self, it is no wonder that women rage. In *The Dance of Anger,* Harriet Goldhor Lerner writes that anger is inevitable when our life consists of giving in and going along, when we assume responsibility for other people's feelings and reactions, when we relinquish our primary responsibility to proceed with our own growth and ensure the quality of our own life, when we behave as if having a relationship is more important than having a self.[2] Rage arises from the anguish and loneliness that is a consequence of our self-sacrificing behavior. It occurs when our needs are ignored and is fueled by the emptiness we feel when one-way giving is expected in our relationships.

This would be a simple matter to resolve if rage didn't put women in a double bind. Our anger arouses the fight in us, but for girls, venting fury is deemed socially unacceptable. So much so that "nice" girls are shamed into suppressing their rage: Think of terms like shrew, witch, bitch, man hater, castrator, hag, and nag. An interesting aspect of our language, comments Goldhor Lerner, is that there is no single equivalent term to describe men who vent their anger on women. Terms like bastard and son of a bitch place the blame for the man's behavior on a woman—his mother![3]

Of course with conditioning lobotomizing the emotional aspect from men's lives, they too are enraged. They're angry about having to live up to their role, and threats to their false sense of superiority can accelerate their rage to physical aggression. For men, the expression of a certain degree of anger is socially acceptable, but women are manipulated into bottling it up. And as we know, suppressing an emotion doesn't mean it evaporates. So powerful is the destructive energy of unresolved anger that it can make us ill, both physically and mentally, or it can cause havoc in our relationships.

Although many of us may be unconscious of the rage festering in our system, it can easily be sparked.

Female wrath is triggered when our emptiness is plumbed by being ignored, dismissed, belittled, humiliated, abused, or negated. Think about how you feel when your spouse walks away in the middle of an argument. Or when a colleague receives accolades for work you have done. Even something as simple as being ignored at the supermarket or dismissed by an auto mechanic can unleash rage.

Anger occurs whenever we compromise our priorities. Everyone has passions, but we know that too many women jeopardize theirs to support the dreams of others, particularly those of their husbands and children. This breeds huge resentment, and a woman may then vent her rage on those closest to her. In a study that shook the feminist community, Murray Straus and Richard Gelles show that women are just as likely as men to be physically violent in the privacy of the home.[4] The study was criticized because many believed it provided male abusers with an excuse to continue battering women. This may be a valid argument, but men's violence is a separate issue, and using it to further deny female anger won't help women manage their rage.

The denial of female wrath means that instead of finding appropriate strategies to channel anger, women either bury it deeper or express it in extreme forms. In *Deadlier Than the Male,* Alix Kirsta identifies numerous studies that confirm the Straus and Gelles findings as well as pointing out the complexity of clearly identifying perpetrator and victim when violence escalates at home. More shocking still is the explosive issue of women's violence toward their children.[5] Denying an equal propensity for violence in women is the most powerful means of furthering the perception of girls as nice and sweet, while attributing boys' aggression to testosterone. As said by Kirsta, "If there is anything more dangerous than our refusal to recognize women's capacity for domestic violence, it is the temptation to manufacture excuses. . . . For women to similarly shrug off their accountability and deny their capacity for free choice and responsible action would be to slow the progress of sexual equality—if not halt it forever."

Men use aggression, or the threat of it, to stay in control, but anger makes women feel out of control.[6] This is why unleashing violent rage is dreadfully discomfiting for women. Even in a nonviolent argument women agonize over the anguish and shame they feel, and often overcompensate for their behavior. Instead of yelling and walking away, women take too much responsibility. Rather than looking at the other party's conduct, we convince ourselves that our own behavior was bitchy or unreasonable. Then we apologize, and wonder why nothing in our relationship changes. This is the cause of much female frustration.

Denial of rage was one of the issues that early feminists tried to open up. On their soapboxes, "libbers" were out there bringing to light behaviors and feelings that women had been suppressing for a long time.

To identify with the feminist vision, a woman would have had to fathom her own rage first. This would have entailed growing out of the princess's dependency and becoming a full-fledged female—embracing wicked witch and all. But this proved too much of an obstacle for most women at the time. Rather than tackle their anger, most opted to shoot the messenger and rage against the women's libbers instead!

### The Right to Be Unreasonable

When pushed too far, why don't women have the same right as others to express their rage?

Mary Valentis and Anne Devane talk about the complications of suppressing this emotion in *Female Rage.*[7] What happens when we bottle up our anger? It simply turns inward, and we start raging against ourselves. Few women realize that the following symptoms are all connected to bottled-up rage: phobias, obsessive-compulsive disorder (OCD), controlling behavior, hypochondria, addictions, anorexia nervosa, bulimia, obesity, self-mutilation, jaw tightening, depression, and high levels of anxiety or panic attacks.

How many women do you know who are well? How many live free of any of these symptoms? Observe women and you'll notice how they're constantly communicating rage. Whether they're complaining about their husband, their boredom, their children's inadequacies, their weight, or their physical imperfections, what women are griping about is how enraged they really are. But instead of dealing with rage, many women create an inner world of illusions of dependency or fantasies of powerlessness, and it is this sense of impotence that makes women complain.[8]

When it comes to our physical well-being, rage can be particularly dangerous. Daniel Goleman quotes research showing that being prone to anger is a stronger predictor of dying young than risk factors such as smoking, high blood pressure, and high cholesterol.[9] In a more specific study, hostility was linked to high levels of a protein that damages blood vessels, increasing the risk of heart attacks.[10] Neither suppressing anger nor venting rage were found to be effective antidotes. Could this be why we are witnessing an increase in heart-related deaths in Western women?

Depression is the biggest silencer of the wrath emanating from our authentic selves. It puts the raging self into solitary confinement, where drugs can become its jailer. Numbed by addictions to prescription or street drugs, alcohol, cigarettes, or the comfort of food, it appears that it's not our lack of self-esteem that's killing us. It is our rage.

Thwarting an instinctive urge like rage also makes us neurotic. These neuroses surface as the first four symptoms listed above: phobias, controlling behavior, OCD, and hypochondria.

### Who's Afraid of the Big Bad Wolf?

A great many women suffer from phobias. They develop young and are sparked by an incident, and although that incident is probably forgotten, what remains is the terror of being left to deal with the situation on one's own.

When we are children the incident coincides with the realization that we are not going to get the support we require. So it's not the spider or the height that frightens us as much as the vulnerability that the event represents. Whatever the symbol is, it becomes a powerful reminder that we are unprotected. We are on our own.

Girls are particularly prone to the development of phobias because of emotional alienation from their mother and the realization that no one is going to meet their authentic needs. It's a sorry state of affairs that the only way girls can get their needs addressed is to act out their rage in the form of a phobia.

Recently, I was on an African safari with a young woman from Scotland. While the ranger was off tracking lions, I got the fright of my life—the woman started jumping around in the vehicle yelling something unintelligible about "beasties." I assumed the hullabaloo was caused by a close sighting of a hungry-looking predator. But no, "beasties" for her took the form of spiders, ants, or any other creepy-crawlies. Evidently one of the offending Teeny Five had come too close for comfort.

Given the choice between a spider on the one side of the vehicle and a lion on the other, she was adamant that she would take her chances with the lion! When I mentioned that incapacitating phobias like this could be easily cured through desensitization, she rapidly changed the subject.

It's worth remembering that people consistently behave in ways that work for them, and it's no different with phobias. Although detrimental, these conditions allow us to remain dependent on others, and they can be handy disguises for the storm blustering inside. The payoff is that neurotic symptoms such as phobias allow us legitimate avenues to take out our anger on other people.

For this young woman each "beastie" was an opportunity to yell at her husband. This is how she gets attention. And if you suffer from agoraphobia, a trip to the supermarket is out of the question. Illness, too, provokes much sympathy and care. If you can't drive across bridges, you become dependent on someone else for transport. With complex conditions like OCD, you can rage at anyone who messes up your perfectly clean or measured-out arrangements.

Another expression of this is the control freak who complains about being exhausted because she's in the driving seat of her family's lives. Women are prone to controlling behavior, often because they can't tell the difference between getting involved, which means working cooperatively, and taking over or dictating, which means having power over people.[11] The payoff of creating dependency is twofold: Firstly, other people's reliance upon you props up your illusion of power, and secondly, when things aren't done your way, you've got ample opportunity to go on the rampage.

After working through this in a seminar, one attendee told me that she understood what I was saying but wasn't prepared to give up her neuroses! Of course not. The payoff is too powerful. But these conditions alienate one further, making life even more lonely and miserable in the long run.

Women may get sucked into this controlling role because men refuse to honor their responsibilities, yet this can have its benefits, too. As we grapple with trust, we create codependent relationships. We hope that this will guarantee our long-term security, but it's also how we end up mothering everyone, meaning that many of our own needs still go unsatisfied. If men are ineffectual, pandering to their poor behavior won't make them change—it just creates further difficulties in the relationship. This is particularly true when it comes to sex—after all, if you're behaving like his mom, it will be psychologically difficult for him to find you sexually attractive.

It's better to allow him to assume responsibility by leaving him to get on with his role in the family.

### Living in a Perfect World

Often control-freak behavior and the need to be perfect coexist, and here the payoff has a double benefit. First, the obsession with perfection is a neat decoy to consume some of that rage energy, and second, being seen to be flawless not only compensates for the "evil" in women, it also gives you permission to criticize those who are simply human.

What perfectionists fail to see is that we live in an imperfect world. So no matter how controlling you may be, perfectionism will always leave you feeling disappointed and let down. Perfection has no measure; at what stage are you going to be able to say "I'm perfect now"? Simply put, it's an unattainable goal, one that only reflects back how imperfect you are.

This sets up a vicious cycle of judging yourself harshly, prompting greater rage, and even more of a need to cover up with perfection. It's why perfectionist behavior gets more severe over time.

These are the lengths we go to for attention or care, and because these behavior patterns offer the false promise of getting our needs met, they're particularly difficult to relinquish. If you suffer from any of these neuroses, understand that the perceived payoff won't benefit you in the long term. By resisting these learned behaviors, you're more likely to unveil the source of your rage, which is the expectation that women sacrifice themselves so that others may lead satisfying lives.

Our neuroses mask our anger, and without them we're afraid that our raging self will burst out and we'll risk being further isolated and ignored. Masking rage simply traps us within it and consumes our energy; even more dangerously, it leaves no room for our subconscious demands to surface. It's much healthier to channel our energy, creativity, and courage into fulfilling our passion, instead of trying to keep the lid on suppressed rage.

### The Sweeter the Smile

It's not only neuroses that cover for our anger, though. Passive-aggressive behavior is another favorite way in which to express rage without having to verbalize it. Passive-aggressive behavior is a way of resisting others, but the person being resisted is clueless as to why they are getting the cold shoulder. The silent treatment is used to avoid conflict, and sulking or withdrawing sex are common weapons to control the behavior of others. What the person being passive-aggressive is really saying is, *If you force me to compromise any further, someone's going to pay . . . and that someone will be you.* For plenty of women this need to indirectly punish others can go on for years.

This kind of behavior may be directed at the world in general. I know of a few divorced women, now in their fifties, who flatly refuse to work. Sure, if you're Jane Fonda and have earned a bundle in your career, this luxury may be yours. But if you're Jane Doe and have become dependent on your siblings, this unspoken refusal to participate may simply be a childish way of saying "Fuck you, world."

Probably the most perilous of all angry women is the one who covers her rage in a veil of niceness. This extreme self-censorship is what a Harvard University psychologist, Carol Gilligan, calls the "tyranny of niceness," because you'd better believe that the sweeter she is, the bigger the rage.[12] Through her smile she is hissing her fury. If confronted she'll be the first to escape in denial. This woman is so removed from herself that her life is one big hidden agenda. As such she is capable of the worst form of betrayal. Respond only to the words of this well-disguised viper and, for your own sanity, ignore the hostility delivered in her tone.

Eating disorders are another complicated manifestation of rage. Overeaters are stuffing down their rage, eating compulsively to distract themselves from events that trigger their anger. Others are eating to feed emotional needs that are difficult to express. One woman may use her bulkiness to assert her presence, while another will use obesity to make herself sexually invisible. The first is raging at the way society ignores women, and the second is hiding her wrath about being dismissed as a sex object.[13]

Anorexia nervosa is a complex affliction that is a powerful way of lashing out at being born female and therefore powerless. Anorexia may begin as defiance, through asserting control over food intake, but ironically the anorexic ends up as society's "perfect woman": weak, sexless, and voiceless.[14] She has starved out her troublesome authentic self and has no energy left to take charge of her life. She becomes what society dictates for women: totally dependent. In the 1990s on college campuses, two out of ten young women were anorexic and six were bulimic; only two out of ten were well.[15]

Self-mutilation is another side effect of suppressed rage. It takes many forms, but most commonly those afflicted regularly cut themselves with a knife or blade. Cutters tend to be driven by self-punishment, injuring themselves in order to connect with their feelings of pain and/or self-loathing through the act of drawing blood.

While the late Princess Diana's eating disorder was well known, it has emerged that she also suffered from self-mutilation.[16] Both conditions have their roots in the rage females feel from their emptiness, and, given the expectations placed upon Diana, this is understandable. To cope with the royal charade, she would have had to completely stifle her authentic self.

It is difficult for any of us to live up to the unrealistic expectations placed upon women. Unlike the women in movies, we're not always beautiful, nice, and congenial. To fulfill our own dreams we often need to be both tough and demanding. If we're to have any impact on this world, we need to accept that aggression and anger are not the sole domain of men. Whether socially acceptable or not, these emotions are equally appropriate for women, especially when our needs are ignored or our rights are trampled.

### Mission Acceptable

One of the most surprising characters in the list of rage responses is the obsession with self-improvement. This is a double-edged sword, for every time our thoughts go toward improvement, our feelings scream "I'm not good enough! I'm not okay!" That's why we believe we need to improve in the first place.

With constant reinforcement, the raging emotional message is much more powerful than the original thought. Tapping our insecurities, it makes us even angrier than before. But in reality, living is not a mission through which we have to prove ourselves acceptable.

This is a predicament I know well. I've spent much of my life using my enormous rage energy to keep proving myself okay. Like a regular Ms. Fix-It, I've rallied to all manner of causes (always there when needed) and neurotically believed it necessary to appear perfectly well -balanced, a position that only made me arrogant enough to offer loads of advice to others, whether asked for or not. What helped was finding my lifework, into which I redirected this energy, but hard knocks, great therapy, and plenty of reading helped me to become more conscious of my motives. Now I know that without having resolved this issue, I would have died believing that my real contributions were not up to scratch.

For many raging women, self-improvement seems such an obvious answer. If we can just change this, shift that, nip and tuck a bit here and there, then the furious attacks on our self-esteem can be arrested. This is pure fantasy. As with depression, what we're really doing is silencing ourselves, fashioning a plastic model that can be molded to perfection.

Self-loathing drives this need to develop a more acceptable shell, yet we must always remember that this dislike for ourselves is learned behavior. It doesn't in any way relate to the truth about who we really are. For many women, our real self is the person whom we are yet to get acquainted with, and getting to know her is a big treat we've got to look forward to.

To get to know ourselves, we must first accept that we don't have to improve anything. What we do need to do is unravel the social crap that has been inflicted on us.

### Empowerment, Not Improvement

Empowerment gets us back to a real sense of who we are. Unlike the tempting promise of self-improvement, empowerment does not provide a fairy godmother's wand. It's more about reeducating ourselves. No longer can we rely on what we were taught by parents, because our world is totally different from theirs. It's also not about what we learned at school or even university—many of these institutions just regurgitate the old rules to make us settle for the mundane.

Empowerment requires nothing more than you experiencing yourself. This means paying attention to how you deal with new ideas or challenges. Noticing what amuses or irritates you. Observing what makes you boost yourself or put yourself down.

This is how you find out what turns you on or leaves you cold. Unlike the pointless fury of prove, prove, prove, this way of life gives you freedom to find out more about who you actually are.

### A Healthy Fighting Spirit

In denying our rage we kill one of the essential components for leading a successful life: our fighting spirit. This spirit is the energy that motivated great humanitarians such as Mother Teresa, Nelson Mandela, and Martin Luther King to fight injustice in this world. It is the same force that gave feminists like Betty Friedan, Susan Faludi, and Eve Ensler the courage to take a stand.

The authors Valentis and Devane state that once a woman accepts her capacity for rage and aggression, she also lays claim to her power.[17] So if making a difference is on your agenda, the bitch inside of you holds much of the passion you'll require. This energy is vital because you'll only get what you want if you fight for it. In effect the bitch holds the sword of personal power. The sword contains your courage, passion, creativity, and determination. But while the bitch is gagged and bound, her energy is dormant and her weapons rendered flaccid and impotent.

Don't confuse the real, energetic bitch inside of you with the voice of female suppression that bickers and nags.

### Release Your Inner Bitch

Unravel your rage by releasing the bitch inside. Accept who you are, bitch and all. Better still, consider the bitch your very best friend. Who else will protect you when others take advantage of your generosity? Ironically, it is only with her protection that women feel safe enough to reveal the softer aspects of our character, like vulnerability for instance.

Self-acceptance also means learning to embrace the imperfections you've raged about, whether it's your weight, age, cellulite, or wrinkles. It's not our perfections that make us amusing, unique, interesting, and memorable. It's our faults, weaknesses, and imperfections. So by denying these, all we're really doing is sentencing ourselves to a bland life.

It's our struggle to accept and overcome our failings that makes it easier for us to connect with other people. For how can we have anything more than a superficial conversation with those who keep up a flawless facade?

Part of self-acceptance is recognizing that we have a right to our feelings (all of them) and to getting our needs met. This requires learning to be more direct about what our feelings and needs are. No matter how much we may wish for it, other people simply won't mind-read what we want. Start with small things and slowly you'll learn to become more assertive. This makes it easier on others than manipulations driven by resentment and rage.

Reclaiming the bitch inside is also the fix we need for our self-esteem: That bitch won't tolerate any of our self-sacrificing nonsense.

Self-esteem is developed by taking risks and embracing challenge—by doing.[18] The "doing" part is essential, because it often surprises you with how able you actually are. So instead of lobotomizing the bitch, use the energy of her anger to make success your best revenge. At least then your rage can be channeled into creative projects more likely to fulfill your passion.

### Do, Don't Dream!

An intelligent way to channel rage is to find a creative outlet for self-expression. Whether it's web design, music, or engineering, women who create are healthier. Even specialists treating cancer are now recommending a creative outlet as a vital component in healing women.

But instead of getting out and doing something, too many women avoid the pain of their rage by living in their intellect. They read dozens of books, attend any number of courses, and talk, talk, talk to heal their self-esteem. The bad news is whether it's my work or anyone else's, just knowing some handy intellectual techniques will do zip to raise your sagging sense of self-value.

Many women use mind games as a foil to avoid the hazards of experience. The fear is that if they do something they may fail, and then the experience will only confirm how deficient they are. In fantasyland failure can be avoided, so they'd rather talk about their dreams than "do." Women in this trap tend to live through other people; they often put unrealistic pressure to achieve on their spouse and children.

Instead of reading or sitting around commiserating, get out and do—and do anything as a start. Of course, you're probably not going to succeed at first, but that's life. Every step we take gives us some new positive ideas about ourselves. This is valuable because how we handle these experiences has the potential to strengthen our self-value. Self-esteem is earned, not learned. It is a perception of ourselves that grows as we gain experience, but it cannot flourish when we are controlled by our fears.

## FEAR: THE TERROR WE FEEL WITHIN

Like rage, fear is an instinctive emotion. It exists to gear us up for the fight-or-flight response linked to our survival. It is interesting to note that humans only have a few instinctive emotions, and a woman's rearing is a catalyst for two of the most potent—rage and fear. Throughout our childhood we will have taken uncountable knocks for behaving against the norm. The result? We associate our real self with pain and fear.

This pain convinces us that our authentic self may really be objectionable and offensive, so the thing we end up fearing most is being ourselves. Again this is learned behavior. It gets cemented into our psyche by the biggest of all human fears: alienation. If we put our real self on display, we risk being alienated even further.

Most fears are generated by memories of losing personal power. Feminine rearing is geared toward forcing girls to give up the idea of being powerful. This leaves women feeling alone, which is why the risk of even more rejection is so frightening. Instead of challenging these learned fears, we unleash our rage upon our authentic self, in an attempt to weaken and destroy it. This keeps us trapped in our false persona, which by definition is flimsy and unstable. Relying upon this phony sense of self makes us even more vulnerable and afraid. But the only real security we have lies within ourselves.

### Who's Pulling the Strings?
Our fear drives us to sacrifice ourselves for the acknowledgment we crave, and that's why fearful people are the easiest to control. Relying upon our inauthentic persona guarantees our dependence on others, which in turn makes us more insecure. It means that those who can provide approval have a great deal of power over us. As such even some of the fiercest women I know are still highly vulnerable to being controlled.

This is particularly true when it comes to relationships with men. Recall that as children we turn to Dad in an attempt to overcome the fear of rejection from Mom. Thereafter we naturally look to men to provide us with the nurturing and approval we hunger after. But many men don't value who we are—they value women as conquests or acquisitions. And because we fear even further alienation, women place too much emphasis on what we naively believe men value most: the physical female form.

Paradoxically, women crave emotional intimacy, but with our fragile psyches overwhelmed with the fears of our false identity, it remains out of reach. Many women use manipulative games to cover for their fear of intimacy. Talking incessantly is one such game, as is verbal bullying, envious sniping, one-up(wo)manship, naysaying, and playing the drama queen or victim/rescuer games. Games such as these are primarily nonverbal. Again, these games have a payoff, for if we allow people to come close to us, they may find out how inadequate we really think we are (see chapter 10).

### Bowing to Authority

In so many different ways, our fears maintain our powerlessness, affecting every area of our life. One such area is our response to authority. Too easily, many women capitulate to bosses, doctors, bank managers, priests, political and legal systems, fashion gurus—anyone who seems to know better than we do. However, surrendering more power to others just deepens our impotence, and in turn stirs more of our rage.

### Getting Our Own Way

Another fear-driven response is our inability to take from other people. Few women are able to ask for help when they need it.

Outwardly we may seem capable and in control, but inwardly we may be crumbling. Many women mistakenly believe that getting help makes things worse because it acknowledges our lack of power. So we battle on alone, generating greater levels of isolation and fear.

Unable to admit our fear and our feelings of powerlessness, we resort to worrying, mostly over things we have no control over. Although worry feels extremely real, it is known as a fake emotion because it covers up for what we're really afraid of.[19]

Worrying has the advantage of consuming some of the nervous energy generated by our fear and rage. In the short term, fretting seems to make us feel better; it defuses some of the pressure building up in our system. So we worry about everything: the safety of our loved ones, our jobs, employees, friends, pets, homes, you name it—women worry about it. Although our overbearing "concern" drives others to distraction, it seems easier to worry than to deal with the root cause of our anxiety, the fear we feel within.

Like many of the actions driven by fear or rage, fretting about others also has a payoff. It can be used to control other people because, in one way or another, our worry will curb their freedom.

For instance, if you're constantly worried about your husband having a car accident, you feel that you have legitimate reason to control when and how he comes home. Your manipulative behavior is disguised as care and concern, so he's never sure how to respond.

Children, too, will appear to acquiesce to your demands rather than carry the burden of your worry, but your partner and children will offer only reluctant compliance as opposed to real cooperation. As soon as your back is turned, they'll do what they wanted to anyway.

Most of these behaviors have our poor sense of self as their root cause. Due to our upbringing, we don't feel good enough at work or at home, socially, sexually, or as a mother, daughter, or wife. To cover up for these anxieties, we often neurotically attempt to hold things together in the hope that no one will notice. As there are seldom times when we can relax our guard, this takes its toll on our system.

Yet none of this has to do with the reality of who we really are—as we've seen, it is simply learned behavior. We can unlearn these habits and regain the power of our womanhood. To do this we need to throw off the impotency of our conditioning by becoming consciously aware of what happened to us as girls. We need to put society's expectations into a perspective, so we can see them for what they are. This will allow us to slowly start acting in ways that internalize our control over our own existence.

### The Success of Failure

When we allow our fears to dictate how we live, we squeeze the life out of opportunities that come our way. Success requires us to relinquish our dependencies and take full responsibility for ourselves. Everything in life has consequences, so we need to ask ourselves whether we choose the responsibilities of achieving what we want or the responsibilities that go with being controlled.

Along with the fear of success, we can equally well be trapped in a fear of failure, and under this influence we attempt nothing new. The resulting boredom and pointlessness we experience is the single biggest slayer of the value we place on ourselves. Although many choose boredom rather than risk failure, the reality is that dealing with our duds actually does more for our self-worth than outright success. So we need to learn to fail superbly.

Failure tests our mettle, allowing us to show the stuff we're really made of. If you collapse in the face of it, your flops will end up failing you. However, failure only works for us when we learn its lesson and use the knowledge to pick ourselves up again. In reality, failing to learn from our screw-ups is the only failure there is.

In seminars I often say only those who've had monumental failures can expect colossal success. Screwing up big-time results from taking risks. Without it, you're left managing only the predictable and mundane, which is hardly likely to generate a stimulating and fulfilling life. In addition, the courage and strength gained from bouncing back are exactly the qualities needed to manage success in the long term.

To deal with our fears we have a number of choices. Tranquilizers are one option, but they can't help us deal with the cause of our anxieties and fear—all they do is separate us from the feelings. This doesn't help us reclaim our life, nor does it restore the control we want over our destiny. Realistically managing ourselves can only happen by dealing with the fear itself.

Susan Jeffers, one of the best-known authors on the topic of fear, offers some sound advice. She suggests acknowledging our fears and going ahead with our plans anyway.[20] When it comes to behaviors that challenge our conditioning, this isn't easy, so it's best to tackle your fears in baby steps initially. Doing so allows other people to gradually get to know the "new you," and it reduces the overwhelming fear women have of further rejection.

Jeffers' advice worked for me many years ago when I was invited on my first radio interview. I was so terrified that my knees literally shook. I knew I had two choices: Either I could cancel and avoid the experience altogether, or I could acknowledge my nervousness and get on with it. While on the show I was acutely aware of my panic but told myself to do the best I could under the circumstances. Thereafter each subsequent interview became easier, and now interviews are an enjoyable part of what I do.

Dealing with fear is never a walk in the park, but if we're to make our lives successful and achieve what we want, we need to release ourselves from its paralyzing grip. Freeing ourselves from fear will eliminate our need for self-sacrifice so we can make our own growth the priority.

I'm aware that for many women, just the thought of making yourself a priority produces large doses of guilt. In the seminar room it always does.

This feeling gets so intense that it's almost tangible. But it makes sense, as alongside rage and fear, guilt is the third part of the emotional triangle that inhibits women from exploring their full potential.

## GUILT: SOCIETY'S GATEKEEPER

While rage and fear force us to silence our authenticity, guilt provides the justification. By locking us into socially acceptable behaviors, guilt is society's gatekeeper. It controls the choices we make and fouls up our destiny. The wild woman knows what she wants but is gagged by guilt. Listen to women's voices—sometimes the guilt gag squeezes so tightly that the only thing surfacing is the high-pitched sound of a little girl.

To integrate our womanhood, we need to understand the consequences of a lifetime of guilt. Guilt, like worry, is not a primal emotion; it is just another fake feeling. It certainly feels real, but guilt is learned behavior. It comes from fear that we're not doing the "right thing," which according to the social norms means we're not being self-sacrificing enough.

Driven by social expectations, this feeling traps us in the "guilt-resentment" cycle. If guilt drives our actions, rather than our own idea of what we want, we become resentful at having to fulfill these obligations. So in effect, we're damned by society if we don't act according to the wants of others, and damned by ourselves if we do.

### Doing the Right Thing

Difficulties with guilt exist because of a changed female role in a world that's not mature enough to handle real women. This is not just an indictment on men. Our continuing dependency on male approval shows that we're not yet fully managing ourselves. So instead of independently getting on with our lives, the dependencies we indulge make us susceptible to the pressure of doing the "right thing."

Yet what is this "right thing"? Where's the rulebook that dictates how we live our lives? One thing's for sure—if it did exist it would be in dire need of an update.

For Baby Boomers who are working mothers, this feeling is fairly understandable. Most of their own mothers believed in the sanctity of staying at home. This was also something the media kept hammering, supported, of course, by the experts and religion. With parents, the media, the experts, God, and corporate business dead against working women, Baby Boomers had to prove that they could manage it all. Still the social norms didn't bend. Instead the propaganda attacking working women escalated.

### Working Off the Guilt

In *Beyond Sugar and Spice,* the authors Caryl Rivers, Rosalind Barnett, and Grace Baruch identify some of the problems for working mothers. When it comes to experts, they talk about social myth masquerading as science. One of the most detrimental examples involved research into how working mothers damage their children.

"In the 1930s and '40s, studies were done of infants in dismal orphanages, where they had minimal (physical) contact and little sensory stimuli. In these deprived environments children, not surprisingly, showed serious emotional and developmental problems. These studies were cited for years as proof that mothers shouldn't work—despite the fact that the orphanages had nothing at all to do with loving homes and working mothers." [21] So much for science.

Today the guilt factory continues. Even in news publications, working women have been blamed for the social ills of society.[22] For women to escape this socially programmed guilt, we need to understand reality. The most comprehensive survey to date on the working mother issue showed in 1999 that a mother's employment does not place children at risk in any way.[23] The authors Barnett and Rivers also detail why working mothers are good for their children in their book *She Works/He Works.*[24]

For example, working mothers provide children with greater economic security, which can improve the home environment. Their children tend to be more independent and have more flexible attitudes toward gender roles, and because Mom brings the external world home, conversations are different, so the children's verbal intelligence is improved.[25]

With more flexible gender roles, boys of working moms grow up with greater respect for adult women. This is certainly something their wives will appreciate. As for girls, having a working mother makes having a career less fraught with conflict. For these girls, mothers work—no questions asked. Already this can be seen in the way girls' play has evolved. Very often their games will involve something about business. As a result working moms are more-appropriate role models for their daughters.[26]

It's quite unlikely that upcoming generations of women will have a choice about working or staying at home, so there's little point in transferring the working mom's emotion to her daughter.

The authors of a journal article aimed at reducing working mothers' guilt write that the only cautionary for moms is the attitude that they hold toward firstly their employment and secondly placing children in care. When moms are unsure about, or unhappy in, their jobs, their insecurities will be acted out by their children.[27] Too easily the feeling of missing one's children can then be confused with guilt. These authors offer a good means to make the all-important distinction: Guilt will manifest in bad thoughts about yourself, and the feeling of missing your children will play out as thoughts about them.

If you're feeling the working mom's guilt, do yourself a favor and calculate how many of your children's waking hours you spend with them. Take into account the time your children spend at school or are playing with their friends. These would be happening whether you're working or not. Mostly when women do this, they find that they spend more than half a child's waking hours with them. This is more than enough. Even if your time together is spent hurrying children off to school in the morning, your household will look no different from that of nonworking moms.

When it comes to guilt, women often find themselves in a catch-22. Too often working mothers feel guilty, while resentment can be the lot of stay-at-home moms. Although escaping this trap may appear impossible, a reality check can provide the relief that's necessary. Mothers who don't wish to work, but are forced to do so by circumstance, feel guilty and are unhappy people. Equally so, mothers who want to work but stay at home are resentful and dissatisfied. So for women, a guilt-free life means taking the freedom to choose whatever life you want.

It was also never intended that one person should take full responsibility for child rearing. Betty Holcomb in *Not Guilty!* makes the pertinent point that it takes a village to raise a child. Whether mothers work or not, children still need input from involved fathers, educated daycare workers, teachers, counselors, grandparents, aunts, uncles, neighbors, and friends.[28]

### There for the Taking

Today women have more freedom than ever before, but we're not very good at taking it. We keep ourselves trapped in the way society tells us we should behave.

Start freeing yourself from guilt by listening for the word "should" in your thoughts and vocabulary. "I should spend more time with . . . " or "I should go to the gym, be kinder, lose weight, have a face-lift." These are not your wishes—they are the social demands that play out in your mind.

"Shoulds" do not communicate what we want. They are just a head trip we use to keep conforming. Certainly they can't add to our happiness, as "shoulds" are impossible to sustain. "I want to . . . " offers a totally different kind of motivation. It's backed by our own energy, not society's demands. So whenever you hear the word "should" in your head, don't respond to it. Instead, ask yourself what you really want. This will help you focus inward rather than being vulnerable to the conditioned emotional cycle, the guilt-resentment trap.

Questioning what you really want will help sort out some of the priorities discussed earlier. It is also the only way to identify your life-work, or what's important to you. No one can dictate this, especially not society. Living guilt-free will also improve your health and relationships. Too often guilt forces us to overcompensate, which is why it's considered an expensive habit. Ultimately the costs to ourselves are great. Make a decision to dispense with guilt, then slowly discipline yourself to stop responding to its unrealistic demands.

As the generations that are straddling tradition and liberation, the best we can do is to be true to ourselves. Although being more conscious may not make you popular, at least you'll be comfortable living with yourself.

Given that our issues are complex, this work may be difficult. Don't be shy to seek help if necessary. Find a female therapist *au fait* with these issues, and view your therapy as a personal exploration instead of a process to fix your problems.

Turn your therapy into a personal adventure by using it to find out more about who you are. This will help you find your passion, which will lead you to your lifework.

Also find like-minded souls and form your own support groups. This work is easier if you're not doing it alone. Of course it's going to be challenging to learn to trust one another, but give it time. Within the group, make a point of staying with your authentic self as best as you can—this will help you avoid the trap of discussing issues from your intellect. Intellectual discussions may be interesting, but they won't help you find out more about your real womanly selves.

To bring about real change we need to dispense with the roles and choose how we plan to live through our womanhood. As you free yourself, you will find that some people will battle to accept you, but the interesting thing about life is that "like attracts like," and the more you shift and change, the more like-minded people you will encounter.

Freeing ourselves also allows us to have some fun. Instead of wasting time and energy raging at yourself, go on the rampage against establishments that no longer suit the reality of women's roles. Become a royal pain. Write letters, boycott companies, challenge the system . . . but whatever you choose, be wild about having your fun.

In *Pulling Your Own Strings,* Wayne Dyer relates a story about his sister who gave him an embroidered pillow that read "I'm Allowed."[29] Giving ourselves permission to live can overcome many of the difficult feelings we've inherited from our upbringing, so perhaps get a similar silk cushion for yourself, but add "Because I am a woman."

## A Fairer Tale: Slow-Wet and the Seven Dorks

++++++++++++++++++++++++++++++++++++++++++++++++++++

One fine day the queen was sewing in the palace. Secretly she detested sewing (and grocery shopping, knitting, cleaning, cooking, and keeping house, too). What she yearned for was an exciting career that would take her out of the palace confines.

But as a young and impressionable princess, she'd been swept off her feet by the sweet words of a handsome prince. "Be my queen," he'd said, "for the rest of your days you can happily stay home, and I will treat you like a goddess."

As she sat alone in her chamber thinking wistfully back on her girlish hopes, she looked up through the glass ceiling. There was the king in council with six of his "old-school-tie" advisers. Today, she'd heard, they were due to debate the delicate matter of contraception. Should such a thing be allowed in the land? Staring through the thick glass, she saw six hands raising six placards. To her horror, the word "no" was written on every single one.

Enraged, the queen realized that these men wanted only one thing: to keep all power for themselves. Their ruling meant that women would continue to be slaves, rearing children and working in the home forever. The queen flung down her sewing—vowing never to pick it up again—and began to conceive of a plan.

"I wish," she said vehemently, "that I had a baby girl whom I could raise to be so powerful that no man would dare tell her what to do."

Soon afterward she delivered a lovely baby girl, who came out of the womb cursing the nurses in her infant voice. "This sex-role stereotyping stops here!" muttered the little mite. "Take all these pink things out of my room straightaway." So proud was the queen that she named her daughter Joan.

Sadly, not long afterward the queen fell ill and died, and the king—unable to live without a wife—quickly married again. The new queen suited him perfectly; she was beautiful, marvelously submissive, and entirely respectful of tradition. In accordance with the king's wishes, the queen went about grooming little Joan in the ways of a true princess. But there was a major worry: "Joan," said the queen, "is a most unsuitable name. We simply can't celebrate the misdeeds of that Arc woman who caused so much trouble."

With the king's consent the queen changed Princess Joan's offensive name to Slow-Wet. "'Slow' because a girl must never imagine she can be clever like a man, and 'Wet' because she mustn't display too strong a personality if she plans to find a good husband," explained the queen.

The queen's dearest possession was a crystal glass bowl. Each day she'd carefully wash it in new SuperBrite until it gleamed magnificently. She was convinced, having watched many a television commercial, that her precious bowl was the very thing that gave her life its deepest meaning.

The bowl, she was sure, had magical powers. Every morning the queen would creep silently and barefoot into the kitchen and ask:

"Crystal bowl in the sink,
Who is most traditional, d'you think?"
And the bowl would reply:
"Thou, O queen, art most traditional of all!"

Growing up under the queen's fine tutelage, Slow-Wet became a model princess. The king was mightily pleased to behold her grace and compliance. All unsuitable character traits, such as wit and willfulness, had been thoroughly expunged. Following in the barefoot steps of the queen, Slow-Wet learned the health arts of making homemade muesli and baking whole wheat bread. Many an evening she spent uncomplaining and alone, bent over her exquisite needlepoint.

Then one day, when as usual the queen asked:

"Crystal bowl, in the sink,
Who is most traditional, d'you think?"
The bowl gave a disturbing reply:
"O Queen, Slow-Wet is most traditional, I think!"

The queen grew pale with rage. She began to hate Slow-Wet with all her heart.

Every day the girl grew more traditional. Soon her home-baked bread was more wholesome than the queen's. Her needlepoint was finer. Her gracious manner, when serving spicy beverages to the king and his advisers, surpassed that of the queen. The princess could whip up banquets fit for a king and on a shoestring budget.

The queen's jealousy raged, and no matter how often she consulted her bowl, she got the same insulting answer. She stewed and brewed, but nothing in her experience had equipped her for what she wanted to do. Eventually in her fury the queen summoned one of the royal huntsmen. "Take Slow-Wet into the forest," she ordered imperiously, "slay her, and make sure you bring her busy little hands back to me."

The huntsman took Slow-Wet into the forest. But he couldn't bring himself to kill the little princess. "She's such a compliant and kindly princess," he said to himself. "How will the kingdom perpetuate courtly tradition if we slay one such as she?"

"Run," he said gruffly, "find the protection of a husband and never return!"

"What will become of me?" cried the terrified little Slow-Wet. But there came no answer. The huntsman had hastened away, knowing that he would be unable to resist a little girl's tears.

The princess wandered aimlessly for many hours until at last she glimpsed a little cottage in a clearing. Cold, tired, and frightened, Slow-Wet peeped inside. "What an odd and messy little place," she thought to herself. There were piles of squashed beer cans, smelly socks strewn across the floor, and moldy leftovers in the kitchen. "What kind of a person lives in such a way?" she asked herself in astonishment, forgetting her fears for a moment. "I can only think," she replied at last, "that it must be a man all alone with no woman to look after his needs. . . . I've heard of poor men living in ghastly places called bachelor pads."

"How small everything seems to be," thought Slow-Wet. Something reminded her of advice the wicked queen had once given her: "Treat your men like little boys and they will act like men!"

"How right she was!" thought Slow-Wet forlornly, for under all the mess and rubble, she could just make out seven tiny beds and seven tiny chairs. Clearly, she thought, this must be the home of seven little boys masquerading as men.

And indeed she was quite right. The cottage belonged to seven dorks who went out all day to work their minds.

As there was no one about, Slow-Wet tiptoed into the little house. She picked up one of the strange-looking magazines lying about. It was filled with unusual pictures of bare bodies in strange contortions. "Odd," thought Slow-Wet and decided it was time for a nap.

That evening the dorks came home from work and lit seven candles as usual. "Goodness me, there's someone here!" cried one of the dorks in surprise when he noticed Slow-Wet. She woke with a start, finding herself encircled by the very curious dorks.

"Why have you come here, my dear, and what can you do for us?" asked one of the dorks. Slow-Wet explained that for some reason the more she'd practiced womanly diligence, the more her stepmother had hated her. As she told the story of what had happened, the dorks grew more and more enchanted by her perfect feminine grace.

"You mean you can cook, clean, wash up, sew, do the grocery shopping, bake fresh bread, and serve beer?" said one of them. "Welcome, welcome, welcome," chorused the seven dorks in unison. "You can live with us forever and ever."

One by one the dorks introduced themselves. "My name is Egotistical!" said the first one eagerly. "I'm Arrogance!" called out the second. "Know-It-All!" shouted the third. "I'm Oedipal!" piped up the fourth. "Aggressive!" "Power-Hungry!" and "Slovenly!" shouted the fifth, sixth, and seventh dorks in quick succession.

In no time at all, the dorks drew up an agreement that would bind Slow-Wet to them forever. Then they carefully explained, "If you pick up after us, clean the house, wash and iron our clothes, cook our meals, serve us, love us, and care for us without making any demands of your own, we'll protect you from harm."

"Sounds fair," said Slow-Wet and gratefully accepted their offer.

Every morning the dorks would leave the house to work their minds. As they left, she'd hear them cheerfully singing, "Hey ho, hey ho, it's back to our opinions we go!"

The more she heard about their work, the more Slow-Wet imagined that it must be a bit like Monopoly, a game in which those who have get to tell everyone else what to do, and if they feel like it they can simply take away everyone else's possessions.

At nightfall the seven dorks would return to their clean and cozy cottage in the forest. They'd be exhausted and dejected after their long, hard day at the game, so Slow-Wet would put on a cheerful face and meet their every need. Slovenly was particularly demanding, but no matter how worn-out she felt, Slow-Wet didn't mind; after all, it made her feel needed and secure.

Nightly, the dorks would entertain her with their antics, and no matter how many times Slow-Wet saw the same old tricks, she'd smile sweetly and make encouraging sounds. Arrogance and Egotistical would generally fight with Know-It-All, and, in between her chores, Slow-Wet would mediate in soothing tones.

At bedtime all the dorks, except Oedipal, would tumble drunkenly into their little beds. Oedipal had a great need to please Slow-Wet. He'd wait patiently while she folded the clothes that the dorks had discarded, then, since there were only seven little beds in the cottage, he'd generously offer to share his own with Slow-Wet.

One day, the dorks went off as usual, and Slow-Wet began mopping and cleaning, singing all the while to keep up her lonely spirits, when there came a knock at the door. She opened the door and there stood an old woman with a kind expression on her face. Unbeknownst to Slow-Wet, this was the spirit of the first queen, her own dear mother, disguised as a job peddler. "Look, Joan . . . I beg your pardon—I meant Slow-Wet . . . " she corrected herself, "out in the world there are lots and lots of exciting careers just right for a skilled girl like yourself." The slightly perplexed Slow-Wet began to feel a kind of hopefulness rising in her belly.

Then she looked crestfallen, saying, "But there's nothing much a girl like me can really do."

"That's no way to talk," said the old woman gently. "You are well able to manage not just one, but seven dorks, and this home is clearly run with executive efficiency; it's obvious that you are more than equipped for a top management position!"

Slow-Wet felt herself blush; no one had ever described her domestic duties in such an exciting way. None of the dorks had even told her that she was good at looking after them. She felt her spine begin to straighten, and she let the broom in her hand clatter to the floor. "Now that I think about it," she said to the old woman, "there are things I'm good at doing."

"Tell me then," said the woman, "what are all these things you can do?"

"First of all," replied Slow-Wet, "I can nearly always get the dorks to stop fighting and cooperate with each other." *Dealing with conflict,* wrote the woman on a little notepad. "Then, if one of the dorks is grumpy or sad, I find out what's upsetting him and help him to sort it out." *Managing difficult temperaments,* wrote the woman. "I also do a lot of other things," admitted Slow-Wet, suddenly beginning to feel quite proud as the list got longer, "like the laundry, the shopping, and I have to make sure the dorks don't spend all their money on payday so it lasts to month's end. I make the cottage breezy and fresh, I clean it and air it, and every now and then wash the curtains and carpets. I've even made the dorks curtains and bedcovers, and I do their mending, and of course all the cooking." *Multitasking, budget management, interior decorating, menu planning, and catering,* the woman added to her list.

"Another thing I do . . . but isn't the list getting a bit long?"

"Not at all," replied the woman.

"Once a month I arrange for us all to sit down and discuss everything that needs to be done. Even if they're my tasks I find out if the dorks are satisfied with my contribution, and I ask them if there are any tasks they would enjoy, but that's when they usually say, 'Time for a beer!'"

The old woman completed the list then held out her hand to Slow-Wet: "Let me congratulate you, my dear, on a commendable résumé; your prospects in the job market are excellent!"

When the dorks came home, Slow-Wet had barely done any of her chores. There was a pile of books on the table, and Slow-Wet had her nose buried in a formidable-looking tome entitled *Executive Skills: Identify How Much You Already Know.*

"What, may I ask, are you up to, Slow-Wet?" asked Arrogance icily.

"Where's my supper?" demanded Slovenly.

"So you think you're good enough to play our kind of business games all of a sudden. Well I've got news for you," said Power-Hungry cuttingly.

"You wouldn't really go out and get a job. Who will love me then?" said a hurt-looking Oedipal.

Stricken with guilt, Slow-Wet stowed away her management manuals and whipped the house into shape. The next day, and for many days after that, Slow-Wet did her chores at top speed then sat down to study until the dorks got home. In no time at all she realized that she wasn't half as slow-witted as her stepmother had led her to think.

Then one day the wise old woman reappeared. This time in her basket she had letters offering Slow-Wet some very interesting jobs.

"Come," said the old woman. "There's more to life than being the penniless servant of seven dorks."

Slow-Wet felt sorely tempted. One of the offers was from the palace. The old woman, who seemed to know an awful lot about everything, informed her that the king had died and that the palace money counter had run off with most of the widowed queen's booty.

Disguising herself as Ms. Efficient, Slow-Wet made haste for the palace. For the dorks, she left a note: "You're big boys now. If you want to live in the modern world, learn to cook, clean up, and look after yourselves. These days a girl's got more important things to do than playing nursemaid to dorks. So, goodbye!"

When Ms. Efficient reached the palace, she found the queen was in a terrible state. She was in the process of consulting her bowl:

"Crystal bowl in the sink,
Who is most traditional, d'you think?"
The bowl replied:

"O Queen, wise up! Traditional roles are lost methinks,
They've gotten you into this mess that stinks.
When will you learn? Men aren't going to be around forever.
Get a job and get clever!"

Screaming with rage, the queen took the little plastic hands, which the huntsman had told her were Slow-Wet's, and with them smashed the crystal bowl to shards. When Ms. Efficient rushed to her side, the wicked queen yelled, "Fix this mess! Fetch me my happy pills; I must rest."

With that the queen stormed off and was never seen again. (It was rumored that she grew more and more miserable and took stronger and stronger happy pills, until she went mad and died of an overdose.)

Ms. Efficient became Regina, Queen of the Land. She set up a feminocracy, which no longer tolerated the kind of scoundrels who were running the dork's dem(on)ocracy. But suspecting that the dorks would be unable to cope, she rushed over to their little cottage and said, "I can offer you employment as man-ual labor-ers, because that's what men are really good for."

Grateful to see their unpaid domestic help again, the dorks gladly agreed, and were soon set to work. After a time, however, Power-Hungry, Egotistical, and Aggressive became enraged because they were no longer in charge. They huddled together to conspire against Queen Regina.

Using Oedipal to incite the other dorks, they spread all manner of vicious rumors about the queen. Calling her dreadful names, they spoke most unflatteringly about her body parts; they giggled with vulgar delight when they secretly referred to her as Queen Vagina, or Princess Pudenda or Vulva the Fifth. They were convinced that attacking her private parts was the very thing nec-essary to topple her.

But Oedipal, who secretly lusted after the queen, was deeply afraid of losing the special courtesy she afforded him. So he took Slovenly and Arrogance aside. He knew that Slovenly needed the queen to maintain his decency, and that Arrogance secretly craved the acknowledgment she so generously gave. Neither of them could consider living without her, nor could they tolerate once again being dictated to by Power-Hungry. So the three of them hatched a plot.

That night they quietly crept over to Power-Hungry's camp and, in great gushing spouts, peed on everything in sight. Noisily comparing the size of their weapons and bragging brazenly about the distances they could shoot, Oedipal's dorks created a stink loud enough to awaken the sleeping Queen Regina. She took one look at the degenerate combatants and merely pointed out, "Warmongering is outlawed in this feminocracy." When the dorks called out rudely, she quietly left the site of their lavatorium and went to seek counsel with the Moon Goddess.

Together they came up with an ingenious plan. Regina would develop a potion using a vial of female hormones infused with the mysterious power of moonshine. Then she would invite the dorks to a party to reconcile their differences.

A few nights later, in came the disheveled, wet, angry, stinking dorks, and Queen Regina thought she caught a whiff of spilt testosterone. To replenish the vital juices they'd squandered, the dorks grabbed greedily at the jugs of moonshine and began drinking heartily.

The more they slugged it back, the dimmer the little light of their one-eyed trouser god became. And that's how the seven dorks gradually grew friendlier and friendlier and more and more considerate.

Soon they were enthusiastically volunteering to support Regina's compassionate humanitarianism. And—with the troublesome little warlords who'd been running everything now silenced—dangerous combat became a thing of history in Queenland.

Ruling over her peaceful and productive feminocracy, Queen Regina made sure that no person ever again meted out the kind of traditional role training that her stepmother had imposed upon her. And the gracious and powerful queen lived happily ever after!

+ + + + + + + + + + + + + + + + + + + + + + + + + + + + + + + + + + + + + + + + + + + + + +

# CHAPTER 4.

# Survival of the Prettiest

**T**he *Big Issue* magazine ran an article on Anita Roddick, founder of The Body Shop, a cosmetics company using natural products primarily sourced from impoverished communities.[1] The article detailed her views on globalization and the irresponsible attitude of corporate business. A reader replied as follows:

"Why can't women like Roddick get off their high horses and understand that there is nothing wrong in women aspiring to be beautiful? . . . Next thing she'll be saying that buying *Cosmopolitan* is a form of women abuse. . . . Frankly, I have had enough of these Marxist/feminist troublemakers. Is Roddick jealous of other women's beauty or does she really believe that women should all look like bag ladies?"

Rather than attacking the person who exposes the lies and unethical behavior of the beauty industry, wouldn't we be better off raging at the businesses that exploit our vulnerabilities?

Yes, both men and women strive to be attractive, but when this desire reaches obsessive proportions it becomes an unhealthy preoccupation. So just how vulnerable does the female self-sacrificing agenda make us to the image industry's fabrications?

## YOU—JUST BETTER

This slogan is just one example of the multitude of advertising fibs making us scramble for the cosmetics counter. Pick up any women's magazine and most of the pages scream image or beauty, detailing myriad ways for self-enhancement. But what percentage of articles is dedicated to female accomplishments?

In *The Beauty Myth,* Naomi Wolf offers a critical analysis of typical women's magazines; in their defense, Wolf claims that they are a woman's sole means of accessing female culture.[2] She may be right, but if that culture's premise is that women can only fulfill themselves through self-improvement, then what are these publications doing? The concept of self-improvement is inherently undermining: It implies that we are not okay as we are. Self-improvement has nothing to do with pursuing our interests, or developing into mature human beings; it's about making sure we reinvent our image with every fashion shift. It's a full-time occupation consuming huge amounts of female energy.

The fashion industry is enticing with its quick fixes and makeovers, all "guaranteed" to turn us into successful and above all appealing women. All you have to do is step obediently onto the treadmill: Get a makeover, cover your blemishes, lengthen your lashes and nails, adopt the latest hairstyle and color, and while in the salon do yourself a favor—check out the Paris winter look, because your boots and that coat you wore just about every day last winter . . . well, we won't say any more!

Get sucked into the self-improvement treadmill and you are falling for the hidden message that you were never okay in the first place.

If your reading diet consists mainly of women's magazines, don't expect to find information that truly promotes female independence. Generally the content of magazines tends to be 60 percent advertising, and even the leftover 40 percent containing articles is often heavily influenced by advertisers. When it comes to the editorial, superficiality is the code, and features that truly wrestle with women's issues are rare.

Cyndi Tebbel, former editor of the Australian women's magazine

*New Woman,* became concerned about the inappropriate portrayal of the female form, so she put a model larger than the anorexic norm on the cover of one issue.[3] She documents this experience in her ground-breaking work, *The Body Snatchers.* Horrified image advertisers pulled out, and her days as editor were numbered. To other journalists the message was clear: Industry aggression will be used against editorial transgression. So much for objective journalism.

## SUBSCRIBING TO THE ONSLAUGHT

The media will usually feign innocence when accused of perpetuating destructive nonsense about women. "We're simply reflecting back what's happening in society," say publishers and editors. What a joke! Women don't spontaneously show up in droves for nips and tucks. So whether the media denies it or not, it does play a significant role in the most pronounced suicidal fad of our time: women starving themselves, sometimes to death.

The media bears a huge responsibility for distorting perceptions, but we, the public, are not innocent either. Given that every month millions of women's magazines get sold worldwide, it cannot be denied that women are eagerly subscribing to the onslaught. Why?

Have you ever noticed how you start putting yourself down when looking through women's magazines? A host of studies have linked the so-called "thin-ideal" portrayed in women's magazines to low self-esteem and depression,[4] body dissatisfaction,[5] restrained eating,[6] and the onset of eating disorders such as bulimia, especially in young girls.[7]

There is no doubt, and the media moguls know this too well, that producing images that make women feel inadequate is extremely profitable. A mere thirty minutes' exposure to television programs and advertising can negatively influence a woman's perception of the shape of her body.[8] Feeling dissatisfied with our bodies is reported to be ten times more common for females than for males. Body dissatisfaction is now considered the norm for women.[9]

Susan Faludi reports on the Wells Rich Greene survey, one of the largest studies of women's fashion-shopping habits in the 1980s. This study found that the more confident and independent women became, the less they liked to shop—and the more they enjoyed their work, the less they cared about their clothes. Only three groups of women could be identified who were loyal followers of fashion: the very young, the very social, and the very anxious.[10]

## ENRICHING YOUR LIFE?

Ultimately magazines supporting female consumerism cost us three times over. We pay for the magazine itself, we pay in diminished self-esteem, and then the biggest cost, we fork out billions for products to alleviate this damage to our self-value. Women's magazines persuade us to overidentify with the physical ("bodyism") and buy into stereotypes like the "thin-ideal" as the only way to attract men's attention. Women may assume that thinness is important to men, but studies show that men prefer curvaceous, pear-shaped women with larger hips.[11]

The popularized ideal woman is so distorted that it's actually unattainable except through costly products and services, such as surgery, the modern equivalent of Victorian corsets. This is what the beauty business wants—the dependence of women on the products and services that only they can supply.

The Feminist Majority—a women's movement promoting legal, social, and political equality—reports that in America alone, the takings from the beauty industry are close to $30 billion a year.[12] So someone is having a lot of fun making money by pulling the wool over our exquisitely made-up eyes!

## LOGIC ASIDE

Our subconscious mind is being bamboozled with graphically retouched visuals, which means that glamour and success never appear old: If a woman interviewed for an editorial is sixty years old, her picture will be retouched to make her look forty. In comparison, our natural wrinkles make us feel defective, so we become increasingly vulnerable to the industry's onslaught.

Notice how the number of miracle cures for fat, cellulite, and aging is increasing. If they were indeed miraculous, we'd be seeing a decrease in the number of large or wrinkled women, and how come those who use these products keep having to buy more of them? Logic may be telling us the obvious, yet the lies are still getting the better of us. How many products do you have on your shelves that have not lived up to their promises?

When it comes to fat, anyone who has rapidly shed some lard knows that the weight inevitably creeps back on again. This is usually with a few extra pounds to remind us of our previous starvation. Yet the spending continues. So, there must be a few wily alchemists out there capable of turning our fat into gold. (Chapter 5 explores why fat has become such a big issue.)

In *The Beauty Myth,* Naomi Wolf exposes the falsehood of the Professional Beauty Qualification, or PBQ, through which females are hoodwinked into assuming that good looks will translate into career success.[13] This form of control will continue for as long as we women allow people who don't look and dress like models to be taken less seriously.

In the past it may have been true that men preferred to invite good-looking women into the hallowed halls of business. But how seriously were they taken? How many Cindy Crawford or Naomi Campbell lookalikes can you name who are currently directors on the boards of Fortune 500 companies? It is said that people with good looks seem to get promoted more often, and earn more money. . . . But a study shows that more-experienced managers are less likely to be biased toward attractiveness, and highly experienced female managers may be immune to this influence altogether.[14]

## THE POLITICS OF IMAGE

In the 1960s and 1970s, women entering business were forced to emulate men and downplay their sexuality. Their attire was severe and asexual, to keep men's thoughts on the ball of business rather than on those in their own lower regions. Decades later men's tendency to focus on the desires of their lower region hasn't shifted. The species survival instinct is said to genetically program men to prefer younger women, as they're likely to be more fertile. Big breasts symbolize fertility, as does fair hair for Caucasian men. In the genetic past of Caucasians, blondness was an indicator of youth, thus offering men the promise of dominating the full span of a woman's reproductive life.[15]

Although few men are consciously aware of it, these outdated indicators of fertility still make women more sexually desirable.

In business, no matter how professional a woman's conduct, the sexual conquest is often top-of-mind for males, especially if the woman is young. After thirty-five, a woman is considered less desirable as a sperm receptacle, which is devastating for those who've relied on their physical sexual allure to get where they want. But for women who wish to have their intelligence taken seriously, age comes as a welcome relief.

As long as we obsess about wrinkles, inches, and calories, are we not condoning men's behavior? When we viciously criticize our sisters for their appearance, are we not giving others permission to judge women on image alone?

Think back to women in powerful posts, such as Maggie Thatcher, Madeleine Albright, and Indira Gandhi. It's an understatement to say that none of these women prioritized the prerequisite PBQ in their careers. But, for their supporters, did their image detract from the power of their positions? Of course, none of these women escaped criticism about their image, but judging from their behavior, they didn't toe the line when it came to the media's superficial demands. These women, and countless others like them, expose the contradiction of the PBQ—looks may get you a few wolf whistles, but will they get the horn blown for your achievements?

The other side of this coin, of course, is a woman such as Madonna. Few could deny that she has a PBQ. Nevertheless, she is still lambasted for overstepping the mark with her forthright sexuality. She attracts labels like "slut" and "whore," and the reaction to her image makes it clear that society dictates some fine lines when it comes to female behavior. Perhaps the supermodels are the only ones who can hack it in this type of society—they are waiflike and good-looking, and their job also requires them to be silent. Methinks this may be what some men really want.

Despite women's progress, or perhaps because of it, the notion of the PBQ is being increasingly emphasized from an early age.

Girls as young as five or six years old are influenced by pop stars like Britney Spears, Beyoncé, and Christina Aguilera. Instead of pointing fingers at men who treat women as objects, these stars are staging their own rebellion by using sexual domination as power. For young fans it's unfortunate that their idols are using the stereotypical PBQ to make their point, because it perpetuates the idea that a woman's main value lies in being beautiful, skinny, and raunchy. But what happens to these girls' self-concept when their bodies mature into more womanly figures?

## SISTERS ARE DOING IT TO THEMSELVES

Recall the Bill Clinton sexual harassment debacle: The fact that Monica Lewinsky was large and Hillary Rodham Clinton had thick ankles and bad hair days was as talked about as was his undisciplined member. In the height of the media frenzy, many women seemed to forget who the victims were.

The late Princess Diana is another tragic example. Owned by the image cops, she conformed to the harsh social expectations. We know she paid a hefty price for doing so, and more and more she is becoming an icon for the misery this overidentification with image can inflict upon any one of us.

The same cruel treatment was meted out to Sarah Ferguson. Although she eventually did conform to the demands of the thin-guard, she was fortunate to have had a more rebellious nature.

For successful women, protecting the privacy of one's image is an onerous task. Look at Oprah Winfrey. For years the vipers have been on her case. But whether she's large or slim, of what relevance is her size to the contribution she is making? While many seem to expect Oprah to do something about her weight, few people insist that her colleague, Phil McGraw, do something about his genetic inheritance, his baldness.

This superficial treatment of women will continue until we take a stand. As long as we indulge in media that perpetuate these ideas, we are sending out messages that their shallow pulp is of value.

## TRANSPARENCY'S IN FASHION

Although young women often use fashion to make subversive statements, it's heartwarming that the more mature a woman becomes, the more she starts to vote with her wallet. Many older women today seem less concerned with the fact that skirt or trouser lengths may be up or down, and has anyone these days got the time to care whether pastels, purple, or orange parade as the "new black"?

Many can see the connection between the increasing inanity of fashion and the upward spiraling of female independence. From the creative absurdities seen on the ramps to street vogue, plenty of women are concluding that fashion's prime function is to mock the fairer sex. Don't just believe me, though—tune in to the dedicated fashion channels. If a good laugh is what you're after, this is where you're guaranteed to find it.

Fashion absurdities seem to make more sense if interpreted as abstract paintings rather than something to sport on one's back. Not even the classic business suit is shown without a nipple peeking—perfect, of course, for that somber boardroom presentation!

But perhaps there's more to the fashion industry than meets the eye.

Unlike men's garb, in which a suit mostly remains a suit, female styling through the years has been dictated by social history. Fads are manipulated, depending on the prevailing political climate, and this climate favors what best suits men. Nowhere is this more evident than after the Second World War.

During the war years many women stepped into industry and made a place for themselves. But the minute the war was over, women were sent back home and fashion became frivolous and impractical, emphasizing feminine delicacy and frailty: Dresses were hourglass shaped, sporting sweetheart necklines in flowery prints. The wearing of overalls and earning of bucks were again reserved only for those with penises. The new reverence for femininity was the main incentive encouraging women to go back to the kitchen sink in droves, and in one of the most callous and calculating manipulations, fashion responded.

And since all jobs were reserved for males, it's no coincidence men of this era also dominated haute couture. Here began the predominance of men in the industry, and while there are many women in fashion, the male slant is but one of the factors that's distorted the female image; the other is the highly profitable diet industry.

Some prominent male designers, like Giorgio Armani, switched from men's to women's fashion, and many followed in their footsteps. A designer I know claimed he switched to women's design because "When it comes to styling you can only push a man so far." No prizes for guessing who the real pushovers are!

However, when it comes to shifts in body image, the issue is not whom men in the fashion industry choose to bed, but rather what they advance as being attractive. Today it's clearly not the full roundness of a real woman's body.

Prior to the recent comeback of breasts, runway models looked asexual and androgynous, their bodies more like those of undeveloped boys than full-fledged females. Often their shoulder blades were more pronounced than their breasts. The most natural parts of the female form, like hips, bums, and tummies, virtually vanished from ramp modeling.

Starting with Twiggy, modern models encapsulate the image of a man's perfect woman—barely there at all! The real irony is that while the female image created by the men of the fashion industry has become the "ideal" female form, it doesn't coincide with what men actually find desirable in real life. Evidently the boys have got the last laugh on this one!

The last natural feminine form appearing as an image icon was that of Marilyn Monroe. Her womanly hips were exaggerated by tight clothing, yet nowadays she'd be considered too fat for a career in modeling. Her body just wouldn't conform to the gaunt and asexual look necessary to model fashion today. When she died, though, few realized that the death knell also rang for the bona fide female form.

## THE DEATH OF THE FEMALE FORM

The transition from voluptuous to skinny happened rapidly. An older woman acquaintance of mine was a sought-after runway model in her younger years. She recalls the switch well: When her bookings started to wane, she was told it was because her breasts were too large for the new skin-and-bone era. Yet in Monroe's time her ample assets were the very feature making her most desirable.

In the 1950s, the weight of a model was 8 percent below average.

Today it's more than 25 percent below. One of the medical criteria for anorexia nervosa is being 15 percent under regular body weight.[16] This means that for girls in the modeling profession, anorexia is a prerequisite. Although some prominent designers have made moves to address this distortion, it's unlikely that the industry will start flaunting normal-size bodies. So a move from 25 percent below average weight to 15 percent or 10 percent still leaves us in the pin-thin category.

Only 1 percent of women have pin-thin physiques naturally.[17] Given this statistic, if the female public follows the "thin ideal," it's obvious that 99 percent have to starve themselves to become "desirably" anorexic.

Like the general population, many models do not fit the 1 percent either, so most have to find ways of appeasing their appetite. Too often this is achieved by an unhealthy dose of drug taking. No longer are these narcotics just diet pills with their harmful side effects; today we're talking serious drugs like heroin.[18]

It's no wonder that "junkie-chic" models look so petulant—if your job demanded having to starve yourself, wouldn't you be grumpy too? When it comes to image, many of the role models we admire are, in effect, asexual drug addicts. So, why are we surprised when our daughters start showing the same tendencies?

## OF BALLOONING BREASTS AND BONY BODY BAGS

Until we change the relationship we have with our body, we cannot expect that our daughters will do things differently. But while we enthusiastically subscribe to the media's portrayals of the female body, our daughters will eagerly follow in our footsteps.

This is especially important as the media today features models who are often fourteen to fifteen years old masquerading as adult women.

Cosmetic artistry is used to make these girls appear more mature, and while they may have breasts, their absence of hips and tummies still shows the bodily form of a young girl.

In an issue of *Shape* magazine, the lingerie feature titled "Feeling Flirty" showed images of a model in poses more suited to a little girl. In some of the images her head was coyly cocked to one side and her toes shyly curled inward, and in another her obviously transparent underwear revealed a complete absence of pubic hair.[19]

What we need to consider is the grave consequences of emblazoning young girls' bodies as the epitome of sexual desirability. By cloaking girls in the mantle of sexual maturity are we not furthering the possibility of their abuse? The media portrayal is "normalizing" immature bodies as the pinnacle of female sexuality, and for young girls who are innocently exploring their own body and their sensuality, the consequences may be dire. This is particularly relevant given the increase in the incidence of date rape and young women's involuntary ingestion of date rape drugs like Rohypnol.

The emergence of soft-pornography images into mainstream advertising is another disquieting trend.[20] While the "come hither" look may now be passé, today's images are of pre- or postorgasmic women, with perfume advertising being the most blatant culprit. Some examples include Gucci Rush (a woman with hair tousled, mouth open, eyes closed in ecstasy, and the image washed with a red tint screaming passion), Dior Addict (woman with bra half-removed, tugging at her G-string, face turned away with only a mirror image revealing her ecstasy), Dolce & Gabbana (man standing behind a woman grabbing her breast with one hand, and in the other he is ready to rip her bra strap, her facial expression: ecstasy).

These examples contain a powerful underlying message: Women need a perfect body, a flawless face, and, of course that particular perfume to achieve the heights of ecstasy.

It's also no fluke that the model's face is invariably turned from view: Firstly it confirms how uncomfortable society is with a woman's sexual potency, and secondly it fulfills the male fantasy of anonymous sex.

Commenting on the era of the 1970s when women became political about womanhood, Naomi Wolf said, "Anonymity became the aphrodisiac of the moment. . . . If women were going to have sexual freedom and a measure of worldly power, they'd better learn to fuck like men."[21]

In an apparent reversal of this trend, Hugo Boss carries the slogan "Your Fragrance, Your Rules." But in the print version the Hugo Boss model is shown on all fours with the submissive expression of a pussycat. So, remind me, whose rules are we playing by here?

The media onslaught also reveals that the more sexual freedom females take, the more the natural and tender version of intimate, loving sex gets pushed aside as dull. So too has the normal state of our bodies become unacceptable. How comfortable would you be seducing a man without your makeup, with your armpits and legs a bit hairy and your cellulite and jiggly bum showing? In no way will this affect your ability to achieve orgasm, nor will it affect a man's performance, but this is not the point. The problem exists in our mind, because we've been programmed to find the natural female form unacceptable.

As a result women put themselves on constant sex alert, ready-shaven legs, well-manicured Brazilian, enticing underwear, and permanent makeup. We can't just be and let our hair down. But letting our jeans down is another thing entirely: For men the best women's clothes are the ones that come off fastest. Fashion poses frequently show zippers undone and straps tumbling off a woman's shoulder. The implied sexual readiness is often taken further by showing the model with her legs wide open, or with her thumbs in her trousers or G-string as if waiting for a command to whip off her remaining clothes.

Although women have taken so much more freedom in all areas, the escalation in mainstream media porn is retrogressive. It's the same old story: Female sexual energy is a potent force of creativity and personal power, so male dominance insists upon denigrating it.

Pornography reinforces the notion that the only thing women are good for is sex, but only as long as sex is something done to a woman; she must remain a passive recipient of a man's desire rather than an active participant. In other words, she has little control over the situation.

Wolf points out the consequences of constantly repeating these images: "A quarter of young women have had sexual encounters where the male denied her control."[22] If women, especially young women, have no authority over their bodies, what chance do they have of protecting their life by insisting on the use of condoms?

Bombardment with "sexy" images is blurring the line between pornography and sensuality. Slowly but surely pornographic images are becoming more acceptable to women, and with an increasing number of female authors writing about women's eroticism, the issue is becoming very confusing. However, there is a big difference between women celebrating the physical, emotional, and spiritual power of their own sexuality and men reducing the value of a woman to nothing more than her sex organs.

As lecherous literature becomes mainstream, so it influences advertising, which is one of the reasons for the return of ballooning breasts. But unlike for Monroe, where an ample bosom was balanced by womanly hips and thighs, for those subscribing to the "thin ideal," big breasts pose a problem. If you slim down to the size of a pencil, your breasts will be two empty pencil cases. But the surgeons have the answer to staying pencil thin and having big breasts all at the same time—implants!

## SILLY-CONES

Breast augmentation is big on the current fashion agenda, but few will believe that the risks are real. The National Center for Policy Research for Women and Families says that, although today's materials are supposed to be sturdier, all breast implants will break eventually.[23] Half of first-time augmentation patients experience complications within the first three years, and many require a high degree of surgical maintenance throughout the implant's lifecycle. Cost aside, breakage poses the danger of chemicals migrating to major organs, which can lead to catastrophic health problems.

Whether implants are filled with saline or silicone, breast tissue can harden around the capsule. This interferes with feeling and makes the breasts very hard, misshapen, overly sensitive, severely painful, or asymmetrical. If removal of the implants becomes necessary (which breakage makes inevitable), this hardened tissue requires the surgical procedure of mastectomy.

Whether hardening occurs or not, implants cause breast tissue to stretch, leaving the patient looking malformed (and scarred) after removal. More dangerous still, some implants interfere with the detection of breast cancer because they obscure the mammography image of tumors.

A National Cancer Institute study found that women who had breast implants for at least seven to twelve years were more likely to die from brain tumors; lung, cervical, and vulva cancer; other respiratory diseases; and suicide compared with other plastic surgery patients. Scandinavian studies reported that women who had breast implants for augmentation were three times more likely to commit suicide compared to women in the general population.[24] This contradicts the manufacturers' assertion that implants improve a woman's feeling of self-worth. Although researchers at the National Cancer Institute were unable to establish whether implants directly caused these problems, their findings are scary enough.

On a lighter note few people are warned that implants are ice-cold in winter, and some women with saline-filled capsules report that when moving they can hear their breasts sloshing around.

Equally absurd are the new pills available on the Internet "guaranteeing" breast augmentation. If they work, heaven alone knows what these concoctions must do to the rest of a woman's physical system. With bosoms vaulting to a new high in popularity, the top-heavy bony body bag has become the new ideal. But when fashion reverts back to revering bee stings for breasts, where will all the breast-augmented patients be?

Breasts aside, what's happening at the butt end of fashion? With the arrival of women like pop star J.Lo, the big happening of 2003 was the comeback of the voluptuous bottom. For those of us already well-endowed in this department, the fact that fashion has finally caught up with our rear ends is vindication. But those with less-well-endowed bottoms are the prey of surgical magicians offering the latest bum deal. Micro-fat grafting transfers fat from one locale to another, but those with no spare tire are plumping up their rear ends with cheek cushions. Could this mean that leaking from both ends will become the modern symbol for being a well-balanced woman in the future?

Regardless of the risks and costs, some women will do anything to achieve the latest fashion in physical form. Lolo Ferrari succeeded in sporting the biggest breast implants on the planet. Along with her zeppelinlike chest, she had many other cosmetic operations. Did any of this make her happy? Evidently not: She died of a prescription drug overdose at thirty-one.

Cindy Jackson literally tried to transform herself into Mattel's anatomically incorrect Barbie. Cyndi Tebbel (author of *The Body Snatchers*) claims that Jackson spent $100,000 volunteering for the knife on twenty-seven occasions![25] Among other things, she had breast implants, tummy tucks, a full face-lift, nose job, ear tucks, liposuction, cheek implants, and some of the fat on her bum transferred to make her lips more voluptuous. I saw a documentary about her, and, not unattractive beforehand, she claimed that the full sculptural overhaul was necessary to rescue her sagging sense of self-value.

Then there is Elizabeth Christensen, who surgically altered her face to look like the Egyptian queen Nefertiti.[26] All that could be said about the result was that she looked like a poorly cloned Michael Jackson.

Many women recast themselves in the image of physical perfection, with plastic breasts and plastic smiles.

It's clear that the media's influence in this area is powerfully detrimental, but what of the surgeons? It's naive in the extreme to expect doctors such as these to have your health and well-being at heart—they're business people!

## PROTESTING AGAINST THE INEVITABLE

Looking flawless doesn't mean that a woman is okay on the inside too, and no matter how marvelous we may appear, no amount of surgery can heal the emotional damage we've experienced. So our desperate attempts to find fulfillment through remolding our bodies can only lead to confusion and disillusionment. No matter whether we've got an A cup or a double D, or if we're in our gardening gear or flannel pajamas, glowing from the inside is what makes us shine.

Nevertheless, in the United States alone cosmetic surgery rakes in some $10 billion per annum,[27] and this is increasing. Whether they get breast implants, face-lifts, liposuction, or vaginal tucks, women are spending huge amounts to protest against the inevitable: maturity. Those who battle to accept their age are rushing for the knife, and by doing so they hope to be a cut above their younger sisters.

Many of us know women who had seemingly simple cosmetic operations that resulted in permanent disfigurement. Even if liposuction had only killed or maimed one woman, it's one of vanity's too many victims. Yet, regardless of the risks, women still rush in.

This misdirected behavior seems to know no bounds. I know of women who have taken out insurance policies for the sole purpose of having their sagging flesh uplifted in their midfifties! These are not wealthy women, but the most adamant among them are those who are currently single. They believe that youthful looks are the best insurance against having to finally become independent.

In addition, the industry has convinced women that they are doing this for themselves. This manipulation was a crucial point in rescuing the "image business" from the damage done to it by feminism. But we need to ask ourselves: If we felt loved and fulfilled in our work and relationships, would we take these health risks and pay so much? And if Rubenesque voluptuousness became the ideal, would those who'd had their hips and tummies vacuumed turn around and demand that the surgeons put all the fat back again?

## THE APPEAL OF PARALYSIS

If the desire for these procedures is motivated by retaining your sexual appeal, perhaps consider the following: When your breasts are as rigid as torpedoes, your face stretched beyond a smile, and your flesh as responsive as that of a blow-up doll, how sexy will you feel . . . and how sexy will he find you?

If you think this is an exaggeration, consider the effect of Botox injections. This treatment doesn't remove wrinkles; it just paralyzes your facial muscles. By doing so you are prevented from creasing up your frowns or wrinkly crevices. Worse still, the paralysis is achieved from the deadly bacterium that makes botulism a lethal form of food poisoning.

Dr. Peter Misra, a clinical neurophysiologist writing in the *British Medical Journal,* wrote, "While immediate adverse reactions to Botox are rare, evidence for the long-term effects has not been gathered."[28] Claiming that Botox could affect the brain, nervous system, and muscles, he appealed to today's guinea pigs to treat the drug with caution.

However, Botox must also affect people's intelligence, because you can receive a "happy hour" treatment at a party where your injections are served up in between a glass of champagne and the canapés, despite medical warnings that Botox and alcohol don't mix. The 4.1 million procedures conducted in 2006 make Botox the leading choice when it comes to noninvasive surgical procedures.[29] Evidently women (and some men) are queuing to disable the most expressive part of their bodies, even though research has shown that for a quarter of women applying for this treatment, psychotherapy would have been a more appropriate choice.[30]

It would seem that the look counts more than anything else, including the discomfort and potential danger. Even more disturbing is the multitude of surgical addicts who now believe the scalpel is a normal part of their maintenance program.

## "CIVILIZED" FEMALE MUTILATION

Although surgery presents itself as a modern and civilized practice, how close is it to age-old social customs that have consistently abused women? Extreme forms of this include female genital mutilation, a practice that still happens in many places, including immigrant communities in North America and Europe.[31] In certain cultures in Africa and the Middle and Far East, until a girl's vagina has been mutilated, she is not considered an adult and is unacceptable for marriage. Barbaric customs such as these may horrify Western women, but what's so different about cosmetic surgery, starving yourself, or the hellishly painful process of vaginal tightening? The big difference is that we are selecting ourselves for mutilation rather than other women in our culture forcing it upon us. Have you seen (or been) a woman recovering from a face-lift or laser skin peeling? If you are still thinking about it, visit the wards and chat with the bandaged-up mummies before doing so.

This is an important way of counteracting nonsense TV programs like *Extreme Makeover.* Realistically, shows like *Extreme Makeover* are about as interesting as watching some poor sod having his appendix removed. But the appeal is that these programs don't dwell on the blood and gore or the weeks of agony it takes to heal from a face-lift or chemical burn. Instead they play up the usual quick-fix myth that you too can be miraculously transformed . . . in about an hour or so.

Naturally, women just don't have pin-thin bodies with bulging breasts and bottoms, and without a little help from our surgeon friends, our upper lips could never reach such vulvalike proportions. What a powerful team the media and the butchers have made!

## WELL WHITTLED VS. WELL-BEING

What's even crazier is that if we're doing all this for men, it's point-less, because most men I know who are the partners of well-whittled women were adamantly against these procedures in the first place. They say they'd prefer real women to cuddle rather than plastic versions served up by surgeons.

This obsession with our bodies reveals our ignorance about what actually excites and ultimately satisfies men in relationships. Ironically many men have become more "feminist" in their choice of an ideal woman than most females expect.

Sam Keen, author of *Fire in the Belly,* says a man will be more sexually attracted to a woman who is powerful and accomplished than to those who are physically beautiful.[32] When men were asked about their top ten qualities in women, they listed the following: intelligence, sense of humor, physical attractiveness, independence, trustworthi-ness, sense of adventure, good values, self-confidence, sex appeal, and kindness.

When asked which of these qualities they would most likely compromise on, physical attractiveness was the first to go—albeit they admitted so reluctantly.[33] So humor, guts, inner strength, and the excitement of growth in their relationship are the emotional connec-tions that are more likely to turn men on in the long run. It's not for nothing that sex therapists talk about the mind as the primary sex organ.

When it comes to our sensuality, what's even more absurd is that after body-enhancing procedures, many women are left with little or no feeling in the body parts that were treated. Slim and wrinkle free they may be, but what's the point when your skin is lifeless and untouchable?

In volunteering for such procedures, all we're doing is showing our tacit agreement with the notion that only youth has value.

## GROWING OLDER WITH INTEREST

I'm enormously excited about the benefits of age. Mature women don't need to curtsey to social demands; we can allow ourselves to manifest the power of individuality that comes with age. Age frees us to explore more of ourselves, which adds greatly to life's adventure. We can be unapologetically cantankerous, and our behavior is put down to age. If we challenge the system our words are considered wise rather than rebellious. Life experience also makes us more discerning and less gullible.

One of the great benefits of age is that the knowledge that comes with it makes the world more transparent, so we can maneuver around systems that baffled us when we were younger. Age allows us to see things in perspective and think more clearly. Certainly, for those opting for success, it's only these empowering benefits that ultimately make achievement possible.

But mainstream media has a vested interest in ignoring or downplaying the benefits of age. Just think of cosmetics. Mostly the manufacturers are targeting those allergic to their age . . . and the biggest suckers here are us Baby Boomers, the first generation simply refusing to grow old. Remember the days when a cheap and cheerful cream was more than adequate as skin protection? Today some women can spend up to $500 for a month's supply. Just the word "antiwrinkle" on the jar is enough to magically inflate the price tag.

Whether you accept them or not, wrinkles speak volumes about how a woman has laughed, wept, loved, and loathed. Certainly any realistic beautician, independent of a sponsoring cosmetics house, will tell you that no amount of expensive cream will wipe off the life experience etched into our older faces.

When it comes to the ludicrous claims (i.e., youthfulness promised in a couple of weeks) made by these exorbitantly priced little potions, Anita Roddick has the final word: Antiwrinkle cream is just God's way of testing who is stupid!

It looks like self-sacrifice has genetically mutated our species into one big bullshit receptor.

So it seems that women are not neurotic about their image, because this is something we genuinely want. Nor are we doing this because men demand it. We're doing so for no other reason except that the modern marketing myth programs women to do so. Certainly this doesn't come from our womanhood, because it's no longer about what's attractive anymore—now it's all about money.

## MILLIONS CAN BE WRONG—OR RIGHT

The facts are simple. There are only a few hundred people controlling the beauty industry. But the greenbacks are in our hands, so we can be discerning about where we invest them. If you doubt claims that a company's advertising is making or disapprove of the way it depicts women, don't buy its products.

Product failure delivers a far more potent message than a protest letter to the company.

You can also set up a dynamic list on the Internet and mass email it to a thousand of your closest friends!

Additionally, you can file a complaint about sexist, deceitful, or offensive advertising with the Federal Trade Commission or the attorney general of your state. This will probably send a few people into a tailspin because your objection puts at risk the hundreds of thousands spent creating these tacky little advertising messages. By filing a complaint one hopes that those involved in sexist nonsense may be a bit more conscious about women in the future.

Another way to make mischief is to send products that fail to live up to their promises back to cosmetics houses. Be creative or downright rude in your letter and demand a response. The easiest way to get a reply is find out who the product manager is by name, address the letter to him/her personally, enclose a dollar bill with your letter, and demand a receipt. You can sarcastically suggest that the money is a donation to their feeble research and development department. The point of the money is that employees are not allowed to accept cash from customers, and, because they won't be able to supply a receipt, they have to return it, forcing a response.

I find it obscene that some $80 billion (diet industry combined with cosmetics and cosmetic surgery) is spent in one country on appearance fraud. This situation occurs in the same world where millions of women are violently abused and are genuinely starving.

For the weight-loss addicts, how about encouraging the World Health Organization (WHO) to organize a campaign to feed famished children from our excess? WHO could encourage dieters to adopt a starving child. You could be sending money to your adopted dependent instead of spending money on more food or unhealthy diet products, or both. Photographs could be exchanged both ways. As you get thinner you would receive pictures of your child looking healthier. This is real feel-good stuff and could help reduce the unhappiness that makes so many people fill their faces.

As so much money is invested in cosmetics, why not also insist that the purveyors of these highly profitable products donate a good percentage of their profits to women's causes? Naomi Wolf details just some of the things the money spent on cosmetics could buy: three times the amount of daycare currently on offer; fifty women's universities; 2,000 women's health clinics; 75,000 women's film, music, literature, or art festivals; or one million highly paid domestic or childcare workers. It could also buy one million support workers for the elderly, 33,000 battered women's shelters, two billion tubes of contraceptive cream, or 400,000 full four-year university scholarships . . .[34] and heaven only knows how much staple food for the women and children living in desperate poverty.

Companies like The Body Shop (which empowers communities worldwide) and MAC (which donates money to AIDS centers) have started the ball rolling, but the reason that this isn't happening on a broader scale is that we are not demanding it. Remember the power of the anti-animal-cruelty campaigns? Although it's a moot point whether animal testing has ceased altogether, the awareness made women boycott the most awful perpetrators.

Now, with the power and simplicity of the Internet, a campaign to force redistribution of profit into women's causes is easy to organize. After all, why should a few company directors (and shareholders) alone profit from our image neuroses?

When it comes to our personal lives, women who put their energy into self-development are far happier than those who strive to be skinny and beautiful. Instead of forking out a lot of money on surgery, injections, or even a cream, buy an inspiring book, sign up for a self-development program, or see a shrink. These latter options will do more for your health and happiness (and your relationship) than anything you put on (or in) your face. Self-development also provides the fodder for a lot more interesting conversation than foundation, antiwrinkle cream, or mascara.

Politically, nothing is a more powerful distraction from the female conscience than focusing on bodyism. So notice how many times a day you think about what you look like. Question whether this is something that really concerns you, or if it's more about what you think is expected.

Far healthier than raging at our physical imperfections is learning self-acceptance—this will save us plenty of money, anguish, and much unhappiness.

The beauty industry treats us like morons, but we can defy it by acting intelligently. If we're not prepared to act, even on a personal level, then we'd better heed the words of Elizabeth Barrett Browning: "If a woman ignores these wrongs, then may women as a sex continue to suffer them; there is no help for any of us—let us be dumb and die."[35]

# CHAPTER 5.

# Looks That Kill

In few areas is women's self-sacrificing tendency as obvious, or as literally suicidal, as in our all-consuming obsession with weight. And this is despite the fact that our female psyche, if only we'd hear it, does not believe that waiflike anorexia is healthy or even attractive. Women obsess about their weight simply because they're bowing to a false ideal.

We've been thoroughly bamboozled, as evidenced by this supposedly tongue-in-cheek T-shirt slogan I saw: INSIDE OF ME THERE'S A THIN WOMAN TRYING TO GET OUT, BUT I CAN USUALLY SHUT THE BITCH UP WITH SOME CHOCOLATE."

Today's weight-loss industry is one of the most successful swindles ever.

When journalist Terry Poulton (author of *No Fat Chicks*) completed a comprehensive investigation into the North American diet industry, she concluded, "What I ultimately discovered is that the whole diet phenomenon is *not* [her italics] about beauty or how much women weigh at all. It's about how much we can be persuaded to spend trying to be thin. The entire process is just a despicable scheme to guarantee annual sales of weight-loss products and services currently estimated at $3 billion in Canada and more than $40 billion in the United States."[1]

## THE BILLION-DOLLAR BRAINWASH

Poulton refers to the diet industry as the "billion-dollar brainwash." Anyone who has seen a weight-loss advertisement will know that these products are promoted with powerful emotional appeal, science that is mostly groundless, and many promises.

No matter what product or program dieters use, in time, 95–98 percent will regain not just the weight they've lost but a good few extra pounds to top it.[2]

## NEVER SATISFIED

With the prognosis for keeping the pounds off at 2–5 percent, you'd think that dieting, as a way of life, wouldn't have much credibility. But women, as we know already, are riddled with guilt and feelings of inadequacy, so all the manufacturers need to do is blame females when their products don't live up to the preposterous promises. And all over the world women lambaste themselves for their lack of willpower. And what if the weight did stay off permanently? Where would the diet industry find future victims to fatten its own coffers?

According to *Never Satisfied,* Hillel Schwartz's social history of dieting, the diet industry gained momentum as a means of increasing the sales of products that were traditionally prescribed for indigestion.[3]

On looking into the origins of diet "medicine," Schwartz came up with some horrifying findings. One of the earliest drugs to be applied to weight loss was dinitrophenol, a derivative of benzene used in dyes and certain explosives.

In the 1930s an estimated 100,000 people took the drug, and while some simply perspired excessively, developed grim rashes, or lost their sense of taste, others went blind and a few died.

Dinitrophenol is an industrial poison that is not flushed by the system; when accumulated it will speed up metabolic rate until the body literally burns itself up. Although it was prohibited in 1938, a shady Texas doctor revived dinitrophenol, and the product made a brief comeback in the 1980s.

In the 1970s amphetamines, commonly known as "speed," were the appetite suppressants of choice. Annually, two billion amphetamine pills were gulped down, and equal numbers of downers (barbiturates) were required to put these medically sanctioned addicts to sleep. Not only are amphetamines highly addictive, but long-term use leads to heart damage, stroke, kidney failure, seizures, psychosis, and sudden death.[4]

You may be reassuring yourself that these incidents occurred because of the pharmacological ignorance of the past. But some of the products emerging onto the market since make amphetamines look as innocent as a package of cheerful M&Ms.

In her book titled *Losing It,* Laura Fraser turned her obsession with weight loss into a passion to expose the diet industry.[5] As an investigative journalist who battled a chronic eating disorder, she personally tested many of the modern diet products. At best she found them to be a massive con, at worst downright dangerous. Whether we're talking paperback diets, commercial eating plans, or new drugs more lethal than those of the past, the findings of both Fraser and Poulton paint a picture that looks far from healthy and even further from attractive.

From the 1980s onward, a profusion of diet paperbacks hit the market. For instance, *Dr. Atkins' Diet Revolution* assured us if we ate vast quantities of protein and fat but held back on carbohydrates, we would thin down to the size of a waif.[6]

Next came Judy Mazel's Beverly Hills Diet, with such a fondness for fruit that temporary weight loss was primarily caused by the frequent occurrence of the world falling out of your bottom.[7] This Mazel spiritedly saluted as a very good sign.

By 1983 there were 360 diet books on the market, by 1995 this increased to 700, and from then on you could take your pick of titles ranging from the mundane to the absurd. Examples of these include The Complete Scarsdale Medical Diet, the I Love New York Diet, the

Diet Type Weight Loss diet, the Pray Your Weight Away diet, and the Macrobiotic Diet (or the Macro-Idiotic Diet as my husband calls it).

Eating disorders pioneer Susan Wooley condemned the juicy Beverly Hills Diet as the first instance of anorexia nervosa being recommended as a cure for obesity.[8] Even so, Mazel's book was a bestseller for many years.

In the 1970s the American Medical Association (AMA) hauled the late Dr. Atkins, a cardiologist, over the coals for recommending not only large quantities of protein but also portions of animal fat that were large enough to be potentially dangerous for the heart. Although the AMA claimed his actions bordered on malpractice, his books kept selling by the millions, and Atkins continued unperturbed writing bestsellers until his death in 2003. The Scarsdale Diet followed similar principles, and as a result of the difficulty digesting such enormous quantities of protein, followers of this regimen suffered high levels of cholesterol, bad breath, constipation, nausea, and weakness.[9] Even so, doctors recommending high-protein diets are still with us today, but now they bash heads with others who are adamant that low-fat, high-carbohydrate eating plans will make fat melt away.

## THE DIET INDUSTRY PLAYS ON

Fanatical dieters don't seem to find any contradictions in the abundance of conflicting information on the market. Too often after a failed diet they simply console themselves with the notion that different body types require different ways of eating. So if low fat, high carb doesn't do it, then fruit must be right. When fruit fails then high protein is it. When boiled eggs and tomato juice also fall short, nil-per-mouth starvation fasts provide the hope they are looking for.

This never-ending roller coaster ensures high levels of failure, and the diet industry thrives.

What the weight obsessed are not getting is that any diet will cause short-term loss of weight, so they therefore deduce that if they had persisted a bit longer, the reduction would have been permanent. Anyone who has been on a restrictive eating plan knows the physical, emotional, and mental hardship that goes with sticking to it. Even those who manage to lose weight initially can't maintain the same starvation routine once they've reached their goal. Restricted eating plans lead to binge cycles, and this means that goal weight is virtually impossible to maintain. So the cycle of yo-yo dieting begins.

The body adapts to this constant cycle of losing and regaining weight by permanently lowering its metabolism, and career dieters then attribute their sluggish metabolism to a medical condition. Instead of breaking the diet/binge cycle, they try to work even harder to compensate for their diet-hammered underactive thyroid. These repeated "failures" also batter self-esteem, leading to bouts of severe depression. Studies have also linked yo-yo dieting to early death from coronary heart disease.[10]

## GETTING CRANKY

One of the most revealing investigations into the consequences of restricted eating is "The Keys Study" conducted in the 1950s.[11] As the originator of U.S. Army rations, Ancel Keys, a University of Minnesota researcher, recruited young male volunteers who were completing alternative service as conscientious objectors. They were physically and psychologically healthy and of normal weight. For the first three months they ate a regular diet of some 3,500 calories a day; they did chores, exercised, and were cheerful.

For the next six months they were put on a diet similar to those recommended by many commercial weight-loss centers—one of semi-starvation. The men lost weight rapidly and became cranky, lethargic, negative, apathetic, and so argumentative that their regular meetings had to be cancelled. They also became moody, irritable, listless, anxious, and depressed, were indifferent to visitors, lost interest in sex, and became so food obsessed that they spent most of their time fantasizing about the sumptuous chow they'd eat once the study was over.

Like many dieters, they developed long, drawn-out rituals around eating and an unusual interest in cookbooks and menus; three even became chefs after the experiment was over. Gum chewing and consumption of coffee and tea became so out of hand that the experimenters had to limit their intake, and some started nail biting or smoking. They also became hoarders of nonfood items, something that is also observed in anorexic patients. On a cognitive level, concentration was impaired, as was comprehension and judgment. They also experienced the physiological symptoms of dizziness, headaches, hair loss, and slowing of heart and metabolic rate.

Even after the men stopped dieting, the symptoms of their misery persisted. What's more, once these men were allowed to eat whatever they desired, they binged. For several weeks afterward their appetite was insatiable, and larger daily portions of food than the normal diet they started with didn't appease their hunger.

Most regained the weight they'd lost, but with one significant difference—many replaced the muscles they formerly had with fat.

The eating plan that caused their misery allowed 1,750 calories per day—for many dieting women this daily intake would be an extravagant smorgasbord compared to the restrictive diets they're surviving on.

Anyone who has stomached a "low-cal" diet will be well aware of these consequences. To lose weight, dieters take untold risks and even tolerate side effects such as hair loss, cold intolerance, anemia, dehydration, irritability, fatigue, weakness, bad breath, gallstones, and cardiac arrhythmia (which can lead to cardiac arrest), as well as loss of muscle tissue (including the lean muscles of the heart). These are the side effects of starving to death.

## JUST ENOUGH TO SURVIVE

In *The Beauty Myth,* Naomi Wolf points out that in the German concentration camps of the Second World War, a ration of 900 calories per day was set as the minimum necessary to sustain human life.[12] Some diets today restrict calorie intake to half of this. The Cambridge Diet, popular in the 1980s, is a liquid protein diet providing a meager 320 calories per day.

When insufficient protein is consumed to sustain physical functioning, the body will cannibalize its own stores, such as muscle tissue and vital organs. Laura Fraser reports that at the time the Cambridge Diet was launched commercially, this product was already responsible for killing fifty-eight people.[13] It is estimated that more than three million people tried the diet, but it took another thirty deaths before the Food and Drug Administration (FDA) forced the by then very wealthy doctors to withdraw it from the market.

As a student in the 1970s I recall all too well the popularity of liquid protein diets. I lived (more like survived) on them myself. But had I known more about their contents I would have been sufficiently grossed out to quickly go back to cornflakes and tasty sandwiches for breakfast and lunch. Liquid protein, in some cases, is derived from products such as animal hides, tendons, bones, glands, or any other waste that can be sourced from the slaughterhouses at rock-bottom prices.[14] These are ground up into the fine powders we purchase—at a premium—and then flavored with enough strawberry, cherry, or chocolate to disguise the foul taste of animal waste. Women still swear by their protein shakes in many different forms, giving new meaning to the phrase "sacred cow." Today some are made from milk proteins, but if you're still tempted to consume these "shakes," it may be worth investigating what they are produced from.

## WHOSE PROBLEM IS IT ANYWAY?

Although both Fraser and Poulton report on the many deaths caused by specific regimens and products like protein shakes, it's of grave concern that no record exists of the total number of women who have experienced diet-related deaths. Death certificates commonly report heart failure, so unless someone is sufficiently concerned, the silent causes of our failing hearts will remain as deeply buried as the tightly sealed graves of the unfortunate women who starved themselves to death.

Regardless of the risks, the diet industry relentlessly continues to convince women that short-term weight loss is a prize worth more than one's career, one's relationships, and one's life. Poulton reports that some women responding to a survey said their most important goal is not professional success, personal fulfillment, a happy home, or financial security, but rather the loss of some ten to twenty pounds.[15]

But the bad news is that in the long term, diets don't make you thin; persistent dieting keeps you fat. Obesity researchers such as Kathy Brownell of Yale University observed that most people stand a better chance of recovering from most forms of cancer than losing weight and keeping it off.[16]

The most tragic consequence of this billion-dollar brainwash is that there are numerous women who'd rather die than be fat. Some consciously take their own life, while others slowly commit suicide from anorexia, replacing food with cigarettes, or constantly popping laxatives, purgatives, and diuretics, and still others consume drugs like amphetamines or heroin.

Although amphetamines have been pushed out of mainstream medicine and onto the streets, they haven't disappeared from today's diet scene. An ingredient widely used in over-the-counter appetite suppressants (and cold and flu medications) is phenylpropanolamine (PPA), a close chemical cousin of speed. Banned in much of the developed world because of its potential for causing hemorrhagic stroke, it is still available in the United States, even to minors.

PPA raises blood pressure, causing anxiety, nervousness, and the jitters. These are symptoms I remember well. When I was younger I recall lying in bed terrified that my heart was beating so violently that it would leap right out of my chest—this after only taking two doses of a similar product.

At the time of writing, the FDA is taking steps to remove PPA from the shelves—but talk about being slow to respond! Fraser reports that in 1970 a professor of medicine at Johns Hopkins University School of Medicine said, "I defy anyone to find another medication that has had so many misadventures so often reported."[17] He went on to state that in the long term the drug is ineffective in keeping weight off and that studies disputing this had been paid for by the diet industry.

In 1989 alone, American Poison Control Centers reported 47,000 complaints, but it took until 2002 for the FDA to act upon the wealth of information it accumulated over thirty years.

A more scandalous tale is the disturbing case against the lethal diet drug Fen-Phen. In *Dispensing with the Truth,* Alicia Mundy weaves such a powerful story of deceit and manipulation that you could be forgiven for thinking you were reading a John Grisham novel with an atypically tragic ending.[18]

Before American Home Products (AHP) (now renamed Wyeth-Ayerst) launched this combination appetite suppressant, one component (fenfluramine) was suspected of causing brain damage in monkeys, and the other (dexfenfluramine or Redux) was annually killing between twenty and forty women in France, before restrictions were called for in that country. After a single research study in the U.S., Fen-Phen was approved and launched as a combination in 1993.

When the combination drug was launched, the manufacturers and the FDA knew that the Redux component could cause primary pulmonary hypertension (PPH), a condition that makes the blood vessels supplying the lungs tighten resulting in the heart having to pump so fast it could fail. PPH is an incurable disease reducing life expectancy to about four years.

After Fen-Phen had been on the market for a while, reports started to filter through about another potentially fatal side effect—chronic heart-valve disease—so severe that a thirty-year-old woman's valves would look like those of a frail octogenarian. While AHP (Wyeth-Ayerst) was enthusiastically marketing the combo drug as a miracle cure for fat, the side effects were killing users. The most well-publicized case was that of a short-term user named Mary Linnen. In 1996 she took Fen-Phen for a few weeks so as to fit into her wedding dress. She arrived at the church not in a wedding dress, but in a coffin, having died of pulmonary hypertension.[19]

Hailed as the latest miracle cure for weight loss in 1993, Fen-Phen is estimated to have been prescribed to more than six million people. After some 45,000 users were believed to have developed symptoms of heart/lung disease and 123 had died, the FDA finally called for withdrawal in 1997.

As a result of a class-action lawsuit, AHP/Wyeth-Ayerst paid out claims to more than 200,000 victims. The longer-term complications in the remaining 5,800,000 users were not known, but claims against the manufacturers continued to the time of writing.

Were the risks worth the benefit dieters gained? Fen-Phen's efficacy was known to be 3 percent. This means that a 200-pound woman would lose just over 6 pounds more weight than if she hadn't been taking it.

## TRICKY TRADE-OFFS

In the year that Fen-Phen was withdrawn, physicians were prescribing Phen-Pro, a combination of phentermine and Prozac. Against the advice of its own committee, the FDA also approved another diet drug,

Meridia (sibutramine). Produced by Abbott Laboratories, Meridia at the time of writing is under regulatory scrutiny because of 397 serious adverse reactions such as the alleged linkage to twenty-nine heart attack deaths. The company denies these allegations,[20] but Ralph Nader's consumer advocacy group—Public Citizen—has called for withdrawal, claiming that the risks of increased blood pressure and heart rate outweigh the benefits.[21] Abbott makes claims about Meridia's potential for a thirty-pound weight loss, yet the Public Citizen's correspondence (with the Department of Health) quotes the FDA as saying the average weight loss in obese people taking the drug for one year was only six pounds more than if they were getting a placebo. When it comes to the public's reaction, evidently the Fen-Phen shock was insufficient to scare people off, because 8.5 million more users are estimated to have taken Meridia. (If you're taking this drug, the URLs for correspondence from both parties have been supplied in the reference section. Read them and decide for yourself.)

Shortly after the flourish of drugs that fiddle with brain chemistry to curb appetite (like Fen-Phen and Meridia), new products started emerging that interfere with the body's ability to absorb fat. Whether these are medical products like Xenical or foodstuffs like Olean (Olestra, Procter & Gamble's low-fat oil for use in snacks and potato chips), there's one consistent little snafu that users may have to contend with—uncontrollable anal leakage.[22] (An Internet wisecracker noted that Procter & Gamble also conveniently produces laundry detergent!)

When it comes to medical products that inhibit the uptake of fat, Roche Pharmaceuticals's website lists the following potential side effects of one of its registered products, Xenical (chemical name: orlistat): oily spotting, flatus with discharge, fecal urgency, fatty/oily stools, oily evacuation, increased defecation, and fecal incontinence.[23] These symptoms, confirmed in a study, are made worse by consuming high-fat meals[24]—something use of the drug may give irresponsible users "permission" to do.

Some over-the-counter products used to trap fat induce a heightened crescendo of farting and can make a greasy substance slide uncontrollably out of one's ass—a bit inelegant when wearing a bumfloss G-string under that sexy little number.

Most fat absorbers and trappers are produced from powdered

shellfish shells, and studies proving their efficacy in weight loss have been inconclusive. About these concoctions sold through infomercials, obesity researchers say, "There are absolutely no studies being carried out to show that these products or any of the ingredients in these products can cause weight loss."[25]

In 2002 *USA Today* reported that between 50 and 100 drugs for the treatment of obesity were in the early stages of development.[26] Due to research costs we can anticipate that only a few of these will hit the market. But in the near future, expect many more companies to promise magical cures and definitive answers to the weight-loss Holy Grail: permanent reduction.

Not to be outdone, herbal product manufacturers also noticed the passing bandwagon and quickly leaped on. Before the ink had dried on the Fen-Phen class-action settlement, the mimic Herbal Phen Fuel was launched. Sales were virtually guaranteed because many consumers naively concluded that goods sold in a health store must be exactly that—good for you. But with products like this one containing the stimulant ephedrine (also known as ma huang), side effects are not too dissimilar from PPA, the dangerous culprit in appetite suppressants. After reviewing 16,000 adverse-event reports, in 2003 the U.S. Department of Health and Human Services (HHS) cautioned about the use of ephedra-containing products, especially under conditions of strenuous exercise and in combination with other stimulants, including caffeine[27]—a stimulant consumed in vast quantities by dieters.

Fraser reports that even something as seemingly benign as a dieters' herbal tea has sent at least one woman to an early grave from heart failure.[28]

We can't expect too much protection from bodies like the FDA, and even less so since legal changes were made to their jurisdiction. Under the Dietary Supplement Health and Education Act of 1994, the FDA does not review dietary supplements for safety before they are marketed and cannot restrict sales unless it proves there is a danger.[29] Whereas previously the burden of proof was on the manufacturer to ascertain the safety of a product, now the FDA has to conduct lengthy and expensive research to prove a product hazardous and pull it from the market. As the FDA is government funded and understaffed, it is highly unlikely that this will happen except in extreme cases.

## BITTERSWEET POISON

An industry that has taken full advantage of the impotency of this toothless protector is the artificial sweetener business. Sweeteners like aspartame are gulped down by 200 million people and are now included in some 6,000 products.[30] According to websites promoting aspartame, this product is perfectly safe, and any information to the contrary is dismissed as unsubstantiated Internet hoaxes. Well there must be a lot of people busy with these hoaxes, because a simple web search reveals millions of hits, many of which are sites quoting research from doctors, some of whom were sufferers of aspartame disease themselves.[31] According to the Department of Health and Human Services, ninety adverse symptoms were listed in 1994. Among others these include mood disturbances (including depression), chronic fatigue, digestive tract problems, eating disorders, headaches, migraines, heart palpitations, anxiety and panic disorders, skin rashes, impotency, menstrual problems, brain tumors, and cancer.[32] Although approved by our good old faithful protector, aspartame accounted for 75 percent of adverse reactions to food additives reported to the FDA. Some of these were serious, including seizures and death. However, since they are listed as a "food additive," these sweeteners are exempt from FDA safety monitoring.

Aspartame is the sweetener in NutraSweet, Equal, Spoonful, Equal Measure, and many diet colas, and just one of the problems is that it contains methyl alcohol. When released into the small intestine, this is converted into formaldehyde (embalming fluid), but worse still digestion further changes formaldehyde into formic acid, otherwise known as ant poison. The pro propaganda assures its site visitors that this chemical is equally present in food, but what it doesn't say is that when it exists in fruit and vegetables, it is combined with other proteins that mediate its effect.[33]

The bulk of the product is made up of aspartic acid (a neuroexciter) and phenylalanine (a neurotoxin). According to Dr. H. J. Roberts—a vociferous critic of aspartame—since this chemical combination was introduced an enormous increase has been witnessed in incidences of brain cancer.[34]

A less-serious side effect of phenylalanine is that it is widely reported to cause sweetener addicts to crave carbohydrates. So it's no wonder that dieters using such products get fatter and fatter. But, take heart, the Aspartame Information Center assures, *Don't be fooled, the bottom line is aspartame is safe.*

## FIRST DO NO HARM?

Where, you may be asking, do medical doctors stand in all of this? While many practitioners are genuinely concerned about their patients' health, there are also those who are more concerned about their pockets. They have jumped at the opportunity to use weight loss as their prime moneymaking vehicle. One of the most highly publicized studies on weight loss was based on data from the long-term observational Nurses' Health Study (this study was launched in 1976 and currently examines the development of chronic disease in women). In a 1995 research project based on this study, Harvard Medical School doctor JoAnn Manson and her colleagues released information to the media that provided compelling evidence for the proposition that being even mildly overweight is associated with a substantial increase in premature death (quoting it to be as high as 60 percent).[35] However, in statistical terms the increased risk was so small that Fraser says, "At 161–175 pounds women did have a 60-percent increase in death rate, but the death rate was so low to begin with that 60 percent more than almost nothing was still almost nothing."[36]

Regardless, the press had a field day sensationalizing the findings, and this figure of 60 percent is still quoted by scientists. There's more to this story, however: The public was unaware that Manson, at the time of the study, apart from being a Harvard Medical School doctor, was a paid consultant at Interneuron[37] (now called Indevus Pharmaceuticals).

The plot sickens when one realizes that at the time, Interneuron was the company producing Redux, one half of the noxious drug Fen-Phen. What's even more interesting is that Abbott Laboratories's website in 2003 cited Manson's somewhat dubious 60-percent risk factor as reassurance for continuing to take their drug Meridia.[38]

The National Association to Advance Fat Acceptance (NAAFA) quotes Thomas Moore's book *Lifespan:* "Most leading obesity researchers are either consultants to diet or pharmaceutical companies, conduct research for these companies, presenting their results at conferences sponsored by these companies, or sometimes all three."[39]

While in many countries pharmaceutical manufacturers have been stopped from waving enticements, like overseas vacations, for doctors and their families, they can still creep in through the back door by offering tickets for medical conferences and the like. Is this perhaps why conferences are often in exotic destinations like Bermuda or Hawaii? As a result it's difficult for innocent patients to know what hidden incentives lie behind the medical advice they're receiving.

One of the most extreme forms of medicine dished up to the overweight is the surgeon's knife. While many defend this practice as necessary to improve health and increase longevity, NAAFA claims that operations like stomach bypasses or stapling can indeed result in weight loss of 20 percent within eighteen to twenty-four months, but—surprise, surprise—weight regain is common, requiring second and third operations. With each additional operation, mortality rates increase. So much for longevity![40]

Terry Poulton, as a victim of such an operation herself, reports side effects such as vomiting after only a few teaspoons of food.[41] Laura Fraser points out that apart from weight regain, victims endure other, nastier side effects, such as pain from the staples and fifteen to twenty bowel movements a day (some of which are uncontrollable, meaning that a change of clothes always needs to be at the ready). In addition, because the food is undigested, foul body odors make social interactions highly embarrassing. When surgical victims experience problems such as these, exercise is virtually out of the question, and some have also experienced symptoms of starvation such as hair loss and kidney stones, as well as secondary infections from their operations.[42] NAAFA reports that operations such as these have been performed on hundreds of thousands of patients since 1954 with many resulting in complications and some deaths.

When it comes to bariatric doctors (the so-called weight-loss specialists), it's not surprising that some of their consulting rooms look like retail stores, with stocks of everything from low-fat cookies (which taste like deflavored cardboard) to weight-loss shakes. These products are supposed to contain all the balanced nutrition needed—so no real food is required. Like those who opt for a staple of low-fat cookies instead of food, many desperate women will allow their need for thinness to override the obvious. In a callously underregulated industry, dieters have consumed laxatives and purgatives, arsenic, strychnine, insecticides, bath salts, hormones, and even weed killer. These are just some of the ingredients that have been contained in over-the-counter diet products, which are consumed to the tune of $5–6 billion per annum.[43] But compared with tapeworm larvae, perhaps these remedies may not be so vile after all.

## BIG, FAT, AND UGLY?

The tragedy of the media-driven cultural myth that makes anorexia appear "normal" is that everyday fat people are the butt of cruel jokes. They are ridiculed, abused, mocked, overlooked, and insulted with terms more commonly used to denigrate farm animals. So much so that many women report that they'd rather lose a limb than be overweight.

Fat women are not just considered to be large, but they are also incorrectly perceived to be slothful, lazy, stupid, ugly, unhealthy, unproductive, selfish, asexual, insecure, socially inept, unfeminine, and lacking in self-respect, self-discipline, and control.

To see this in action you don't have to look any further than *The Jerry Springer Show*. Whereas thin people are harangued for their infidelity, the audience—members of which are often far from slim-jims themselves—will spit venom at a large woman's fat.

After being subjected socially to such frequent rejection and heartless punishment, even the most resilient person would suffer profound emotional damage from the constant battering of self-esteem. So not only do the overweight have to carry the burden of excess adipose, but they also serve as the punching bags for a brutal society. NAAFA has substantiated discrimination reports with employment surveys showing that fat people are not hired or promoted as often as their average-size counterparts; they are paid less but have to pay more for their insurance, and in some cases they are fired for being fat.[44]

In the land of the free, these women have little recourse to law. The only legal protection available is to use existing disability laws, but too often being overweight is seen to be a voluntary condition, thus negating the nature of a disability claim.

Even if the law offered protection to large people, it could not prevent the underhanded discrimination meted out by those bigoted about size. But tagging the overweight with unfair judgments is as absurd as discriminating against short people or those with big feet.

A survey of physicians and scientists showed that genetic factors might be responsible for up to 70 percent of a person's weight.[45] So, many people's original sin was nothing more than opting for their genetic line. Regardless, the naturally large often suffer enormously in their hopeless attempts to reduce the body nature gave them to more "acceptable" proportions. As we've seen this only makes one fatter, but regardless of this, desperate women spend every last penny trying to escape the punishment they fear most: imprisonment in the wretchedness of a large frame.

## LIKE MOTHER, LIKE DAUGHTER

Many women are transferring their misguided notions about the ideal body to their daughters. In a seminar I conducted, a really skinny woman was genuinely puzzled that her daughter was at risk for anorexia. Yet in conversation this delegate discussed little other than her weight, dieting, why she could or couldn't eat this or that, and her thin and fat wardrobes. In a study of five-year-old girls, researchers at Pennsylvania State University found that daughters of dieting mothers were more likely to have ideas, concepts, and beliefs about dieting at an early age. So much so that 40 percent of primary-school girls reported having tried a diet to lose weight.[46]

The researchers discovered that overweight girls suffered from a lowered self-esteem as early as the age of five—and they also underestimated their intelligence and physical abilities.

Mothers will do everything to protect their offspring, including risking their own life, so why do they serve as a mouthpiece for an industry that could potentially kill or maim their daughters? All this while there's not a shred of evidence to prove that naturally thin women feel any better about themselves. It's only those who've shed a few pounds who experience moments of euphoria before the next oncoming binge.

## FATTER BY THE MILLION

The absurdity intensifies when one considers that although an estimated 50 million people spend billions on commercial weight loss every year, there is no sign whatsoever that Americans are getting anything but fatter.

According to the *Journal of the American Medical Association (JAMA)*, 30.5 percent of the adult population is now considered obese (body mass index in excess of thirty) and 64.5 percent is overweight (BMI in excess of twenty-five), an increase from 55 percent in 1994.[47] So much for dieting! BMI levels of 18–25 are considered normal, and if you're interested in calculating your own BMI, use this formula:

Weight (pounds) x 704.5 divided by (height [inches] x height [inches]).

While quick-fix vendors justify their claims on the basis that some 300,000 Americans die of obesity every year,[48] the debate is far more complex than the diet industry makes out. Of course obesity is a health problem, but while some say unequivocally that in and of itself obesity will kill you,[49] outspoken critics of the diet industry—like Paul Campos, law professor at the University of Colorado—claim we are not getting the full picture.[50]

Firstly, the BMI poses some problems, as it only takes into account height and weight, not ratio of muscle to fat. Although this index originated with and is widely used by the insurance industry to calculate risk, Campos claims that according to this measure, Brad Pitt and George Clooney are overweight and Sylvester Stallone is obese! Secondly, the research (including the figure of 300,000 deaths from obesity) also fails to control for other unhealthy behaviors like inactivity, poor nutrition, previous dieting behaviors, weight fluctuations, use of weight-loss drugs, and access to medical care. When these factors are accounted for, Campos suggests that an unhealthy lifestyle may be the main contributor to early death, and obesity is just one of its symptoms.

Although the National Institutes for Health (NIH) insists on weight loss as a goal for obese individuals, *Radiance*[51] (a size-acceptance magazine) claims that even the NIH admits that there is little information regarding the health benefits or risks of long-term intentional weight loss.[52] As a result, the article continues, some health professionals are recommending that instead of encouraging obese people to achieve the impossible (permanent weight loss), health professionals should help them to improve their overall health and reduce the risk of chronic disease.[53]

The research of Steven Blair (research director at the Cooper Institute), arguably the world's leading expert on the relationship between activity levels and overall health, points to some interesting findings.

Fit men and women are protected against the health risks of being overweight or obese.[54] In a study focusing on men, fat fit men lived as long as those who were lean and fit, but a thin unfit man's risk of dying was twice that of a fatter fit man.[55] And when it comes to how much exercise is necessary, even couch potatoes shouldn't be frightened off by the finding that thirty minutes of moderate activity on most days (like walking for instance), is enough to experience the health benefits.[56]

For both the overweight and those obsessed with dieting, the new paradigm suggests changing behavior rather than focusing on weight loss. Small daily changes like increasing activity levels and eating more fresh food have motivational advantages. Unlike the devastation of being dictated to by the floor scales, these regular successes are more likely to make you feel positive about the effort you're making.

## A LOSING BUSINESS

It's interesting that figures for supposed obesity-related deaths are plentifully available, while those who die from diet-related complications don't matter enough to be counted.

Alongside the weight-loss industry, there are of course many parallel businesses benefiting from the fallout. Aside from the funeral parlors and legal eagles who fight the cases of the dead, dying, and maimed, the pharmaceutical companies not only profit greatly from producing weight-loss drugs, but they also score from the increasing demand for over-the-counter products like laxatives and purgatives. This is not to mention the antidepressants and tranquilizers needed to appease the misery of dieters.

The food industry is also gaining, since diet pills promise all manner of reassuring ways to miraculously purge fat, thus tempting people to eat more. Profitable too are the millions of compulsive eaters with their expensive binge cycles—in some extreme cases this can be up to ten times per day—and the dentists profit from purging because of the stomach acid's damage to the teeth.

The fashion world thrives on the notion of "thin" and "fat" wardrobes, and a whole industry has developed to coax dieters into caring for their body.

Fitness centers and sports clothing and equipment manufacturers are laughing all the way to the bank.

But no matter what you do, your natural size is your natural size, which means most of us, even at our so-called ideal weight, don't look anything like Madonna. And Madonna herself looked a lot more "homely" before she embarked upon her four-hour-a-day exercise regime. Many women trying to emulate figures like hers have developed what is now commonly known as "exercise anorexia"—this form of anorexia takes up an inordinate amount of energy and time.

Only a permanent change in lifestyle will result in permanent reduction. So like your mom told you, eat plenty of fruit, veggies, and grains and do moderate exercise, and your body will slowly return to its natural state. More than an old wives' tale, this advice holds weight with agencies like the Federal Trade Commission (FTC), too.

## SPOTTING THE SCAMS

The FTC offers some useful tips on spotting false weight-loss claims. It says that an ad is probably a diet rip-off if it promises:

- you can eat your favorite high-calorie foods and still lose weight.
- you can lose weight without diet or exercise.
- a product can block the absorption of fat, carbohydrates, or calories.
- a product can make you lose more than three pounds per week.
- a product will work for everyone.
- a product will cause you to lose weight permanently.
- any patch, cream, gel, et cetera., can help you lose weight.

If ads making these claims are not dealt with with a healthy dose of skepticism, then the FTC warns that the only thing you're guaranteed to lose is your money.[57] Report diet scams to the FTC (www.ftc .gov); it has had success in permanently gagging numerous weight-loss swindlers.

## OF FAT AND FASHION

Being brainwashed to spend money is just one side of the skin-and-bone story: The other resides in a deliberate manipulation to limit women's newfound sexual freedom.

For this, let's take a quick walk back into the past. A century ago women's bodies were large and buxom, and although cellulite makes many shudder today, it used to be desirable and was affectionately called a woman's "silken layer."

While in the upper classes there was a movement afoot associating a slimmer body with wealth and status, there were many who had no option but to carry the refrigerator on their hips and thighs. The corset was born in order to allow anyone to emulate the slimmer waist of the upper classes. In the Victorian era, the slimmer waist created by a corset accentuated a woman's well-developed bust, buttocks, and hips—everything that announced that she was a full-fledged sexually functioning woman. Sexuality in a woman was no threat then, as she was homebound and entirely dependent upon her husband.

Fat is categorically understood by the subconscious as fertile sexuality, and the indoctrination about dieting started at the same time as women got the vote and rudimentary forms of contraception hit the market.[58]

The "flappers," so called because they left the buckles of their shoes undone, were the first generation of sexually rebellious women. The social disapproval for their overt expression of sexual desire subjected this generation to the pressure of being thin for the first time. As members of the fairer sex were not supposed to be seen indulging their body in any way, the mantle of a slimmer and therefore seemingly underdeveloped body gave the impression that beneath their overt sexual rebellion, they were still just innocent young girls. And so being slim became a social metaphor for displaying sufficient self-control to be a good girl.[59]

After the Second World War a refeminizing process encouraged working women to put down their factory tools and go back home, giving birth to the even-more-rebellious Baby Boomers.[60] The 1960s saw new developments in contraception and, with this, the second stage of the female sexual revolution. But for young women who'd grown up believing that virginity proved you were a "nice" girl, the fun of the rebellion was dampened by the guilt associated with sex.

In the British television series *Absolutely Fabulous,* the Baby Boomer character Eddy epitomized this guilt: Every time she had sex she felt the many disapproving eyes on her, so much so that her mother's retinas became the best form of contraception. Fearing the alienation that went with social judgments like "slut" or "whore," and afraid of the wrath of God himself, women dealt with their fear by raging against themselves. Some overate in an attempt to curb their sexual appeal, while others showed how controlled they could be by not eating at all.

As the sexual revolution gained momentum, so the popularity of flesh-revealing attire, like the bikini, grew. But the more fashion exposed naked female flesh, the more women were required to shrink physically, and the less sexual their bodies became. Once again the metaphorical sexual corset had tightened, and out of the ashes of a voluptuous Monroe came the stick figure of Twiggy. Her diminutive ninety-five-pound frame and childlike form caused a never-seen-before media frenzy.

Even the stodgy *New York Times* had something to say, reports Poulton. Its description of Twiggy as "just like your next-door neighbor, if he happens to be a skinny twelve-year-old boy," showed an uncanny sixth sense of things to come.[61]

Finally the corset strings had pulled tight enough to achieve the desired result: an asexual female form. Although Twiggy herself exited from the modeling scene quite quickly, her boyish figure called the fashion shots for more than forty years.

With marriage no longer an institution that binds people together forever, the sexual corset serves as a powerful chastity belt, virtually guaranteeing fidelity in women. Anyone who survives on a long-term starvation diet will report the damage this does to their libidos, so not only do pin-thin females appear asexual, but their lack of interest in screwing has also succeeded in putting the kibosh on female sexual freedom. With women trapped in the mental cycle of maintaining a child's body (some with bulbous implants both back and front), what chance do they have of growing up? Not only does our preoccupation with weight inhibit the natural development of our body but—given that it takes nothing less than obsession to maintain an immature form—it's also an impediment to us maturing beyond the dependency of our teenage years.

Men who need to demonstrate that they are in control can have a perennially childlike princess to play the official role of wife, while at the same time they may be seeking the sensual pleasure of a more voluptuous woman.

## FAT IN THE HEAD

What makes women vulnerable to the industry's claims is the old thing of feeling that we're not good enough anyway. Poulton quotes an insight from a woman who knew what it was like to be both thin and fat—the actress Elizabeth Taylor: "The large amounts of food I ate were a substitute for everything I felt I was lacking in my life. But what was really starving was my self-esteem . . . "[62]

Eating-disorder survivor and author Geneen Roth has written many helpful works, including *Feeding the Hungry Heart*,[63] to deal with the most debilitating condition of all—being fat in the head.

Without the courage to rage against a society that puts a metaphorical chastity belt on our sexuality, or the energy to fight an industry that raids our pockets, we wage war on our bodies instead.

Because women have been encouraged to overidentify with one aspect of themselves, they now believe that they are nothing more than their physical looks, a sure recipe for stunting emotional, not to mention spiritual, growth.

As said by Timothy Freke and Peter Gandy in *Jesus and the Goddess*,[64] "as long as we think that the real self is the body, we are spiritually blind."

Roberto Assagioli, known as the father of transpersonal psychology, has some powerful advice for those who overidentify with one aspect of themselves, as in bodyism. In *The Act of Will,* he suggests constant reaffirming ourselves as follows: "I have a body, but I am not my body," or, alternatively, "I have beauty but I am not my looks."[65] Repeated frequently, this can replace the self-punishing sermon of the mirror, and turn you into the nurturing mistress of your body.

So, if like the majority of women, you don't like what your body looks like, at the very least start appreciating the miraculous things it does for you, daily.

# CHAPTER 6.

# The Wicked Witch
of Business

Successful businesswoman. What mental image does the term conjure up for you? A picture of an outstanding community member who commands respect? Or is it one of a ruthless, pushy bitch trying to emulate men?

It's now more than fifty years since women actively entered the portals of business, yet cultural fantasy still portrays career women as oddities. "She's a tough cookie" is just one of the patronizing terms to describe experienced, intelligent, mature, successful women. But are similar comments made about male captains of industry?

While successful businesswomen may get a certain grudging respect for the power of their position, unlike businessmen they are seldom admired for who they are and what they've achieved. Instead of accolades, working women, and especially working mothers, often get slapped down and criticized for neglecting their dutiful role.

Decades of conservative culture have made sure that the blame for the breakdown of family values and hence the moral fabric of society sits fairly and squarely on the shoulders of working women. Symptoms of social malaise like high divorce rate, or issues with children such as drugs, delinquency, and learning problems, are laid at the door of the working mother. And the greatest wickedness of the modern-day working "witch" is her failure to sacrifice her energy to men. So instead of the flaming pyre, she gets burned at the stake by the media.

In women's magazines the modern witch is fairly well disguised as a belle in a business suit. But in the hit movie *Fatal Attraction* she was depicted as being stark raving mad. Although *Fatal Attraction* takes us back some fifteen years, was the crazed working mother in the more recent motion picture *American Beauty* that different?

In the movies, career women are seldom portrayed as normal females getting on with their lives. They are more typically seen to be selfish shrews who are depressed, neurotic, insecure, sex starved, vicious, immoral, and callous.

Even in a film with the promising title *What Women Want,* Bette Midler takes the role of neurotic shrink, and Helen Hunt, who supposedly plays the high-powered exec, is really no more than the love interest, a working princess.

Instead of fighting for herself, Hunt's character succumbs to the manipulations of Mel Gibson's character, and, once he's sabotaged her efforts, she waits for him to rescue her. The ending shows Hunt falling into Gibson's arms with the promise of "happily ever after" fulfilled. Since when are betrayal and emotional abuse what women really want?

## WHAT WOMEN DON'T WANT

A few decades' worth of portraying businesswomen in this way is what it's taken to keep the shackling stereotypes alive and well, as they are today. And if you think the movies are damaging, television is worse. How much is your opinion of working women fed by shows like *Desperate Housewives, The Office,* or *The Apprentice,* all of which highlight the notion that the priority of women in business is men? The standard television portrayal of working women is superficial and silly.

In the few instances where women are not depicted as shallow, they're typecast as the other extreme, the hard-nosed superbitch. As for courtroom scenes, have you ever noticed how ruthless female lawyers are appointed to defend the bad guys? And how righteous male attorneys invariably triumph over them?

Not only are successful women typecast as the wicked witch, but those who don't conform to social norms get attacked about their sexuality. When Janet Reno was appointed as the first female attorney general, there was much speculation about her sexual orientation. This was because she was in her fifties, had never married, and had borne no children. Surely those who forgave Clinton's misdemeanors should understand that whomever Janet Reno sleeps with has about as much impact upon her effectiveness at work as Slick Willy's poor control over his dick?

## BACK TO THE BROOMS

When the dyke label doesn't fit, women are accused of using their sexuality to get to the top. You'd think by now as a society we'd have matured a little beyond the mattress theory, yet two very recent examples spring to mind.

A woman I know, after running a highly profitable business for more than twenty years, received hate mail accusing her of doing it on her back. I have a male cycling companion. After we were seen having a postcycling breakfast by one of his colleagues, rumors in his organization spread like wildfire that my contract with the company had been earned in the sack!

The shameful reputation forced on females in business is still being perpetuated by ultra-right-wing conservative movements like Christian Coalition of America, Focus on the Family, Family Research Council, Concerned Women for America, Eagle Forum, and Promise Keepers.[1] Under the banner of "family values," these groups are anti-abortion, antichildcare, and, of course, overtly antifeminist. As such, they disapprove of women stationed behind the boardroom table, preferring them to be positioned behind the mop or vacuum cleaner. In the United States this would mean losing nearly half of all paid workers, and one wonders what the conservative plan is to compensate for this massive loss of productivity in the economy.[2]

## KEEPING THE FAITH

Promise Keepers is an example of a religious ultra-right-wing men's movement. Among its objectives is to encourage greater responsibility in men. You may grin with glee at this necessary and noble mission, but the bottom line for Promise Keepers is to restore men to their "rightful" role as the traditional head of the family. Does this sound like men trying to become more actively involved with their wives and children?

This movement claims to have hosted more than 3.5 million men at its conferences, so it's evident that regaining power is something men hunger for. But given this great attempt to restore male authority, the irony is that most women didn't pick up the ball of financial responsibility because they wanted to play the dominant role in the family. A large percentage of women who work do so because they have to. Now, as the matriarchal power of our society starts to come into its own, it's a little late for conservative groups to persuade men and women to regress to traditional roles.

Surely these movements would make greater headway helping men to cope with joint power sharing, rather than lashing out against the feminization of our culture? In order for us to experience progress, men need to be taught maturity and cooperation in their relationships—after all, it's unlikely that turning the battle of the sexes into a full-scale war will create a healthier future for men, women, or children.

Although right-wing ideas about women are deluded in very obvious practical ways, they still have a powerful influence. A group called Mothers at Home (a conservative organization supporting stay-at-home moms) cites polls that claim 55 percent of children are likely to suffer if mothers work outside the home (1991) and that 73 percent believed children fare best when they have a mother at home (1990).[3] These polls are in direct contrast to the latest research about the effect of working mothers on their children (reviewed in Chapter 3), but they are still touted on the websites of groups such as these.

While some individual women do find joy in swapping their high-powered careers for kids' parties and school runs, right-wing information fails to address the real problem: inflexible working hours for both men and women and inadequate daycare for children.

But we shouldn't forget that flexible working hours could interfere with the idea of generating wealth at all costs (and therefore national productivity), and childcare costs plenty of money.

The fact that millions of women worldwide may choose their business suits and offices because a career is a source of fulfillment for them is completely ignored. The National Institute of Mental Health says that employed married women with children (whose children are in satisfactory and affordable childcare) experience less depression, anxiety, and other forms of psychological distress than do married women who do not work outside the home.[4]

Given that the arguments against working women are put forward mainly by conservative lobbyists, it's not too difficult to sniff out the familiar strategy of reversal. Instead of addressing the real issue of male disinterest, it's easier to hoodwink society by attacking the most industrious group of all, working moms.

Simply put, working women are not the cause of the ills in our society. Do you really think that if all women were to stay at home, we'd see an end to children's learning problems, rape, drugs, gangsters, and violence?

Aren't our social problems largely a consequence of the priorities laid down by the gender that gets to make the rules? Traditionally, men follow power and money—they don't generally put the social needs of humanity first. So how would it be if women and men worked together to rewrite the rules? Work/life balance initiatives have started creating awareness among men, but only when a critical mass of males recognize the impact of gender politics upon their own lives can we begin to imagine a better balance between the energy of ambition and the good of society. Maybe then we'd never see another war or famine or an abused child again.

## FATHER INVOLVEMENT

The breakdown of family values is a societal problem, and while men hold on to their socially dominant position, they must bear a huge amount of responsibility for it. Male disinterest and neglect of their wives and children is profound. How many men still come home and expect their working wife to feed them and see to the kids? A comprehensive literature review conducted by the National Center on Fathers and Families (NCOFF) confirms that fathers' involvement with children is minimal to say the least.[5]

The complexities of fatherhood are influenced by a man's own upbringing, his attitude about being a parent, the demands of his career, and social, economic, and cultural factors. But on the whole, dads tend to see their role as a child's playmate, whereas mothers take full responsibility for caregiving.[6]

Even with women's changing roles, one of the many studies concluded that the idea of shared parenting has changed more dramatically than has the behavior of fathers at home.[7] This means that men imagine that they are heavily involved, but, as a further study confirmed, when both parents are employed the amount of responsibility assumed by the father is actually negligible.[8] If in a reasonable relationship the father is not very involved, in an unhappy union it is worse, with the man withdrawing not only from his wife but from his children as well.[9]

When fathers are involved with their children, their interaction tends to be mediated by the mother.[10] As a result men often claim that the one major obstacle to their participation is a woman's reluctance to trust their competence. Pepper Schwartz in her book *Peer Marriage* confirms that it is "one thing for women to yearn for an involved father and quite another to acknowledge that fathers have the same rights and access as the mother."[11] Although the inability to let go of their role is a common accusation hurled at mothers, the NCOFF review sheds some light on this issue.

Many men do not know how to relate to their children except through their wife; when married they are present yet passive, but if a separation occurs, this pattern of limited involvement is carried through, reinforced by the modest contact they have with their children.[12] In marriage many men prefer to play the role of "mother's helper" rather than act as a full parenting partner,[13] and a father's involvement with children is more dependent upon support from his spouse than the other way around.[14] Although the review confirms that fathers who are single parents (through death of the spouse or custodial rights) are capable parents, it would seem that it may not be the wife's reluctance to trust his competence, but rather that her presence leads fathers to believe they are off the hook.

Although social guilt about the negative effect of a mother's employment upon a child's development will continue to be laid upon working mothers, the significant role that dads play in their children's growth is often ignored by right-wing propaganda. NCOFF quotes a survey conducted by the U.S. Department of Education that suggests that children with involved fathers are more likely to achieve high grades in school and less likely to repeat a year.[15] Not only do involved fathers influence children's intellectual development but they also have a positive effect on both their social competence and ability to empathize with others. In the same review, involved fathers were found to reduce sex-stereotyped beliefs and promote a more internalized locus of control.[16] Additionally, fathers play a vital role in helping adolescents avoid problem behaviors such as drugs, delinquency, and violence.[17]

It is significant that NCOFF admits that research into the role of fathers is minimal compared to the studies conducted on both working and stay-at-home moms. But even though the number of studies is limited, the studies suggest that male neglect is an important factor that must be considered in a child's development.

The disturbing fact that we need courts of law to forcibly extract maintenance from divorced fathers is proof enough of this negligence. Also, have you noticed how few businesses house a daycare center for children? Yet the office bar is a central feature. Let's talk about priorities, shall we?

So instead of conservatives and traditionalists examining their priorities, they've found a handy vehicle for blame—working women. Of course it suits men when women take full responsibility for the family and home, but why is this still the case with dual-income parents? Dual income means dual responsibility, and this is what men are shirking. But it's easier to put working women down than to pick up some of the load.

Although a small percentage of mothers work to afford luxuries in the home (like brand new vehicles, satellite TV, and overseas vacations), the majority of women work because they have to. In 1995 the Women's Bureau at the U.S. Department of Labor found that 60 percent of working mothers are married to men who earn less than $15,000 a year.[18] How can these wives afford to be stay-at-home moms?

## A LONG HISTORY OF THE WORKING WOMAN

Since women have in fact always worked, the debate about whether mothers should work or stay at home is slightly absurd. Even as far back as the hunter-gatherer era, females produced 75–80 percent of their community's nourishment.[19] Of course, hunting wasn't about work only—it was a form of male bonding and entertainment. The meat provided by men was considered no more than an enjoyable luxury, not the bulk of the community's nutrition.

Today a man's place of work remains the venue for his bonding and entertainment. Think of the prevalence of television screens in offices. Certainly these were not installed for women to watch their soaps . . . and have you noticed how business comes to a grinding halt when important sports matches are screened? With our corporate offices awash with bars and televisions for male merriment, can we really say that all that much has changed from the hunter-gatherer era?

I'm sure you've heard the refrain that women would make better managers if they relied on their archetypal "female" qualities rather than trying to emulate "male" roles like hunter or conqueror. But don't people need the whole range of "male" and "female" qualities to succeed?

While it may be accepted in theory that management requires both "male" and "female" qualities, there's still enormous prejudice in practice. When men move toward more-cooperative "feminine" conduct, such as participation, they are acknowledged for their maturity, but when women use their "iron balls," their behavior is deemed unacceptable.

Isn't it interesting that women are also the ones accused of not understanding the difference between being assertive and being aggressive? Many men judge neither behavior to be socially acceptable in females, so perhaps it's not us women who need to learn the difference!

Also, when women break the taboo surrounding male superiority by criticizing macho behavior, they are accused of being man haters or ball breakers. But just because I may have opinions about men, why is it assumed that these views make me anti-male?

To illustrate how laughable things have become, a toning-down program has been launched in the U.K. for "Bully Broads." It teaches so-called ball breakers to be "ladies first," encouraging strong women to speak softly, to hesitate or stammer, and, if necessary, to cry in meetings. One can only presume that this behavior is supposed to cushion the blow real women deliver when truly speaking their minds.[20] Of course, bullies of either gender are tiresome, but instead of training women to go backward, it would be more helpful for women to become masterful in the art of persuasion.

Unfortunately few people have the maturity to pay attention to actions that refute the stereotypes they've absorbed. Most prefer to seek out behaviors that confirm their preconceived ideas.

## SOMEONE, SOMEWHERE, THINKS YOU'RE A BITCH

No matter how nice you are, if you're a successful woman, somebody, somewhere will accuse you of being a bitch. In an attempt to avoid this, many female managers fall into the trap of needing to be liked, but in leadership this is particularly dangerous, as it encourages brownnosing. If staff members are sucking up to you, you won't earn the respect required to encourage superior performance in them. Good leadership sometimes requires being tough, and if you're unable to be so, you make yourself vulnerable to the manipulation of team members.

People-pleasing is once again the culprit here, and in leadership this behavior is ineffectual; not only does it perpetuate the stereotype of the weak woman, but it will also doom you to the ranks of middle management forever.[21]

Stereotypes stick because they contain a small element of truth. This element is then blown out of proportion, and eventually it becomes the whole picture. Female socialization, especially the notion of self-sacrifice, is not the best preparation for your role in business—it leads to internal conflict and hence insecurity. And the solution to business success is not just a matter of allowing our suppressed female qualities to emerge and strengthen. We need to balance our female and male qualities to live comfortably in our own skin.

So why do we find this such a challenge?

From an early school-going age, boys are thrown into situations where they are taught to compete in games where winner takes all. They play rough-and-tumble sports and are encouraged to fight for themselves. Girls, on the other hand, are taught not to fight at all, since their needs, as they've been taught from the cradle, are unimportant.

The resultant rage that females often carry is then turned in on themselves.

In business that makes women particularly tough on themselves. Not only are females poorly prepared emotionally for their role in the workplace, but they also have to work twice as smartly to get half as far. And if this isn't enough, they also manage the home.

According to Susan Maushart's *Wifework,* working wives today continue to perform 70–80 percent of the unpaid labor in the family.[22] Why? If women were to charge the state for this labor (the real work of raising the country's next generation) it's likely that industrialized economies would crumble. Again witness how the self-sacrificing agenda continues to prop up a system that lets men off the hook and harms women.

With women under pressure both at work and at home, it takes a great deal of self-control for working women to simply manage the stress of their day-to-day lives. As a consequence, those who are hard on themselves tend to be intolerant of other people's vulnerabilities and inadequacies, those of both men and other women. This is what makes some women appear harsh, judgmental, and inaccessible.

## GIFTS THAT HARM

In seminars I ask women to draw up a list of behaviors they find unacceptable in others. This list usually reveals more about their own self-criticism, of course, than it does problems with their colleagues and staff members. It reveals the areas that women find intolerable in themselves. Just loosening up on the harsh judgments you make about yourself will ease the unrealistic pressure you may be putting on yourself, your colleagues, or your team members.

If you find the opinions of others offensive, the only way to deal with them is to view their messages as feedback. If it feels uncomfortable, this state is alerting you to the emotional difficulties we women have created by not accepting who we are. Areas we shun in ourselves become sensitive buttons just waiting to be pressed by other people.

Healing requires understanding ourselves beyond the level of the myths of the social programming we've learned. This is about our individuality, not our conditioning. By exploring this individuality we free ourselves from the stereotypical rules and roles we've absorbed from society. Many mature women say they wish they'd learned earlier to get over being nice. For them, caring less about what other people think would have made it easier to accelerate their careers.

Self-acceptance also unleashes more of our gifts and talents. Too often, useful behaviors were squashed in childhood because they were deemed unacceptable. Throughout my schooling I got into trouble for things like talking too much, questioning the system, and answering back. Today I rely heavily upon these gifts.

Think about behaviors that have been crushed in your life—other people judged these actions unacceptable, not you. Retrieve them and you may find that they are the very gifts needed to give your career a boost. In the same way, put other people's feedback into perspective. Men, in particular, find it difficult to be objective about strong women. They battle to get past the stereotypes and judge you accordingly. Weigh their comments and, if they don't resonate with what you feel about yourself, ignore them.

Attempting to straddle social acceptance and personal ambition is the working woman's Achilles' heel. Note that being sensitive to the feelings of others is not the same as being unduly affected by their opinion. When we are highly sensitive to other people's opinions, we allow the glass ceiling to impede our progress. When we fulfill our ambition, we stand alone. But keeping one foot in each camp just makes us ineffectual in both.

If we choose to go it alone, embracing the totality of who we are helps us make headway. The more we retrieve of ourselves, the stronger we become and the less we rely on social approval. Truly accepting that others may never approve of us is part of the process.

If you're battling with sentiments such as these, remember this thought: What other people think about you is none of your business. This is important, as internalizing control gives us the strength necessary to pick up the ax and smash through the glass ceiling, which is the only way we are going to get past this superficially imposed barricade. And don't expect that men will be opening their arms to welcome us in, given that even in the 21st century, most women are still stuck in middle management.

According to the Research Center of the Feminist Majority Foundation, a survey tracking the number of women executives shows little improvement in twenty-five years. At the current rate of increase, it will be some 125 years before women reach equality with men at board level.[23]

## MANAGEMENT BY MOMMY-WITCH TACTICS

Further problems exist for women in business because the frustration women face has led to a peculiar style of management. Women who have been groomed emotionally to be a good wife and mother take this "maternal" habit to work. They nurture staff members, counsel personal problems, and rescue those acting like little birds sporting broken wings.

In this context this "rescuing," which looks like the old female self-sacrificing behavior, is actually a dysfunctional means of accruing power over people. While staff are revealing their frailties, the female manager seldom shares her own deeply felt vulnerabilities with team members. This allows her to manipulate, using the other person's Achilles' heel to her own advantage.

However, when the poo hits the fan, women switch from nurturing mom to rampaging witch. All hell breaks loose when their pent-up rage is unleashed upon the unsuspecting. It is interesting that it's usually control freaks who display this behavior, but it does make sense: Controllers are so busy micromanaging other people that they have little energy left for their own self-control. This is particularly evident when overcontrolling women are under a great deal of pressure. High levels of stress make self-control difficult, so the witch throws her toys when she thinks she is not being taken seriously enough.

Women with this style of management are unreasonable too often, and it works against them because after a while, no one listens. This sets up a vicious cycle, because as we know, ignoring a woman just fuels her fury. Throwing habitual tantrums is not the same as "making friends with the bitch inside of you." A woman who uses this style of management is employing the tactics of the bitch to protect her insecurities, and is regularly reacting to personal slights and petty issues. Both waste energy. Instead, keep the real force of the bitch to fight against injustices, and, if used sparingly, this power will be taken seriously.

This style of behavior probably arose because a girl's upbringing teaches her to be conflict avoidant. So, instead of reprimanding people for each misdemeanor at every opportunity, female managers swallow their feelings by telling themselves that the issue was too petty to address, or too unimportant. Rather than dealing with each annoyance calmly, women let their irritation build and then blow up, one of the unhealthiest outlets for rage. This just confuses staff members and breaks the trust necessary to build the relationships that lead to top performance.

Two critical factors separate good leaders from average managers: inspiring the best performance in each individual, and being authentic. Neither is possible until we heal the insecurities and rage that drive our actions. Perfectionism destroys creative input from others, while micromanaging clearly shows staff that you do not have faith in them.

So what do we do to become authentic managers? It's back to healing the conflicts of the traditionally raised lonely, confused, unnurtured little girl who lives inside us. If her needs remain ignored we simply cannot develop as authentic people, and that means we can't be authentic managers either.

Forcing our feelings to grow up is a frustrating and difficult task. It also takes plenty of patience and time. This is particularly true of feelings that grew out of damaging early experiences. The best we can hope for is to heal the wound and live with the scar.

## HIDING FROM SUCCESS

Women may think they want success, but when it comes down to it, many will make sure it doesn't actually materialize. This has to do with being in the cooperative rather than the competitive mode. Many girls are raised with the idea that being kind and considerate is prized over thrashing the competition. So for women, winning is problematic, because by definition it shows we're looking after number one.

Because this is the way we're all socialized, female accomplishment often brings resentment instead of accolades from other people.

Consequently, many women feel uncomfortable about success that could potentially make them stand out from the crowd.

During seminars, many working women remember earlier experiences that taught them to shun success. One woman recalled the day she threw in the towel on a promising show-jumping career—as a sensitive twelve-year-old she simply didn't have the emotional wherewithal to manage the flak her success was attracting. She reports that as a professional woman today, she'd rather hang back with the crowd than stand tall on her own.

While cooperation and empathy are glorified as female skills, and highly valued in business, neither are primary attributes that have turned anyone into a great achiever. After all, what successful business do you know of that is run by those who accentuate empathy and cooperation? These may be secondary attributes, but few get to the top without the commitment and determination to fight for what they want.

The learned emphasis on cooperation is also the reason women don't wish to put themselves forward. We've been taught that our needs are unimportant, and we are inhibited about fighting for ourselves when it comes to a promotion, a well-deserved increase, or even a project we may wish to work on.

Undervaluing ourselves and our achievements is so entrenched that businesswomen's associations often have difficulty attracting applications for their award ceremonies.

So it's no surprise that women worldwide also earn less than men. According to the Bureau of Labor Statistics, women in 1999 earned 77 cents for each dollar earned by a man,[24] and this is still the case at the time of this writing. Although we've seen that this injustice is partly due to women's inability to negotiate, Senator Hillary Rodham Clinton is championing the Paycheck Fairness Act, legislation that's meant to prevent pay discrimination.

In a country claiming to value equality, the fact that pay discrimination still exists is scandalous, particularly as women—at some time or another—are far more likely than men to be the sole supporters of their families. A 2003 Bureau of Labor update reported that the earnings gap is industry dependent; male industries (such as construction and manufacturing) pay higher wages.[25] It's also a poor reflection on our society when one considers that among the most highly paid women are supermodels and prostitutes. Are these perhaps the most valued female occupations?

## UNDERPAYING PAYS

The underpaying of women has enormous economic benefit. Feminist economist Marilyn Waring notes that the free labor women offer generates 25–40 percent of a country's gross national product.[26] In the same way as chains were used to control slaves, a woman's hammered self-esteem guarantees a pool of cheap labor. Too many women settle for less than their real market value because poor self-esteem makes them so grateful that others will either employ them or offer them a contract. Business managers know just how much this pool of cheap labor pushes up profitability, so why would they change a system where many females are willing to work for a pittance? But without the shackles of our self-denial, women would become more demanding about increased salaries, improved benefits, more-flexible working hours, greater promotional and educational opportunities, and more recognition.

Ironically, "flexibility" has become the excuse that some women use to justify unequal pay because they claim lower salaries come with benefits, like more time off for children. But the facts remain the same: Women are not solely responsible for a couple's offspring and businesses whether they like it or not—form part of the social fabric. Since many corporations operate solely from a profit motive, pressure needs to be applied to integrate work/life balance strategies to cater for the demands placed on working parents, both men and women. First, there is a solid business case for work/life strategies and second, it's simply archaic to expect females to accept lower pay in order to have enough freedom to provide more labor at home.

If you're in the boat of underpaid people, do your research. Find out what men in your industry earn and negotiate. If necessary, group together with other women, but whichever route you choose, insist on equality in your company.

Naomi Wolf reports that there are many economists who believe that the future for unions is female and that these unions are the solution to the "feminization of poverty."[27] She quotes one economist as saying, "The fact that unionized women workers earn, on average, 30 percent more than nonunionized women workers speaks for itself."

The issue of equal pay doesn't apply only to salaried women. Too often self-employed females fall into the trap of underselling their services, and understandably business takes advantage of this.

I have noticed how one male client, at least, compared my earnings for conducting a seminar to his own salary—he commented that my bill was a lot more than his monthly earnings and asked whether I'd be prepared to conduct another session free of charge as compensation. My response is not worth noting!

Another pressing issue is that of sexual harassment. The American Psychological Association reports that almost half of all working women experience some form of sexual harassment in the workplace.[28] Underreporting of harassment incidents shows that many women would rather tolerate men's inappropriate sexual behavior rather than risk their jobs. I have known of women who have called upon the law for protection but have wound up on the losing end. Men know the benefit of out-of-court settlements, and, while the woman may receive some financial compensation, the male perpetrator ends up retaining his position . . . and strengthened by his victory is only more likely to offend again.

If things are to improve for women, it is evident that we need to learn to stand together as well as stand with men who are sympathetic to the cause.

Although the world may have implemented the mechanisms for equality, not much will change unless we collectively become more demanding about using the tools we have at our disposal. One such mechanism is the Convention on the Elimination of All Forms of Discrimination against Women (CEDAW).

The UN General Assembly adopted this convention in 1979, and at the time of writing, 170 countries had signed and ratified this convention. By ratifying it, countries are legally bound to live up to their commitments. The full text can be accessed on the Net (www.un.org/womenwatch/daw/cedaw/cedaw.htm), and it is a document that women can use to make more demands.

However, the great "land of the free" is one of a handful of countries that has signed but not ratified this agreement, and is unlikely to do so. As such, the United States keeps company with the only other two countries that have not ratified this agreement: Iran and the Sudan.

Although Bill Clinton made the right noises about moving toward ratification, in effect he did as little as George Dubya to make it happen. George Junior is well supported by neocon men on this one, but it is surprising that women like Phyllis Schlafly (a vociferous opponent of feminism) take issue with a document designed to free their own gender. Schlafly and others like her cite interference with conservative family values as their primary objection.

## EXPECT EQUALITY

To eliminate personal discrimination, a good rule of thumb is to enter each situation with the expectation of equality. Many women who reach the top of their field advise this. They don't rise to the bait thrown out by men, and they negotiate issues that negatively affect them. If you anticipate being treated like a second-class citizen, your beliefs will show in your behavior, and you offer an open invitation for men to ride roughshod over you.

Many women wage an inner battle between what their "inner adult" wants and what their "inner little girl" thinks she deserves. This makes us vulnerable to being manipulated by superiors—all our bosses need to do is reinforce our mistakes, failures, weaknesses, and inadequacies, and this feeds our belief that we don't deserve greatness. If we accept their judgments, we further weaken our position, making it all the harder to negotiate with dignity.

Again, expecting society to change is naive; what social shifts require is that we heal the damage that makes us demand so much less for ourselves.

## TRUSTING OTHER WOMEN

Strong, achieving women often complain that female colleagues are more likely to put them down than to support them. There are two reasons for this.

Firstly, according to Mary Daly, many working females have the wrong idea about strong women. In the name of female bonding, Amazons in business are expected to be self-sacrificing for their sisters rather than self-affirming.[29] If they're not, other women feel disappointed, as this means they have to fight for themselves. So rather than take responsibility for their emotions, they lash out at the self-affirming woman. Feasibly, the only thing a strong woman, who has secured a top position, can do is make the space for other females to follow through.

The second reason lies in the difficulty women have in trusting one another, which, as we've seen, arose directly from the inconsistent nurturing from mom. This generalizes to an unhealthy mistrust of adult females, which means we fight against each other instead of fighting the system for ourselves. So let's throw out the self-defeating behavior patterns, become more aware of our own expectations, and relearn trust in women.

Trust can only be developed where open communication exists. This means we need to stop "the tyranny of niceness" and get real in our interactions. Trust takes time, and if, as a leader, you are to earn it, your authentic behavior will need to be consistent. Start in uncomplicated areas and the new learned behavior will then be easier to generalize to your other interactions.

The trust issue is important. Lack of trust is the reason why females fail to group together and use the unstoppable power of the collective. Collective power has halted many untenable political systems, and women can use it to demand equal pay or put an end to practices that prejudice women, like sexual harassment. Here again, the only way we'll succeed in capitalizing on the power of the collective is by waking up to the needs of our unnurtured little girl, so she doesn't sabotage our adulthood.

## SOOTHING YOUR INNER CHILD

One of the most effective ways of dealing with the distress of the inner child is to have regular internal dialogues with her. Picture yourself at a young age, and speak to this child as you would any other kid who is feeling frightened and lonely. Let her know that she has no responsibilities and that the adult in you will face the challenges of the grown-up world.

Also reassure her that you will protect her in any battle. In this way she is freed to offer you what children give best—fun and creativity.

Another of the conflicted little girl's greatest fears is rejection. As a successful career is still not accepted as the norm, women's achievement virtually guarantees rebuffs and further alienation.

To fulfill their earlier unmet need to be accepted and belong, women often prioritize close relationships over and above their careers. For many who are not yet disillusioned with the promise of a rescuing prince, marriage promises them the key to a fabulous life. This view makes career success even more problematic. Too often working women don't go for gold because their accomplishments are likely to threaten their men. For those who are single, achievement is feared. They are afraid that success may make them appear too independent to a prospective prince.

## TRADING AMBITIONS FOR MEN

It is difficult to believe that women trade their ambitions for men, yet the consequences that females fear are well-founded in fact. Again Susan Maushart provides the research.[30] She shows that the better women fare in the workforce, the worse they seem to fare in marriage. Earning more than your husband or being better educated than him are risk factors to marital stability and can ultimately result in divorce.

Men behave badly around female achievement. Even though many fantasize about a successful wife, few cope with the reality. Female success emasculates men, because it shows up their inadequacies—so much so that some men completely collapse around their wife's growing achievements. They become increasingly purposeless or ineffectual, and abuse is at times an unfortunate recourse.

Given that only a small percentage of females remain single, and an even smaller number choose to be single and childfree (although these numbers are growing), it appears that the majority opt for marital "bliss."

However, 50 percent of marriages end up as a divorce statistic.

This shows that sacrificing one's career for matrimony is a risky investment, one that is unlikely to pay dividends in the end.

So unlike men, whose careers receive a boost from marriage and children (they earn 30 percent more and are promoted more rapidly[31]) there are no simple solutions for ambitious women.

For the majority of working women, it seems that marriage and career success are still not compatible. This means that until women demand that men mature sufficiently to embrace female success, we can't have it all. Certainly we can't have it all at once.

Sure it may seem unfair that women have to do the work to get past male ignorance, but there are hidden gifts and advantages. These produce powerful female entrepreneurs. Career women work "to make a difference," so it's interesting that young women entering business seldom entertain the thought of becoming an entrepreneur. Many end up doing so, though. When working conditions stymie this need to make a contribution, their thoughts start turning toward their own ventures.

## JUMPING SHIP SUCCESSFULLY

In a 1998 study conducted by Catalyst, a New York–based nonprofit research and advisory organization for the advancement of women in business, four major reasons were cited for females leaving corporate America at twice the rate of men: lack of flexibility (51 percent), glass ceiling (29 percent), unhappiness with work environment (28 percent), and feeling unchallenged in their job (22 percent). Only 5 percent reported being made redundant by downsizing.[32]

According to the National Association of Women Business Owners (NAWBO), one in eighteen woman is a business owner, and 60 percent of start-up ventures are female-owned businesses.[33]

What both figures show is that corporate organizations are making little attempt to retain top female talent. With significant growth in the number of female-owned start-ups, it is evident that big business is unconcerned. Perhaps making a difference is too far removed from the money/power values they prioritize.

Women-owned businesses are the fastest growing segment of the U.S. economy.[34] Having conducted seminars with both corporate and entrepreneurial women, I've noticed there appear to be five main reasons for the success of female entrepreneurs:

Firstly, unlike men whose needs are catered to by the system, the struggles we've been through strengthen us. Challenges force learning. So the more difficult experiences one has had, the greater the potential for knowledge gathering. This knowledge is easier to translate into success than academic book learning.

Secondly, women fed up with corporate frustrations do not jump ship impetuously. They take their time to strategically formulate a well-thought-out blueprint for their new business. Once ready to roll, female-owned businesses tend to be more thoroughly planned. This helps women overcome the early hurdles and stands them in good stead when life's unavoidable surprises show up.

Thirdly, with the need to make a difference as the foundation of the company, women enter commerce with a ready-made passion. Unlike male-dominated enterprises, a woman's business mission is not something that needs inventing as she goes along. It is dictated by her passion. Passion is contagious, and this heartfelt mission makes it easier to inspire other people. From the thinking of emotional intelligence, it's well-known that the ability to gain cooperation is one of the fundamentals of success.

Fourthly, women leave employment because they are exasperated by the limitations that thwart their passion. Consequently, they are under no illusions about returning. With no backdoor option, they tend to have a deeper commitment to their new venture. This keeps women entrepreneurs focused and provides the determination to overcome the difficult challenges that lie ahead.

Fifthly, when it comes to the success of female-owned start-ups, another common characteristic is that few businesswomen allow their ego to determine their needs. Unlike some men who acquire expensive trappings for the sake of appearances, many female entrepreneurs' beginnings are humble. In the early days of their business, a home office furnished with borrowed desks and equipment cast-offs is adequate. This considerably reduces their exposure to risk.

Although companies owned by women account for some 38 percent of businesses in the United States, female entrepreneurs receive less than 4 percent of the $36 billion invested annually in venture capital.[35]

Evidently, financial institutions remain ignorant of the lower risk involved in lending money to women-owned businesses. Because of the institutions' reluctance to support female-owned ventures, women have become more creative. Their determination simply won't allow this obstacle to keep them from progressing.

Although women-owned businesses collectively employ more people than all the Fortune 500 companies, The National Council for Research on Women says that two-thirds reported problems when working with financial institutions.[36] World over, women struggle to obtain support through the conventional channels, and as a result, many are self-financing.

David Silver in *Enterprising Women* states that the women he interviewed started their business with personal savings—some as little as $1,000. (Just cutting back on antiwrinkle creams could make this possible!) Others got off the ground through sweat equity, or by borrowing from friends or family members. Typically these loans were paid back within a year of borrowing.[37]

Where these avenues were unavailable, the creative opted for supplier financing and negotiated upfront payments on early deals. Bartering of products and services also helped new entrepreneurs to acquire equipment and furnishings. Others took advantage of available financial channels like a second mortgage or credit card borrowing.

## DON'T BANK ON THE BANKS

Banks! Need I say more? From their attitude it's difficult to believe that financial institutions make their money from client borrowings rather than from us squirreling our savings with them.

Although service levels have improved marginally, the approach of banks is still one of a power game, making customers grovel for their services. This is especially true when it comes to female-owned businesses.

Like the advice given by well-hardened businesswomen, go in with the expectation of being treated as a valuable customer. Never let bank managers disempower you with their bureaucratic bullshit.

Given that the challenges faced by female entrepreneurs are colossal, their success is even more impressive. We've seen how women in America manage the single biggest economy in the world, and according to the Center for Women's Business Research, the number of women-owned businesses continues to grow at twice the rate of all U.S. firms—14 percent compared to 7 percent nationwide.[38]

Faith Popcorn claims that in 2000, women-owned and female-run businesses stood at 9 million enterprises.[39] These businesses employ 27.5 million people, one out of every four U.S. workers, and generate $3.6 trillion, which Tom Peters puts into perspective by showing that this exceeds the GDP of Germany![40]

Whereas a few decades ago women tended to opt for typical female interests in their businesses, the Fortune 500's top 100 women shows diversity more reflective of the broader economy. Now women are having success in traditional male fields like manufacturing, engineering, and agriculture. Combine this business success with the clout of our economic spending power and it's naive in the extreme for advertisers to still refer to women as a niche market or special-interest group!

Regardless of industry, it's interesting that women business owners also consistently employ a more gender-balanced workforce. Certainly they engage women at higher rates than the national average.

Figures supplied by the same Center for Women's Business Research show that women business owners employ roughly half women (52 percent) and half men (48 percent). Male-owned businesses, on the other hand, still favor male employees by nearly a two-to-one ratio.[41]

With such poor preparation for competing on an equal basis, it's awe inspiring that women have achieved so much. Although off the starting blocks later than the boys, these women can outrun those who are better equipped for the race.

Against the odds, we now not only have many flourishing female entrepreneurs, but we're also witnessing plenty of women successfully heading up major multinational corporations.

With large, male-dominated corporate companies collapsing around us, a strong female influence is more necessary in business than ever before. Men are unlikely to address matters of corporate governance realistically, for was it not their thinking that got companies like Enron into trouble in the first place? Women now have great opportunities to forge even more significant inroads in business. To make a difference we need to resolve our personal issues so that we can test our ideas against the system. Of course, many will fail, but it's only the lessons we gain in the process that will lead to some exciting new ways.

As we've seen before, current changes in our world of work are far better suited to a female's lifestyle. Despite the backlash the working woman's time has come, and with greater flextime, more home offices, teleworking, and contracting, the virtual workplace is a boon to women. This new way of working is more reliant upon networking—a natural female skill.

When it comes to the Net, women are the driving factor in e-commerce. Women entrepreneurs are the fastest-growing market, as they are most likely to do their purchasing remotely. Dun and Bradstreet reported that women business owners are more likely to purchase goods and services on the Internet than their male counterparts—for their businesses (46 percent vs. 34 percent) and for personal use (42 percent vs. 25 percent).[42]

This means that women-owned businesses in this fast-growing sector have a head start when it comes to understanding the needs of their customers.

With factors like the increasing number of women swapping corporate for their own enterprise, as well as the collapse of big business, one can be hopeful that we'll soon see statistics of women making greater progress in the transition from middle management to executive level than the 125 years suggested by the Feminist Majority's Research Center statistics.

When this is combined with the power of the matriarch in the family, it is evident that women are making great headway in restoring our rightful place in the world.

Sure men will continue to protect their vested interests by feeding the stereotypes. But we know that this typecasting is aimed purely at arresting our ambition. The more we go about conquering the self-sacrificing behavior that disempowers us, the freer we'll become. To rise above the stereotypes, we need to accept that prejudice exists and live the way we choose regardless of the role society keeps dictating for us.

By definition, being normal means living an average life. So if success is what you want, it requires having to accept that you are one of a select group that is choosing to be abnormal. If this means having to tolerate the label of wicked witch, then at least let's use our magic wands to full effect. I've learned from experience that sticks and stones may break my bones, but being labeled a bitch can't harm me.

# A Fairer Tale: Slenderella

+++++++++++++++++++++++++++++++++++++++++++++++++++++++++

Long ago in a faraway land there lived a beautiful and kind-hearted young girl called Slenderella. She was very lonely and sad because her mother had died and her father had married a new, mean-hearted wife. Slenderella's stepmother had two ugly daughters—a hopeless one called Desperado and an unsightly one known as Grotesque.

As if that weren't bad enough, soon after he had remarried, Slenderella's father suddenly died. The orphaned little girl was now at the mercy of her stepmother and two awful sisters. Green with envy over Slenderella's pretty face, Desperado and Grotesque made a point of being as spiteful as they knew how.

The stepsisters spent most of their days lounging about reading glossy mags and watching television. They were riveted by anything to do with celebrity gossip, beauty contests, and cosmetics. But like everyone else in the land, Desperado and Grotesque knew well that handsome princes marry only exceptionally beautiful princesses. And their mirrors showed quite plainly that both of them had a far from pretty face. Slenderella on the other hand had been blessed with the type of desirable feminine looks that magazines and men found irresistible.

From a young age Slenderella had been groomed to always do her utmost to please other people. But the harder Slenderella tried to fulfill every wish of her stepmother and ugly sisters, the meaner they became. Slenderella was innocent of the fact that she would never be able to give her sisters the one thing they wanted more than anything: to be as beautiful as she was. But still she kept on trying.

One evening after Slenderella had washed up and swept and done the ironing, her stepmother said, "All girls must do housework, but you also need to work for your keep." So that evening the cruel stepmother and her daughters put their heads together to decide how Slenderella could be put to better use.

Next morning, the stepmother woke Slenderella up and

announced: "To pay for your keep, you will serve as personal beautician to Desperado and Grotesque." And the ugly sisters quickly added, "Day in and day out you will work your pretty little fingers to the bone to make us more beautiful than you."

From then on Slenderella did her utmost to give her grotesque sisters the type of female faces that appeared in the glossy magazines they kept shoving under her nose. She learned all about face creams that can transform any skin into glowing silk, and she studied the techniques of making up eyes and lips so that they sparkle alluringly. She learned how to shade the heaviness out of her sisters' jaws. She even became an expert in home-based cellulite reduction. Day in and day out she toiled, applying one miracle potion after another.

Then one day a grand-looking envelope arrived in the mail. "It's from the palace," announced Slenderella's stepmother breathlessly, ripping open the gilded envelope.

Slenderella had just begun applying hot beeswax to remove some unsightly hair from the two sisters' faces, so she listened as her stepmother read out the official message.

"The king is having a ball!" she said excitedly.

"I know!" remarked Grotesque. "Ever since the queen died he's had difficulty controlling himself. So who's he shagging now?"

Before anyone could answer, Desperado muttered cynically through the beeswax on her lip, "Tsk, tsk . . . wasting all the taxpayers' money on loose women again, I suppose!"

"No! No!" said their mother impatiently. "This is some sort of beauty contest. The king is looking for a wife for himself and some new fluff for the philandering prince to play with. Oh my dears, this is just marvelous! Now I can get both of you off my hands at the same time."

"Am I invited too, stepmother?" asked Slenderella.

"You! Certainly not!" gasped her stepmother. "The thought of such a thing! With your feminine looks and low self-esteem we couldn't risk it; the king and prince wouldn't give a second glance at my daughters if you put in an appearance. No! You are to stay at home. Now, get cracking and prepare them for this momentous event."

"Hah hah!" laughed the two sisters spitefully.

"Oh!" said Slenderella sadly, "I do wish I could go to the ball."

In the weeks before the ball, Slenderella toiled harder than ever to make the ugly sisters beautiful. But no matter what she did they remained ugly. "Look what it says on the packaging!" Grotesque would screech. "'Guaranteed—a flawlessly glowing skin.' You must have done something wrong, you useless idiot!"

In despair early one morning, Slenderella took the last few pennies her father had left her and went herself to the big cosmetics house at the far end of the little town to see what she could find that might solve her problem.

At the store her eyes grew bigger and bigger; never before had she seen so many different possibilities for beautifying women. Quickly she read all the fascinating slogans. To her great relief, she found all sorts of marvelous products that would definitely make her sisters look like the beautiful models on the packaging: *Be slim in just a week. Facelifts in your own home.* And there was more . . . *Thicker hair with Build & Grow. Beautiful nails in a matter of minutes.*

So Slenderella swept up armfuls of these seductively scented magic jars and hurried over to the gold-plated counter. The bill was far more than she could afford; she had to think quickly: "Put it on my stepmother's account," pleaded Slenderella. She told herself that with these magic potions, her sisters would most certainly catch the eye of the king and prince, who would then end up paying the bill anyway. In the days before the big event, Slenderella meticulously followed the instructions on the potions she'd bought. She applied all the gooey stuff in the exquisite little pots. But as the pots got emptier and emptier, the sisters remained as ugly as ever.

With just two days to go before the glittering affair, Slenderella was getting desperate. Her sisters, behind their layers of goop, were incandescent with rage. Slenderella thought she may have to run away, because there seemed to be nothing left that would make her sisters beautiful, but suddenly she was struck by a brain wave: masks!

Working her fingers to the bone, Slenderella—with the delicacy of a surgeon—crafted two exquisite masks. By now she knew her sisters' faces so intimately that she was able to mold shapes that fitted them like skin. To each mask she applied layers and layers of garish color, and finally, by ingeniously using a little pencil, she fashioned the most gorgeous full lips.

The day of the ball finally dawned, and Slenderella spent hours and hours carefully fitting each of the sisters with the beautifully handcrafted masks. For the first time ever the sisters were delighted with the mirror images.

"Look," said Grotesque excitedly to Desperado. "It's me, just better!" But to Slenderella the masked sisters merely said, "Weeks and weeks it took you to do what any beautician could have done in a day!"

When the coach arrived to collect the beautifully masked sisters and their mother, Slenderella looked on hopelessly. And once they were out of sight she sighed to herself, "Oh, I did so want to go as well."

"What for? It's only a silly meat market," said a mysterious voice.

"Who's that?" asked Slenderella, looking around.

"I'm your fairy godmother," said the voice. And with that a strange woman walked up to Slenderella and very gently cradled the sorrowful slip of a girl in her warm, comforting arms.

"You're so kind," Slenderella said, "But why do you have to be a fairy?"

The fairy godmother tenderly explained, "Good, kind women never appear in tales that prepare young girls for marriage and motherhood. So let's just pretend and I will grant you any wish you want."

For a little while Slenderella thought. After a time she said, "Well I've got wonderful looks and a great body; how about lots of self-esteem and a good brain?"

The fairy godmother sat down. "We have work to do," she said. "I will need all those well-thumbed magazines you've been studying, your Barbie doll, the sweet-smelling little pots with their fibbing slogans, your tea set, and any other toys that prepare you for domestic entrapment."

So Slenderella ran off and quickly gathered up the things the fairy godmother had asked for. Soon they were all collected in a big pile in the middle of the floor.

With a single whisk of her magic wand, the fairy godmother set fire to the whole lot. While the flames danced she told Slenderella, "All these wicked things are just make-believe. In the real world, women have more to offer than their looks and domestic competency."

Slenderella was astonished. Never before had she heard such violations of the sacred social code. Before long, the big blaze was reduced to a few glowing cinders. Slowly, the fairy godmother bent down, and, gathering some of the ashes with her magic wand, she forged the most beautiful crystal pendant Slenderella had ever seen.

As she was doing so, she chanted a magic spell: "Out of the ashes of social conditioning, I recreate your self-esteem."

Putting the delicate crystal around the girl's neck, the fairy godmother said, "This is your new freedom. Parade it proudly as a symbol of your self-esteem." In an instant Slenderella started to glow. With all those wicked little hypnotic accessories burned to cinders, she was starting to feel her natural power returning.

With that, Slenderella was ready for the ball. One more whisk of the magical wand and *POW!* the bright and confident little girl found herself standing so close to the handsome prince that she could smell his pheromones.

To the left and right of him were the masked Desperado and Grotesque, whom he now began to ignore. To the sisters' growing disgust, the prince slowly moved toward the enchanting Slenderella.

But, to her great surprise, as soon as he hit the magical glow of her newfound self-confidence, the prince bounced right off. Taking fright, he quickly fled back to the safety of the masks.

Enraged, Slenderella tore the shiny crystal from her dainty neck and flung it so hard that it shattered into hundreds of tiny pieces across the ballroom floor. Swiftly her glow started to fade, and the more it dimmed the closer the prince came.

Soon the prince had Slenderella in his arms, and together they were whirling round and round the dance floor. So enchanted was the prince that within a matter of days the two were married.

But, after a short time, Slenderella began to tire of the prince. It became obvious to her almost instantly that all the prince really wanted was a pretty attachment for his arm, and his philandering continued unabated. Secretly Slenderella decided that since the prince was incapable of loving a real person, a masked one would probably have been better after all.

Thinking wistfully about her shattered self-esteem, Slenderella began to weep. As the tears fell one by one, a little bunny, which had been hiding in the corner, hopped closer and closer to the disappointed princess.

While the bunny was mopping up her tears, more rabbits began hopping into Slenderella's chamber. Through her weepy eyes she could just make out a glow in the darkened room. Indeed! Something very mysterious was happening.

One of the bunnies was carrying a small hand-stitched bag. In it were all the shards of her magical crystal pendant. Upon seeing this, Slenderella jumped up and shouted for joy.

"We found all the tiny pieces, and if you hold just one of them, the magical glow will return," said the bunny clutching the little bag. "For we have a job for you. One that only a girl with lots of self-esteem can do."

Carefully, Slenderella took a piece of the sparkling crystal and put it around her dainty neck. As the glow returned, all the bunnies gathered in a circle and started to tell her their sad stories. To make those sweet-smelling jars with their fancy slogans, they had been put through some horrendous forms of torture, they explained:

"I had to eat fourteen pounds of cherry-red lipstick," said the bright pink one.

"Yucky-smelling shampoo dribbled into my eyes for weeks on end," said another through her bleary peepers.

"Fur-peeling creams were smeared all over me," said the bald one.

And on and on the woeful tales went.

After Slenderella had heard all of the rabbits' sad stories, she wiped the tears from her own eyes and began to think of a plan. Instead of attending to the needs of the prince's left arm, she would become an activist.

Without delay, Slenderella divorced the philandering prince and set about inquiring into the business of the big cosmetics house at the far end of the little town.

In the depths of night, she secretly inspected all the records in the store's enormous registry. Then she came across something that alarmed her greatly. Both the king and the philandering prince were in fact the real owners of the store. "So they are the ones who are behind all this terrible cruelty and these outrageous lies," she exclaimed to herself.

Aghast, she rushed back to consult with the exploited bunnies. Together they began to plot against the two royal fiends.

"But, it's so dangerous," said one of the rabbits with some urgency. "We'd better go underground." And with that all the little bunnies began burrowing. They burrowed and burrowed and didn't stop until tunnels linked each house to their secret central warren. Then from the safety of their burrows, they embarked on their plan.

Every day, the rabbits would pick a new dwelling and scurry through the tunnels to visit the lady of the house. First they'd carefully explain their plight, then they'd give each woman a tiny piece of the little crystal. Once they had visited every home except one, there were virtually no women in the town who would set foot in the nasty store.

Soon the gold-plated counter in the shop began to tarnish, and, one by one, traders peddling beauty products began to close down. First the magazine collapsed, then the fashion house closed its doors. Next, the toy makers—who concocted the Barbie dolls and all those offensive little domestic atrocities—suffered the same plight.

Day by day the king and prince were becoming more and more perplexed and enraged. To keep the royal coffers from drying up, they advertised and advertised, but all to no avail. Nothing could get past the newfound self-esteem of the women in the land.

Now that the campaign was in full swing, Slenderella decided to pay her stepmother's house a visit. She found Desperado and Grotesque in the most terrible state. Theirs was the only house in the whole town that the bunnies had decided to ignore. Now, they sat miserably alone with their cracked masks and no self-esteem.

Quickly Slenderella patched them up, and how thrilled they seemed. "Hurry over to the palace," she instructed, "the king and prince are waiting for you." Faster than anyone could say the word "deception," Desperado and Grotesque were at the palace door.

For months now the ladies of the land had ignored the king and prince, so on seeing the two delightful masks, the men began oozing charm.

Now Slenderella's plan was ready for its final execution. With Desperado and Grotesque firmly behind the regal doors, she gathered all the esteemed women in the land. Together they quietly crept through the tunnels the bunnies had burrowed and made their way right inside the palace walls.

Peeking through the slightly opened door, they could just make out Desperado and Grotesque cooing loudly as they lapped up the king and prince's attention. Then suddenly Slenderella and the townswomen burst into the room.

Capturing the king, the prince, and their new consorts, they bundled them over to the cosmetics house at the far end of the little town.

To this day the royal fiends and the miserable sisters are still housed there. It has been said that the king's legs have been waxed so many times he is almost as smooth as a baby's bottom. And the prince—well, his beard is part of a new test for a nauseatingly painful electrolysis procedure. As for Grotesque, students learn the basics of plastic surgery by practicing on her abundant warts. And Desperado is a perfect candidate for testing the endless stream of new tranquilizers and antidepressants.

In the land of the esteemed women, Slenderella lives happily on. Never ever again will the sweet-smelling jars tell their little fibs. And no bunny will be used for testing ever again. . . . (Now if you believe that, you'll believe anything!)

+ + + + + + + + + + + + + + + + + + + + + + + + + + + + + + + + + + + + + + + + + + + + + + + + + +

CHAPTER 7.

# Princess without a Cause

J ust because women's bodies are designed to bear children, does this mean that our biology must dictate to us for the rest of our lives? Who said mothers need to be their children's taxi service, fast food outlet, Laundromat, daycare, tailor, researcher, nurse, cleaner, information bureau (as in, Where's the cereal?), entertainer, bank, and punching bag?

Although few mothers would agree, parental responsibility requires only two things: making sure that our children physically survive to adulthood, and loving them. And loving certainly doesn't mean sacrificing our own life so we can, like a modern valet service, be at the beck and call of our children in every possible way. But this is where many women get confused, having been groomed to believe that loving others means 24/7 room service plus delivering whatever else may be demanded, whether it suits you or not.

Year after year mothers keep providing services that their children are well able to do for themselves—packing school lunches, tidying rooms, and checking the bus schedule—and all this for kids who are more than able to organize a party and find whatever they desire on the Internet.

So what's going on here? Isn't it supposed to be good for children to take appropriate levels of responsibility, making them resourceful and self-reliant? Haven't we learned that independence will be of far greater benefit to our children than the unrealistic expectation that others will always wait upon them hand and foot? As said by Dr. Phil McGraw, "When we do too much for our children, they don't learn to master anything." So, is our relentless sacrificing of ourselves for their good, or is it our way of trying to feel better about ourselves?

Before you interpret this as a criticism of the warm and generous way in which mothers give of themselves, consider it as a comment on the one-sided way that society forces mothers to take ultimate responsibility for the well-being of children. The burden placed on mothers is total, so it's no wonder that many end up feeling that anything less than total self-sacrifice is not enough.

## FINDING YOUR OWN WAY

I know many women find these ideas difficult to swallow because the self-sacrifice myth demands that children become their lifework. But no matter how much you love your offspring, it's impossible to find happiness by living through other people.

Living through children (or partners) makes you dependent upon them for your life satisfaction. As with all forms of dependence, when the loved one is unable to deliver, the dependent person feels resentful. This complicates our relationship with ourselves and with the ones we depend on for meaning.

When a mother fulfills her own needs through her children's success, it places a terrible burden on the children. By being themselves they may risk disappointing their mother. The dilemma between living their own life and meeting Mother's expectations is too big an emotional trade-off for a child to bear. Younger children usually conform to Mother's plan for their success, but by the teen years they'll start refusing to cooperate. So even if it's just for the children's well-being, women need to find their own deeper sense of meaning and something gratifying to do.

This by no means implies that children should not be a priority in a woman's life. A 2003 Gallup Poll reported that when people were asked about the most important thing in their life, 96 percent ranked family higher than health, work, friends, money, religion, and leisure.[1] In the heartwarming documentaries about 9/11 survivors, those interviewed said that the most significant thought in their mind during the trauma was getting back to their children. Neither men nor women talked about their career or fortune as being the prime motive for survival. So of course in a parent's mind, children will be the most important consideration. But does the fact that your children occupy a central place in your heart mean that you must give up your own development for their sake? Why does it have to be either child rearing or self-fulfillment?

## IT TAKES A VILLAGE

All societies have their roots in the extended family and community lifestyle, which provided many parental options. It permitted adults to give the best part of themselves to the children. When one person got tired or irritated or had PMS, she could withdraw and others would naturally take over as caregivers. Communities provide a rich diversity in terms of personalities, age, skills, talents, and interests, making life more colorful for the children.

The relatively recent advent of the nuclear family means that the responsibility previously taken up by a whole community rests on one person's shoulders—Mom's. This is unrealistic. Although busy women can now pay other people for assistance, Ellen McGrath, author of *When Feeling Bad Is Good,* claims that only 57 percent of American women who can afford household help actually have it.[2] Anywhere in the world, help with daycare, extracurricular activities, baby-sitting, and laundry is both practical and necessary, but working women who call for help often judge themselves to be ineffectual mothers. This reveals just how much the self-sacrificing agenda is linked to a woman's image of herself as a mother and nurturer. Yet the job of child raising was never intended to be the sole responsibility of one person.

## DRUGS AND ROSES

The fact that neither society nor women themselves consider a female's identity or needs to be important is evident in the overwhelmingly high incidence of women's depression. In the United States nineteen million women suffer from depression annually, and (as seen in Chapter 3) females are twice as likely as males to suffer a major depressive episode.[3] Married women have higher rates of depression than unmarried women, but the reverse is true for men.[4] Although genetics and hormonal changes are risk factors, research has demonstrated that a significant factor in a person's vulnerability to depression is the tendency to treat one's own needs as secondary to those of other people.[5]

Dana Crowley Jack, a leading researcher on women's depression, says that women silence themselves in order to cultivate and maintain intimate relationships. We do so by censoring our views, devaluing our experiences, and repressing feelings like anger. She also believes that being dependent on someone else and trying to fulfill the demands of being a good wife and mother combine with low self-esteem to make women more vulnerable to depression.[6]

McGrath notes that the rate of sexual and physical abuse is much higher than was previously suspected and is a major factor in women's depression. In her report she says that depressive symptoms may be long-standing effects of post-traumatic stress disorder.[7]

With major changes in our lives, many women now desire more than the happy-wife-and-mother role. Often those who are discontented in the role, but continue to play it, find themselves severely depressed. Rarely do they understand why. After all, society promises girls that marriage (preferably to a wealthy prince), with a good home and a bunch of children, will be fulfilling. But what the depression is showing is that the notion of prince and red roses can only exist in a fairytale.

## UNHAPPY PILLS

Millions of women are unhappy and discontented, but for these sad millions, will medication make their lives better? According to McGrath, women are incorrectly diagnosed as being depressed about 30–50 percent of the time.[8] As a result, antidepressants are one of the most prescribed drugs in the world, second only to antibiotics. Globally the market is worth $12 billion and, in the U.K. alone, the demand for antidepressants has more than doubled in the last ten years. Worldwide, women account for 70 percent of these prescriptions, and McGrath is concerned that with improper diagnosis and monitoring, drug misuse is a very real danger for women;[9] especially considering that approximately 30–35 percent of people taking antidepressants do not respond to this form of treatment.[10]

The Harvard School of Public Health warns that depression is likely to become the noncommunicable disease posing the leading global concern by 2020.[11] So instead of buying antidepressants, you could probably cheer yourself up far more by purchasing shares in the companies that make them!

The effect of antidepressants is moot. In the first of two studies, Dr. Irving Kirsch, a University of Connecticut psychologist, and his team found that at least 50 percent of the drug effect is due to what's called the placebo response.[12] A placebo is a sugar pill that contains no active ingredient; in other words it has no medical effect. In a more recent study of the six most prescribed antidepressants, approximately 80 percent of the response to medication was duplicated in the placebo control groups.[13]

So drugs—without intensive therapy—can't help us reclaim our power. All they generally do is make us oblivious of the fact that we are powerless. However, for those who want to kick the antidepressant habit, this should only be done in managed care, as in psychotherapy.

It's an interesting phenomenon that human beings learn more through painful circumstances than through pleasurable ones. This is something that is accepted in Eastern philosophy. However, in the Western world we have stopped understanding the function of pain, so instead of using discomfort to pay attention to our life so that we can learn more about ourselves, we use drugs to numb the feedback that our body is desperately trying to give us. This inhibits our ability to understand why we are ill or depressed in the first place.

With so many women addicted to killing their anguish with antidepressants, tranquilizers, sleeping pills, or potent analgesics, one must conclude that something is drastically wrong with women in our society.

## HISTORICAL HYSTERIA

Many people, including medical practitioners, have latched on to a highly simplistic interpretation of Freud's early ideas. This has unfortunately allowed them to lump a huge range of symptoms experienced by women under the title of hysteria. As a result, women visiting family doctors are three times more likely than men to be treated with tranquilizers and antidepressants.[14] The irony is that toward the end of his career, Freud himself confessed to understanding little about women.

Dependence on drugs is not only a burden, but it is also disempowering in most cases. The ease with which our society turns to drugs to solve women's lifestyle and psychological problems is truly alarming. In the short term, masking pain allows people to cope, but if all pain, whether it is physical or emotional, is simply medicated away, then we will never get to the bottom of what gave rise to that pain in the first place. Perhaps the drug companies and threatened male egos of our society actually want women to turn themselves into pill-popping zombies. For if we were to work through the pain, we'd emerge stronger, wiser, and more determined to realize our innate power.

Most women don't need to be labeled and treated as hysterical, they just need to wake up to the fact that accepting society's stereotypes and knee-jerk solutions is killing them. Depression is, after all, an expression of someone who's dying inside. A common cause of women's depression is burnout from giving too much of ourselves, whether at work or at home, which brings us right back to the pitfalls of our addiction to self-sacrifice.

## WHAT ABOUT ME?

We know that girls are taught that giving is noble, but no one warned us that when our own basic human needs are not fulfilled, we simply run out of energy. And when we're totally exhausted, we can't look after ourselves or anyone else at all; we get sick or we go crazy. But most women manage to get through their days on a kind of perennial medium level of exhaustion. This means they aren't comatose, so they can still go through the motions, getting the kids to school, managing the household, and for many holding down a job. But how much of this is done while being ratty, impatient, and short-tempered?

So when you're constantly worn out, how effective are you—especially as a mother? Realistically, no one can achieve what they want to unless they prioritize their own needs. I don't know about you, but for me, constantly being tired and ineffectual is hardly a sensible way to live!

Like men, most women need a life beyond 24/7 child minding. But feminine socialization tells us that if we have personal needs beyond our domestic, mothering, and wifely roles, then we are not only being too demanding but we are neglecting our womanly vocation. Many women try dutifully to deny their own needs, only to find out that one way or another they will surface. Unmet needs, like neglected children, tend to make themselves noticed through difficult behavior, withdrawal, physical illness, or depression. The very high incidence of depression among women today is an extreme expression of the fact that we are not getting our own needs met. So what can we do about this?

## CONVEYOR-BELT LIVES

I believe that everyone on the planet is here to do something they consider important. It's a normal human need, but this is something that husbands and children cannot always fulfill for women. More often it's something we need to do for ourselves.

From Martin Seligman, the founder of "Positive Psychology," we know that the pursuit of happiness is really quite simple. Although many people pin their happiness hopes on having more money, better looks, or greater status, Seligman's research shows that only one thing creates lasting happiness: knowing that our life is making a contribution to others.[15]

It's about leaving a legacy that tells other people we have lived, that our lives mattered. This is our lifework, and it is not a selfish need—it's simply human. Certainly it does not deny the critical role played by children, but rather reinforces the importance of living a balanced life, where your needs are met too.

For women, satisfaction and success do not necessarily mean finding a mundane job with meager pay. Too many do this just to keep the wolf from the door, but mostly this form of self-expression just reinforces our feelings of impotency. Seldom does a routine job satisfy our need to make a difference. Work is our adult form of expressing who we are, and the best is to find something you love doing that others will pay you handsomely for.

For those who have the luxury of not having to earn money, work can take many different forms. But most importantly, it expresses who you are now and who you would like to become in the future. What it requires is finding an outlet for your creative potential. When I talk about creativity, I'm not necessarily referring to the artistic version. Anything you create, be it a computer system or a letter, can be an avenue to satisfy this need.

But, before we go any further, it may be helpful to define success. While many perceive success as the generation of wealth, it's more useful to understand it as achieving whatever it is you are aiming for. This provides the freedom necessary to shift careers, exchange work for homemaking, or become a lazy layabout; what it means is you having enough life experience to know what you want.

## IDENTIFYING YOUR LIFEWORK

Interestingly, most people find their lifework through the process of elimination. It's seldom something that comes in a flash of inspiration.

Prior to conducting seminars and writing books, I worked as a supermarket cashier, a bank clerk, an administrator, a salesperson, secretary, waitress, market researcher, public relations consultant, team manager, scriptwriter, and video producer. I know that none of these are ways I wish to continue experiencing myself in the future.

Yet each of these experiences taught me something valuable that equipped me, in one way or another, to fulfill my passion. Likewise, your studies (even if they were unrelated to your current profession) and every past job have provided important elements in your preparation. Where you are right now is a critical stepping-stone. It may or may not be earning you much money, but it could be an essential part of your learning.

Instead of writing off the diverse experiences you may have had, value each one as important for whatever it taught you.

To get a handle on this, write a list of each job you have worked at, including those you worked at during high school or college. Then, next to each job, list the experiences and skills you gained. Too often we take skills we learned a long time ago for granted, but often the most interesting careers can be fashioned by combining the wide range of skills you have learned with your gifts and talents and the things that interest you most.

Knowing what we want is complex for women, as so much of our thinking is driven by social expectation. To help you identify what these issues are in your life, it may be useful to start from the beginning. For women, the rules of the game determine that females are biologically equipped to bear children. This leads to three key choices:

1. Women can defy their biology by opting not to have babies at all. For the childfree this is a choice, while for others fertility issues keep them childless. Whether desirable or not, the roles here are more clearly defined, requiring women to identify other avenues to provide their life satisfaction. In situations such as these, the options and consequences are numerous, but they are entirely different from those of women who choose the maternal role.

2. Many women opt for children because maternity is the role expected of them. Often they have no clearly defined feelings about having children, but do so either because of accidental pregnancy or the social expectations of their culture, husband, parents, and/or in-laws. These are often reluctant mothers who are obliged to accept maternity as part of their role.

3. Women who long for children will welcome babies who are either surprises or are planned. These are dedicated mothers whose life is often defined by the activities of their children. They enjoy their children and believe that the only acceptable way to parent is largely to give up their own life. If they have a career, their work is usually structured to allow enough flexibility to fit in with their children. These women are often successful in what they do, but because of time pressure, some question whether their career is fulfilling their need to make a difference.

For choices two and three, the reality is that children need adults to take care of them—whether male or female. But to do so, practicality determines that someone's got to bring home the bacon. In all three of the above categories, women again have a number of choices. There are women who:

    i.  are satisfied to be looked after by their partner,
    ii. have to work to supplement the family budget, or
    iii. prioritize their career as a means of making a difference.

## THE JUGGLING ACT

The most satisfied women tend to be those who:

    a. don't have children by choice because they've prioritized their career (1-iii).
    b. are dedicated mothers, choosing to be supported by their man (3-i).
    c. are dedicated mothers who also make a difference in their career (3-iii).

In all three categories these women are doing what they want and are able to make the most of their choices in life.

The area of caution for childfree women is that of getting out of touch with the "real world." For dedicated moms, it's the reality of being financially dependent on someone else and the problems associated with the empty nest syndrome—what happens when your children leave home?

The biggest challenge for women with young children in the third category is combining the demands of being a dedicated mother with prioritizing her career. Men find this one easy to manage, because they generally have a wife, but for women this situation presents some difficult conflicts. While men trust their wife to be a good mother and housekeeper, women who appoint competent caregivers are still considered neglectful of their children!

For a woman, the trickiest difficulty is to reconcile having two priorities—her career and her parenting role. The two can seem at odds and, at times, completely contradictory.

Life demands carefully traded-off priorities—and usually this balancing act happens every day. This is such an overwhelming challenge that at every women's conference there is always a section on balancing work and family. Often an experienced businesswoman is invited to tell her tale. However, mostly the speaker seems to want the audience to believe she's a well-disguised superwoman—albeit somewhat sympathetic. Never have I heard anyone talk about the tough reality of making difficult choices.

For women, this is life, and managing the balancing act requires brutal honesty with yourself. If your career is more satisfying than minding your children, admit it at least to yourself, even if you are not ready to admit it publicly. This will make structuring your life easier.

I'm not suggesting that children be ignored in favor of career demands, but when you know what is good or best for you, you can put effective structures in place to meet today's tough demands. You can also start making more demands on your man. If you don't, the trade-offs you make will be driven by guilt, making them ineffective. Consequently you won't know which support system to depend upon.

## PRIORITIZING FOR PEACE OF MIND

It's taken a long time for me to acknowledge that my career is more of a priority than my husband. This doesn't mean that I don't care, and it's got nothing to do with how much I love him.

It's more that work is a lifelong security—unlike many husbands, our careers are unlikely to run off with someone else, divorce us, or die. Accepting this rather than pretending makes balancing life's demands far simpler.

Balancing the daily trade-offs in your life means having the courage to carefully choose your priorities. You just can't be a superb mother, highly attentive wife, and top-achieving businesswoman all at once. Some things will have to give. Usually, when these decisions are unclear, what gives is the woman herself. Either our health suffers or we crack up mentally. Both are severe consequences, and sometimes they are life threatening.

You can avoid these debilitating consequences by taking an honest look at yourself. Observe your own behavior and take note of the things that you willingly put your energy into or that excite you. Undoubtedly this will reveal what's important to you.

Now, ruthlessly set about restructuring your life so that your activities are driven by what is most fulfilling. If you believe this process will offend others, then leave them out of discussions about it.

While balancing work and family is a necessity for highly ambitious mothers, only a small percentage of women falls into this category. An even smaller percentage is those who don't have children (by choice or through circumstance) and are supported financially by their partner. Women in this category risk being most dissatisfied of all. With little to occupy their time, boredom leads to high levels of frustration, and often they tend to take out their rage on those closest to them. Controlling behaviors like perfectionism and obsessive-compulsive disorder can develop, as an attempt to assert some authority over their lives. Not many women can sustain doing the same thing over and over again, whether it's a weekly beauty regime, cleaning house, shopping, or watching daytime television. Women who choose this way of life often do so to avoid testing themselves in the world. They sidestep experiences because the hazards seem too great. However, unless they find something to get their teeth into, they will continue to make their own lives and those of their partners a misery.

Women who don't have children but have a job purely to produce an income are seldom better off than their bored sisters. Even though they earn an income, their needs remain unsatisfied. The same applies to dedicated or reluctant mothers who have to work simply to supplement the family coffers. Dedicated mothers who are forced to work by their economic situation are resentful, because they cannot fulfill their need to be with their children. Reluctant mothers feel trapped both at home and at work (if it's just for the money), as neither are choices they've made for themselves. Mothers who are intelligent and ambitious but stay at home to fulfill the wifely/maternal role expected of them are equally frustrated.

## ENSNARED BY OUR PERCEPTIONS

Millions of women are trapped, either by economics or social expectations. Both their circumstances and their own emotional beliefs ensnare them. A way out of the trap is to start exploring one's own personal history.

Try the following exercise to find out more about the cultural beliefs you absorbed about female roles in society.

Write down what you perceive to be your mother's views about her role and what she could expect from life. Do the same for both of your grandmothers and great-grandmothers. Even if you didn't know your ancestors, through family discussions you will have learned something about them. What's most important is not the reality of their life, but your perception of their thinking. These perceptions hold greater relevance because they are the beliefs you absorbed from your family. They were ideas and concepts that people lived up to and, when very young, you assimilated them, almost by osmosis. In your analysis, look for patterns of similar behavior in the women in your family.

Next write down the issue in your own life that concerns you most. Generally, women find that the dilemmas they are facing are directly related to the beliefs passed down by their ancestors. As such, your forebears can provide much insight into your current situation. These are the social myths you may be applying as rigid rules for yourself and could be the expectations that keep you trapped in an unproductive emotional cycle.

## ROUNDING UP THE USUAL SUSPECTS

The handy host of excuses we use is another trap that keeps us stuck where we are. Not having enough time may be a reality for many women, but it can also be a powerful excuse. Others could include, "I can't because of . . . [check where applicable] my husband's career, his layoff, my children's extracurricular activities, aging parents, the demands of my lover, my bastard of a boss."

Or, if you prefer, "no money, no domestic help, no energy, no confidence, I'm a single parent, I'm too tired, too lazy, too old, too young, my stress levels, my illness, I travel a lot, I'm under too much pressure," and so it goes. For sure no one could say we're not inventive!

Excuses are handy because we mistakenly think they let us off the hook. But the more you use them, the more they point to the fact that you have difficulty making decisions. Life is about choices and setting priorities—and this is where we often stumble since we've been reared to believe that everything is a priority except ourselves. Be warned though, habitual excuses eventually turn into lifelong regret. Even if women's circumstances change, they often cling to their habitual wail. I've known women whose children have left home, whose husbands have retired, and who now have time and money to explore their interests, but they keep up the same old lament: "I never seem to find the time." Sadly, not finding the time to live is what they'll be known for when they die.

Excuses slip off our tongue easily because mostly we're not conscious of using them. But whatever your excuses, they'll eventually rob you of your life. So if you know you have a standard set of excuses, write them down on a piece of cardboard shaped like a gravestone. Title this boldly with these words: "Here lies the dreams of [your own name], that couldn't be achieved because of the following excuses [and list them]." Place this on your bathroom mirror or someplace where you'll see it regularly.

When we murder our excuses we have to face tackling the tough choices presented by life. Of course this takes courage, but every one of us has more than enough bravery for what we need to do. If you believe that you lack courage, it's just that you haven't yet had the kind of life experience that draws it out. In the book *Ten Stupid Things Women Do to Mess Up Their Lives*, Dr. Laura Schlessinger defines courage as fear plus action.[16] Whether it's shifting your priorities or finding a new career, if you're feeling like the only one who is afraid, take heart. Every success story started out with large doses of anxiety, prompting plenty of action.

## TAKING HEED OF YOUR WAKE-UP CALLS

When we remain stuck in a comfort zone for too long, life has a funny way of jolting us out of it. Here are examples of some of life's wake-up calls: being fired or laid off, failure, illness, loss, accidents, trauma, frustration, divorce, decade birthdays, the empty nest syndrome, and depression. All experiences in life, whether we label them good or bad, teach us something about ourselves, and wake-up calls compel us to live more consciously.

Mostly, wake-up calls act as catalysts for change, forcing us to make decisions. They show us we can't continue in the same way and must act to address the issues in our lives that aren't working. As part of your process of self-discovery, spend some time thinking about the wake-up calls you've had. Avoid focusing on negative lessons like how stupid you may have been to get yourself into the situation in the first place. They say "shit happens" but, more importantly, "life happens," and blaming yourself will teach you nothing valuable. Instead, write the situations down and next to each one draw up two columns: (1) List the changes you've made as a result of these incidents, and (2) list all the good things you've learned about yourself because of these experiences.

Often, events such as these show us that we are stronger than we thought we were, that we're more determined than we'd previously given ourselves credit for, or that we are more creative than we expected. Once people complete this exercise, they are often amazed at just how brave they have been. Too often we take the courage we've shown for granted because we simply expect ourselves to get through tricky situations. But when we acknowledge our bravery, we can use it to remind ourselves how strong we are when next we get into hot water.

Having reviewed the foundations for your lifework, it's now time to discover what your personal mission may be. Everyone has something important to do, and as said in the movie *What the Bleep Do We Know!?,* most people just don't take the time and trouble to find out what it is. Donald Trump's version is a bit blunter. When asked why so few people find their passion he said it was because most people are too darn lazy.

While working through the information, you may wish to consult people who are closest to you. Feedback is often necessary for women, as we were taught that admitting to the good things about ourselves is vain or boastful. Yet when it comes to the depth of self-analysis required to discover one's mission, modesty is not an attribute that will help you become more self-aware.

## SELF-ANALYSIS

The process starts with an analysis of who you are now. Different circumstances draw out different aspects of our character, and analyzing these gives us a good idea of the different faces we show to the world. It will reveal the many qualities you have. When completing this section, avoid glib labels like accountant, business owner, designer, or mother, because they won't tell you anything about who you are. Instead use adjectives—words that describe your behavior.

1. Who are you when you're at home? (relaxed, uptight, efficient, punctual, lighthearted, bad tempered, etc.)

_____

_____

_____

2. What type of person are you when you're at work?

_____

_____

_____

3. What type of person are you when you're with your original family (parents, siblings)?

_____

_____

_____

4. Who are you when you're with your friends?

_____

_____

_____

5. Who are you in your community (clubs, charity work, church groups, PTA, etc.)?

_____

_____

_____

6. Who are you when you're alone?

_____

_____

_____

    This exercise will provide you with a broad picture of the foundation for who you want to become. Review what you've written to explore the varied sides of yourself. Which aspects are you most comfortable with?

    Next let's go a little deeper. The more information you put down for each category, the easier it will be to finally script your personal mission statement.

7. What are your interests?

_____

_____

_____

8. What type of books stimulate you (categories, not specific titles)?

_____

_____

_____

9. What type of movies appeal to you (categories, not specific titles)?

_____

_____

_____

10. What type of TV programs do you most enjoy (categories, not specific titles)?

_____

_____

_____

11. What type of magazines do you read (categories, not specific titles)?

_____

_____

_____

12. Do you have any hobbies?

_____

_____

_____

13. What are your personal gifts (things you do naturally well) or talents that other people recognize in you?

_____

_____

_____

14. Identify your most important skills (things you've learned to do). (Refer back to the exercise completed on skills you've picked up in the jobs you've worked in.)

_____

_____

_____

15. Which things are you good at, that you also like doing? (These are your strengths.)

_____

_____

_____

16. Identify the things you don't like doing; these tend to be our weaknesses.

_____

_____

_____

17. What are your current ambitions?

_____

_____

_____

18. How do you spend your leisure time? What do you do for fun?

_____

_____

_____

19. What nourishes you? What makes you feel stimulated or energized? In other words, what makes you feel most alive?

_____

_____

_____

_____

20. What gets you out of bed in the morning?

_____

_____

_____

21. What are you superior at doing, i.e., better at than most people?

_____

_____

_____

22. List five peak experiences or highlights in your life.

_____

_____

_____

23. What topics do you talk about passionately to other people? (These are topics that interest you, not complaints.)

_____

_____

_____

24. If you lived or live on your own, how would/do you fill your time?

_____

_____

_____

25. If you won millions of dollars and never had to earn money again, what would you do to express yourself in the future?

_____

_____

_____

Examine the lists you've made here. You should start seeing similarities throughout, except for question 16, which addresses your weaknesses. If your ambitions stand out as being completely different from what comes up in your other answers, then perhaps you made these decisions without taking your passions into account. Too often we make decisions about our future with our intellect but are unlikely to fulfill ambitions that we don't feel a burning desire to achieve.

The other area that may be out of kilter is your skills set, because skills are things we've learned to do. If the skills you've listed seem different from the other areas, and these skills describe your current job, this could reveal why you may be unhappy. For example, if the skills you've developed are around detailed, meticulous work and you are an accountant, but the rest of the analysis shows creativity, big-picture thinking, and strategizing, then this could indicate that you've followed the skills you've been taught rather than your real passion.

Instead of packing in your job immediately, take time to look at how you could employ the skills you've learned in areas that have more natural appeal to you. Can you integrate them into a life purpose that's more meaningful? It's possible if you draw on your creative-thinking ability.

Examine your response to the question 20. If your answer is something like "to earn a salary" or "to get the kids off to school," motivation will be difficult for you. If this underscores the lack of passion in your life, then it clearly is time for you to initiate some big changes. Make well-informed decisions by carefully working through the self-analysis and reviewing it regularly. This is important, as little will improve in your life if you simply exchange one mundane role or job for another.

To find your passion, review the analysis you've completed so far and look for the elements that make you most enthusiastic. It's interesting that the stem of the word "enthusiasm" is *en theos,* meaning "inspired by God." So it's a good indicator of your natural passion. When you feel enthusiastic the message is clear; you're close to your purpose. If you live your passion, your vitality will motivate you naturally. Without passion your life will be driven by willpower alone. You'll know this is happening if you have to drag yourself out of bed in the morning. So what does it for you?

26. ENTHUSIASM: What are the things that make you enthusiastic?

_____

_____

_____

VALUES: Values are the guidelines we live by. They are deeply rooted beliefs that have a powerful influence over us. Values are formed early in our life, and they function unconsciously, piloting our decisions and actions. They're so deep rooted that we respond to them without even being aware of what's driving us. But we need to know consciously what they are because we only feel satisfied when our decisions are aligned with our deepest values. Only by understanding what these values are can we get a grip on our behavior patterns. This gives us the awareness to consciously take charge of our lives.

27. What are the key principles or important values that drive your life?

_____

_____

_____

28. How do you translate these principles into action?

_____

_____

_____

FUTURE PROJECTIONS: The present is filled with the counsel of the past and the signposts of the future. It's the starting point to make tomorrow's dreams a reality. Explore your dreams now by toying with the gift of your imagination. Take yourself on an imaginative adventure by visualizing your life in ten or twenty years' time. Let your mind play with all sorts of possibilities. Have fun with this, because your imagination is not constrained by reality checks, so your mind will be free to explore all sorts of new ideas. At the same time keep in touch with your feelings. When you're finished, write down the ideas that excited you the most.

29. FUTURE DESIRES: What are your future desires?

_____

_____

_____

30. CREATING YOUR MISSION STATEMENT: To write your mission statement, you'll need to review the work you've done so far. Use the steps below to summarize your personal exploration.

a. STEP ONE: Self-analysis

Which of your personal qualities are you most comfortable with (from page 168)?

_____

_____

_____

Summarize in a word, phrase, or sentence the interests, gifts, strengths, and the things you are superior at that you detailed in the exercises from page 169 to 171: questions 7–15, 19–21, and 23–25.

_____

_____

_____

List three adjectives that describe you at your best.

_____

_____

_____

What is the most important thing that you want to be remembered for once you're dead and gone?

_____

_____

_____

## b. STEP TWO: Enthusiasm

Write down the three things you feel most enthusiastic about (from page 172: question 26)

_____

_____

_____

## c. STEP THREE: Values

Write down whatever you value most (from page 173: question 27)

_____

_____

_____

## d. STEP FOUR: Role models

What qualities do you admire most in those people you hold in high esteem?

_____

_____

_____

e. STEP FIVE: Visualization

Write a sentence or phrase describing what you desire in your future. Use the visualization from Futue Projections on page 173:

_____

_____

_____

LOOK FOR TRENDS: Next, review the summary you've just completed and look specifically for similarities. These patterns are there for a good reason. It's no surprise that you've landed where you are today. To reiterate: Throughout your life your mind has guided your experiences to prepare you for your unique contribution. The trends you see now alert you to the area where you can make a difference in the future. If you're people oriented, you'll see this written all over the summary sheet. Likewise, those who have a technology bent will see this occurring repeatedly.

WRITING YOUR MISSION: To use your mission statement as the guideline for your life, it'll need to be short. You simply won't remember a lengthy paragraph, so keep it down to a maximum of four or five words. The trends you spotted in your summary sheet provide the starting point for you to play with some phrases. Use terms that are meaningful to you. No one else need understand them. This is _your_ mission statement. Make sure it excites and inspires you.

PERSONAL MISSION STATEMENT:

_____

_____

_____

Over the period of a few weeks, apply your mission statement to your life and check whether it fits or not. Keep reviewing and changing it until it feels right. Once you've discovered it, use it to test the decisions you make about your life. Have it in your mind always and keep reviewing your actions against it. Constantly check whether you're living according to your purpose.

## MAKING TIME

Likewise it's important to run a check on your financial health and your physical and spiritual well-being. Your body is the vehicle that transports the rest of you around, and your spiritual health is an important source of nourishment. Women lead busy lives, leaving no time for contemplation. If you've fallen into this trap, you will have had great difficulty answering the question "Who am I when I'm alone?" To grow and develop we need to have quiet time when we can relax and be ourselves with no one making demands upon us. Make a point of allocating time that you can spend enjoying being alone each day, and be ruthless about taking it.

Given that women's lives are busy, you will need to make time for reflection. To do so, identify areas where you can let go. As discussed, women have problems with being overcontrolling, and it is in these areas that you could let others pick up the ball. Then—without interference—sit back and watch them run with it. When we're overcontrolling, we destroy other people's initiative and creativity. In order to free up some time for yourself, let go, and after a while you may be surprised at how resourceful other people can be.

Knowing what you want and purposefully setting out to achieve it is a more gratifying way to live than coasting through life. It's also the prophylactic necessary to help you avoid debilitating emotional conditions like depression. Despite the powerful role played by the fairytale version of life, finding yourself and acting upon your own passions is a far more likely route to living happily ever after than being carted off by the prince.

Consider deeply what your contribution is going to be. As Hillary Rodham Clinton said, "Women are always being tested . . . but ultimately, each of us has to define who we are individually and then do the very best job we can to grow into that."

# CHAPTER 8.

# Does God Really Hate Girls?

One hundred American virgins offered to appease Bin Laden."
"Daughter sacrificed after man plays Russian roulette with God."

"Judge orders woman to marry her rapist."

"Chained Iraqi women taken back to U.S. as soldier's wives."

"Wife proves virginity with bloodied sheets."

"Father forced to buy back daughter after she refuses to be sex slave."

These are recent media headlines that reflect the transcriptions of archetypal biblical tales into modern scare tactics. They are shocking enough in the biblical context, but what's really alarming is that they can so easily apply today: Virginity tests happen in the British royal family and in parts of Japan and Africa. Mass rape happens in war-torn

Iraq, Afghanistan, and Chechnya, not to mention in prisons on an ongoing basis. Women whose husbands violently rape them, and children whose fathers and brothers sexually abuse them, are returned to the custody of their rapists. Women who protect themselves by killing murderous husbands are jailed and, in some countries, put to death. Destitute parents are still known to sell their daughters as sex slaves.

These inhuman events originate in the patriarchal social orders upheld by the revered books that millions still follow to the letter, and most deem to be holy. Men are esteemed while women are subjected to all manner of barbarous customs.

In the Judeo-Christian and Islamic holy books, which hold sway over billions today, the stories emphasize the masculine role of powerful prophets, forceful kings, strong rulers, wise men, influential disciples, potent tribal elders, an all-knowing male clergy, and God himself. With the holy books continually exalting men and relegating women to the role of obedient supporter, it's no wonder that many females question both the underlying message of the texts and the way they are interpreted. Without exception these texts were written by men on behalf of a God, perceived to be male. The once-powerful role of women is reversed in these texts, and this is where we find the origin of passive behaviors like self-sacrifice.

There are a few exceptions where women broke the rules. Take the story of Judith, which is contained in the Apocrypha (these are books translated from the Greek texts included in Catholic Bibles but not in Protestant and Hebrew versions).[1] Judith saved the Hebrews from the siege of Holofernese, one of Nebuchadnezzar's generals—a siege that could have caused the destruction of the Jews. But unlike Moses, who has been immortalized for a similar feat, Judith was rewarded with the beheaded Holofernese's silver plates and his tent (Jud. 15:13–14). Can we be satisfied that these texts reflect the truth about the male/female character?

## TRUST AND OBEY

Like most other women, I grew up within the edicts of a male-dominated religion. Even if you don't consider yourself religious, it's quite likely that within your family's last two or three generations, theological beliefs laid the foundation for the different degrees of power men and women held. Without too much questioning, these ideas get passed through successive generations, and so hordes of pious women for generation after generation accept that their righteous role is to take a back seat. Perhaps their conviction is divinely inspired, or perhaps there's more to this story.

Before we go any further, it is important to note that this analysis comes from a political rather than theological point of view, and its focus is on the function of power in religion. So it is not intended to be a comment about the spiritual value that many people derive from their religion.

## THE POWER AND THE GLORY

Regardless of the fact that much has shifted in terms of traditional sex roles, the outdated rules contained in the holy books remain virtually unchanged. A "good" woman is still one who is willing to sacrifice herself. So much so that "selfishness" in females remains a punishable offense. This thinking has a long history, but over a few millennia not much has changed—the doctrine makers, who are still almost exclusively male, simply reinterpret their canons to uphold male dominance in the modern context.

When I asked a devout Christian about managing household finances, he said that even if a woman earns more than her man, she should be obliged to hand her full salary over to him, untouched. Probing further, I discovered that instead of joint decision making, she should gather the bills, even write out the check payments if necessary, but he has final signing power and therefore final say.

This is the modern interpretation of Paul's words, which emphatically state that a man is head of the household (Eph. 5:21–23). It is but one example—there are many others that smack more of men keeping control than of the Creator scripting a rulebook about how women should or shouldn't behave.

## IS GOD A MAN?

And who said this Creator has a penis anyway? Men get past this question by suggesting that God is not a sexual or even a physical being—but if not, then what is it that makes him so unarguably male?

Some may believe that even posing such a question is heretical. Yet the history of human spirituality shows that God wasn't always viewed as masculine—in fact, many eons ago, he switched gender from female to male.[2]

Although religious people may be aware of this alternative perspective, many have been hoodwinked into believing that such a notion is the work of satanic forces. They justify this on the basis that a certain Bishop James Ussher (1581–1656) traced biblical genealogy back to Adam and Eve and concluded that the world began on Sunday, October 23, 4004 BCE. Ussher's contemporary at Cambridge University—Sir John Lightfoot—added the time of day: 9:00 AM.[3] Based on this "fact" the existence of the Goddess is easy to deny as her religion is thought to go back beyond 50,000 years, a period that doesn't exist for Christians. Some Fundamentalists even go so far as to think that ancient fossils, like the Taung Skull or Mrs. Ples, were placed on the earth by the devil to further his evil agenda.

While there is no end to this kind of debate, it does illustrate the underlying agenda of those who vociferously defend one or another unsubstantiated dogma.

Marija Gimbutas—archaeologist and author of *The Living Goddesses*—reveals that the imagery of ancient art is overwhelmingly female. With birth and regeneration attributed to the Goddess, figurines, sculptures, pottery, religious paraphernalia, and both tomb and temple architecture often depicted a woman's reproductive parts, such as the vulva, uterus, and womb. Some 100,000 artifacts have been retrieved from Europe alone, which led researchers to believe that ancient people worshipped a female Goddess, the bearer of new life.[4]

In *Beyond Power,* Marilyn French reveals that retrieved female figurines far outnumber those of males.[5] Immortalized over time, these female figurines tended to be well rounded, and their swollen stomachs suggested pregnancy. Although men are physically larger than women, these female artifacts were bigger than those found representing men. Artifacts from early human history embodying males had genitals that were downplayed, and some even appeared androgynous. Although phallic imagery exists, it only entered the picture in more-recent times.

## THE GODDESS AGE

In her book *When God Was a Woman,* Merlin Stone explains why new life became associated with a female deity.[6] Although unthinkable today, archaeologists and anthropologists speculated that the ancient people made no connection between the events of having sex and becoming pregnant, and, if one explores this idea, it's actually quite plausible. In prehistory, sex was seen as a recreational activity, and given that nine months would elapse between the two events (with probably much sexual activity in between), the birth of a baby was more likely to be seen as a miracle. Some societies believed that men contributed only by opening the womb of a woman, but children were placed in the mother's uterus as a gift from the Goddess.[7]

Monica Sjöö and Barbara Mor, authors of *The Great Cosmic Mother: Rediscovering the Religion of the Earth,* show evidence that the Goddess originally existed in African societies that were matriarchal. As the planet's earliest inhabitants, Africans traveled widely, taking with them the religion of the Goddess.[8] In modern museums, iconic artifacts of this ancient Goddess have been collectively given a Christian slant by being called the Black Madonna.[9]

Although the Goddess was responsible for creating life, she had far more power in her people's eyes than the mythical stork we joke about today.

The Goddess was seen as both creator and ruler of the universe, and as a divinity, she was revered as the source of all wisdom, justice, and healing. As the embodiment of Nature, she had the power to bring forth life and take it away, and she was also seen to be a strong, courageous warrior and prophetess.

Archaeological findings in India, Old Europe, and Asia suggest that the Goddess ruled from as early as the Stone Age up to classical Greek and Roman times. Creation myths and stories show her to be present in all the major societies from the Americas to China.

During the lengthy period of her reign, women were perceived as the sacred embodiment of the Goddess, and they were imbued with many of her powers. With a particular emphasis on fertility, the Goddess was invoked by a woman's sensuality, and holy women in places of worship performed rituals, many of which involved priestesses in sexual acts. Although sacred sex was subsequently labeled "prostitution," it was neither a matter of money nor lust but a means of connecting with the divine.[10]

Speculation has it that only women were considered sacred enough to reproduce their own kind, and, as a predictable consequence, a child's paternity was irrelevant. Children were cared for in communities, and the structure of societies was matrilineal. With the aid of modern science, the blood type of ancient bones can be determined, and this revealed that adult females and children in the same cemeteries were related, but that the men were not relatives of either. According to Gimbutas, this is to be expected in a matrilineal society where the mothers and daughters maintained residence and ownership of property.[11]

Cemeteries in ancient Greece were known as the Place of the Mother, and matrilineal custom determined that names, titles, and possessions were also passed down through the female line, as, of course, was royalty.[12]

Stone also points out that ancestor worship was likely to have been the basis of sacred rites, as it still is in many cultures today, and the earliest ancestors were acknowledged through the maternal line of the Divine Ancestress. As such, the female deity was not perceived to be a separate cult, nor was she worshipped as one of a number of idols or Gods. The Goddess was the clan mother, the final word on spiritual power.

Over time these religious beliefs continued to evolve. Each region, area, or town worshipped its own Divine Ancestress, which is why the Goddess was known by many different names. In Africa one manifestation was known as Mawu-Lisa,[13] and Jean Markale, author of *The Great Goddess,* says that the name Cybele was widespread across Europe. In Egypt she was known as Isis; and in Greece she was variously worshipped as Artemis, Aphrodite, and Demeter; in India as Devi, Kali, and Shakti; in Rome as Diana and Ceres; as Anahid in Persia (Iran); as Ishtar in Babylon (Iraq); Astarte in Canaan (Palestine); and in China,

Korea, and Japan she appeared as Amateratsu. The Celts called her Brigit Anna, and creation myths in the Americas revere the feminine in birth and regeneration.[14]

While some may believe that Goddess worship was confined to small areas, Elizabeth Gould Davis, author of *The First Sex,* confirms that all the archaeological findings together prove that feminine pre-eminence was a universal and not a localized phenomenon.[15]

With females carrying a high rank in society, a woman's relationship with power was likely to have been markedly different from that of today.

From the early inhabitants of Africa through Spain to Asia, Goddess worship meant that women held uppermost social status; they were head of the family, chose their husband, and permitted divorce. Their actions were independent of men. In some Anatolian (Turkish) societies it was a man's job to look after the home, and women held positions of power. Females took part in business and financial affairs, and in many instances functioned as the breadwinner of the family.

The Roman Goddess Ceres was known as the "lawgiver," and her priestesses functioned as judges, the way magistrates do today. Women were also the spiritual leaders in charge of all religious customs, and as political advisors, they had the most powerful influence over state affairs.

## VARIATIONS ON THE POWER THEME

Although many matrilineal societies offered women an elevated social standing, females didn't command power to the same extent as those who lived in societies that were matriarchal in their formal political structure.

In matrilineal societies, women and men, for the most part, were content to cooperate with one another. However, in some matriarchal societies, like the one in ancient Crete, it is thought that women ruled over men, and, although there is evidence of males taking positions such as "king" or "chief," these roles were only secured by marriage. The baton of male leadership would have been passed on through the daughter's line, and the youth who married her would succeed as a male leader.[16]

Don't be mistaken that the reign of the Goddess was a romantic golden era when life was gentle and congenial. Detractors of Goddess theories, like Lotte Motz *(The Faces of the Goddess)* and Cynthia Eller *(The Myth of Matriarchal Prehistory: Why an Invented Past Won't Give Women a Future),* do not deny the existence of female divinities, but they say it is neither helpful nor accurate for women to be limited to a history where females are portrayed purely as maternal, nurturing, and peace loving.[17]

As said by Sam Keen, a prominent writer on masculinity, when God was a woman she was a terrible mother, as bloody as God the father.[18] She taught that all living things were sustained by death and that blood was the fertilizer of life—hence both animal and human sacrifices.

Keen claims that Kali (Goddess of creation and destruction in Hindu mythology) was represented as having a plethora of breasts and a necklace of skulls, concluding, "If Nature is the Goddess we must claim both her dark and demonic sides and not merely her nurturing qualities."

In the same way as acknowledging our anger and reclaiming the female potential for violence are important aspects of our healing, so too is accepting the shadow side of the feminine. This is critical to our liberation, because simply perceiving women (ancient or modern) as one-dimensional nurturers keeps us stuck in the disempowering "nice" stereotype.

Even if the Goddess was both nurturing and violent, or whether she was supreme spiritual ruler or one of many deities, Stone maintains that in early societies women held power, and men took a back seat. And so it was that for thousands of years females were elevated in social status, and the Goddess reigned supreme.

Why did things change? The deity switched gender not because the Goddess abdicated her reign, nor because she lost a winner-takes-all battle with a masculine God, but because males usurped her power by storming the pastoral lands where she reigned.[19] The gender of the deity and therefore of spiritual authority—as history shows—is determined primarily by the human gender that holds the cards of social power.

## MEN INVADE THE GODDESS LANDS

The literature places the beginning of the invading male-dominated religious order at around 4,000 BCE, and incursions continued up to classical Greek and Roman times.

The warring males belonged to the Indo-European or Aryan group, the same line that inspired Adolf Hitler to strive for his version of a superior race. Aryan men began their invasions from the northern regions of Europe and Asia. Whereas the pastoral people used metal for tools and ornaments, the militaristic invaders produced weapons. They were the first to ride horses, and their method was gradual infiltration, involving a series of conflicts over many hundreds of years.[20]

These men were thought to be physically larger than their southern counterparts, leading to myths (still present in tales today) about the existence of giants. Their main target was the destruction of the female-dominant social order supported by Goddess worship. The emphasis was not so much upon a divine battle of the sexes but more about the rights that the female deity afforded women, with particular emphasis on the political hot potato of land ownership.

Stone argues that the origin of this religious order, fighting in the name of the male God Yahweh (Jehovah), was the belief that angry, erupting volcanoes personified early male Gods. Stone supports this by demonstrating the number of active volcanoes prevalent in the Near East and Middle East, from which these tribes originated. In the area stretching from Turkey (Anatolia) to Azerbaijan, there are thirteen volcanic mountains, including Mount Hasan, Mount Ararat, and Mount Suphan.[21] Alexander Waugh in his book titled *God* supports the idea of the ancients practicing volcano worship by showing that archaic Gods, such as the fire fiend Vulcan and his Greek equivalent Hephaestus, were portrayed with smoke and sparks blasting from their nostrils.[22]

The biblical Moses was educated in the Egyptian house of Ramses II, who was a follower of the Pharaoh Akhenaton's sun God, and it is thought that this was the inspiration for constructing a similar deity for the Hebrews.[23]

There are numerous references in the Bible that reveal the image of God as a glowing mountain. When Moses was recounting the incidents that took place at "Horeb, mountain of God" he reminded the

Hebrews, "So you came and stood at the foot of the mountain and the mountain flamed to the very sky, a sky darkened by cloud, murky and thunderous. Then Yahweh spoke to you from the midst of fire; you heard the sound of words but saw no shape, there was only a voice" (Deut. 4:11–13).

In the Hebrew Psalms, we find:

"He rains coals of fire and brimstone on the wicked" (Ps. 11:6).

"Then the earth quivered and quaked, the foundations of the mountains trembled (they quivered because he was angry); from his nostrils a smoke ascended; and from his mouth a fire that consumed (live embers were kindled at it). . . . Darkness he made a veil to surround him, his tent a watery darkness, dense cloud; before him a flash enkindled hail and fiery embers" (Ps. 18:7–12).

"Yahweh . . . How much longer must your anger smolder like a fire?" (Ps. 89:46.)

"A fire precedes him as he goes, devouring all enemies around him; his lightning lights up the world, earth observes and quakes. The mountains melt like wax at the coming of the Master of the world" (Ps. 97:3–5).

When it comes to the origin of the word "Yahweh," Stone notes that it has no Hebrew origin, but comes from the Sanskrit word *yah-veh,* meaning "ever-flowing."

Many of these male invasions are documented in the first half of the Old Testament (the Hebrew wars against the pagans). But instead of focusing on warfare, I want to look into the reasons for women's subjugation, especially the necessity of branding female sexuality as the source of evil.

If women under the reign of the Goddess were granted the privileges of power, such as property, economic independence, and significant rank in the political, religious, and social orders, the only means men had of gaining power was to mark their territory with widespread destruction. Reports of Aryan devastation range from the destruction of divine sites of Goddess worship to the absolute annihilation of pastoral land where females held power. In the conquered lands, the sacred sites of the Goddess were replaced with edifices to worship the male God Yahweh.

About Canaan (Palestine) the Bible says, "You must destroy completely all the places where the nations you dispossess have served their Gods, on high mountains, on hills, under any spreading tree; you must tear down their altars, smash their pillars, cut down their sacred poles, set fire to the carved images of their Gods, and wipe out their name from that place" (Deut. 12:2–3).

However, if the biggest issue at stake was the gender of the deity, it could well have been possible for men and women, within a male-dominant religion, to continue living cooperatively—as they had supposedly done under matrilineal social orders. But the issue was far broader than determining the sex of the Creator; it was about a politically motivated territorial crusade in the name of the Gods of war.

Today we still live with the devastating repercussions of males assuming superiority over women, but in ancient times convincing the masses didn't happen easily; it took many hundreds of years. So deeply immersed were the pastoral people in their religious activities that the only hope of changing their ideas was through the spiritual storytelling medium. Therefore, an important part of male indoctrination was to reverse or change the spiritual meaning of female symbols and mythology.

## THE SERPENT—A SYMBOL OF WISDOM

Under Goddess rule, female spirituality was typically symbolized by serpents and dragons. The cobra was the hieroglyphic sign for the Goddess, which can be seen on ancient Egyptian headdresses, and with snake symbols representing insight and wisdom; many artifacts show Goddesses holding serpents in their hands.[24]

Mawu-Lisa, the original African Goddess, was imaged as having a snake in her belly, and this continued through the Hindu tantric tradition of *kundalini* (the name is derived from the Goddess Kunda, also known as Cunti) in which the rising of a mythical snake in the body unites the self with the infinite.[25]

Once the invaders conquered land, the meaning of these symbols was subverted: From forces of good, they came to denote everything that was evil. The fact that we still see princes slaying dragons in fairytales, and the fact that in biblical stories snakes represent Satan, shows how effectively these ancient symbols were remodeled into dark forces.

In mythology, men had to be portrayed defeating serpents and dragons to exemplify the power of their good God over the dark force of evil, the Goddess. Examples can be seen in Greek mythology, in which Zeus and Apollo conquered serpents. Stone believes that this allegorical association may have survived through to the legends of St. George and the dragon, and also to St. Patrick and the snakes.

Over centuries these reversals in mythology watered down the all-powerful Creator-Goddess to a female divinity assisted by male Gods and human kings initially, and then finally enslaved her as the domesticated fertility Goddess ruled by a masculine deity.[26]

## MEN CHAIN WOMEN TO THEIR GENDER

The primary issue was not spirituality but usurping political power. In order to become the sole recipients of privilege, males had to destroy the socially driven matrilineal order and replace it with a politically driven patriarchy. If the passing down of inheritance, property, and business rights was the very issue guaranteeing female entitlement, the legal standing of children as maternal was the primary factor that maintained female power. It was also the biggest obstacle to establishing patriarchal domination, which was why the political question of paternity became central.

The biggest problem the patriarchs faced was that men are unable to bear children, and so the only means of securing paternity rights (making patriarchy feasible) was to own the women themselves. Restrictive rules governing a woman's sexual behavior were crucial to enforcing patriarchy. These rules were not primarily about curbing promiscuity; they were designed to give men control over female reproduction and therefore over their offspring.

Male-dominant religions were the first to impose virginity upon unattached women and to make marital infidelity for women an offense punishable by death.

Most orthodox religions continue to ban contraception today, and most religions vehemently oppose abortion (so much so that their fanatical representatives maim and kill abortion doctors). Ignoramuses in legal systems make women responsible for their own rape, marital rape remains inappropriately handled, the taboo on sex before marriage is making a comeback, and even the corset of thinness has become the modern burqa by hiding the obvious nature of a woman's sexuality.

While control of women was mainly an attempt to own reproductive rights, men justified their behavior by turning female sensuality into the source of all evil. The once-revered vagina fell from grace, to be replaced by phallus worship. In Ecclesiasticus (Apocrypha), a biblical instruction manual about the rules of living, one finds the following statement that reads like a curse:

> From woman is the beginning of sin
> and because of her all must die. (25:24)

This book adds that no wickedness comes anywhere near the wickedness of women, and a husband's only reprieve is to dine with his neighbor, where he can heave his bitter sighs. When it comes to a wife supporting her husband, only bad temper, insolence, and shame will result. On the issue of children, the birth of a daughter is considered a loss—and if she turns out to be badly behaved, both parents are advised to disown her. Spiritual enlightenment aside, it is patently clear that the holy books contain the rules required to suppress the diverse forms of power females originally held.

## PENIS ENVY—A WORN-OUT THEORY

As the phallus still holds center stage today, it shouldn't have come as any surprise that the father of psychology, Sigmund Freud, attributed most women's problems to penis envy. Instead of naming oppression as the cause of female misery, Freud viewed female difficulties in a way that must have been colored by his enchantment with his own appendage—exaggerating the psychological importance he placed upon the penis.

The biblical positioning of women (especially female sexuality) as the source of evil offers men a "valid" excuse for their misogyny. It suits holy men to believe that women are prone to promiscuity and all manner of evil, because men are then only doing their duty in making sure by any means possible that these wayward wenches are kept in hand. I've heard adamant religious men say that the only reason men sin or stray is because of the evilness in women!

Fabrications about female sexuality have successfully manipulated generations of women into keeping their legs crossed. A wonderful example of the Victorian perspective on women and sex is provided in Barbara Kingsolver's *The Poisonwood Bible:* "Each pregnancy drew God's attention anew to my having a vagina and him having a penis and the fact that we'd laid them near enough together to conceive a child."[27] (The shame of it!)

Despite the second female sexual revolution of the 1960s, young women today are still ashamed about their sexuality and fraught with guilt about breaking "God-given" laws about sex.

But applying just the slightest bit of gray matter to this issue shows that the theory of female sexuality epitomizing evil is somewhat lacking in credibility. How is it possible that the all-powerful Creator of this vast and intelligent universe would allow the reproduction of his own creation to be under the controlling force of evil?

More believable is that this view not only gave men control over women but also conveniently provided them with an excuse for gratifying their own lust. With minimal moral limitations placed upon a man's sexual behavior, men have been slow—to say the least—in developing control over their carnal desires. Just think of the television evangelist Jimmy Swaggart (who got caught "entertaining" a prostitute) and Bill Clinton, who now admits "I did it because I could." Both men, right up there as leaders of the boy bunch, initially blamed "that woman" for their own lack of self-control. And many of their followers believed them. But simple logic tells us that if men think about sex as often as they claim to, and if they have no self-control, then they must be far too distracted to take charge of important matters—like world affairs for instance.

When men originally staked their claim over female sexuality, those priestesses who continued to practice their Goddess custom of ritualistic sex were called harlots, and the Old Testament warned men to stay away from them. Also referred to as "alien women" and "sacred prostitutes," these are widely speculated to have been the temple priestesses of the Goddess religion. In 2 Maccabbees of the Old Testament (Apocrypha), harsh judgments are made about pagan sex rituals. "The Temple was filled with reveling and debauchery by the Pagans, who took pleasure with prostitutes and had intercourse with women in the sacred precincts, introducing other indecencies besides" (6:4–5).

One of the greatest warnings to men comes in Proverbs (7:24–27), where males are instructed about the evils of seductresses: "And now, my son, listen to me. Pay attention to the words I have to say: Do not let your heart stray into her ways, or wander into her paths. She has done so many to death, and the strongest have all been her victims."

Today, labels like "slut" or "whore" are still hurled at women who disregard the prissy sexual code. Although such judgments may seem ridiculous, this type of patriarchal disapproval is crucial in maintaining male domination.

Reducing women to men's slaves and sex objects continues the illusion that men control the power of the feminine, her sacred sexuality—and even better if these dictates are supposed to be ordained and sanctioned by the highest power we know, God himself.

## THE GODDESS SURVIVES

For patriarchal leaders claiming a male God, the task of convincing peace-loving pastoral people to adopt an aggressive masculine deity was so onerous that it has never been totally accomplished. In parts of Lithuania and Latvia the female deity survived to the 20th century,[28] and even today some Goddess traditions are maintained among communities of Wicca worshippers, the modern revival of paganism using magic, nature, and a female deity. Incidentally these communities are on the increase.

Although the male political crusade was highly aggressive, Goddess worship coexisted with the male-dominant religions for hundreds of years.

As the oldest religion today, Hinduism is the only major faith in which a functional Goddess survives, but with the Indo-Aryans oppressing Goddess-worshipping people as lower castes, they subdued her powerful role too. Christianity and Islam are Abrahamic doctrines and as such have Hebrew roots championing the virtues of a male God and male superiority.

From about the second millennium BCE, we see an early version of formalized patriarchal chauvinism emerging. Here paternity was secured as a certainty by advocating different moral codes for male and female sexuality. For instance when it came to the Ten Commandments, men needn't have worried about coveting their neighbor's wives, because they were allowed as many of their own wives as they wished. Marriage was polygamous, and while King Solomon had 700 wives and 300 concubines, women were stoned to death for infidelity. However, if a man raped a woman, she was obliged to marry her rapist, and if a woman's husband died, she was forced to wed his brother—with the specific inclusion of the all-important paternity clause: that the children bore the dead man's name.

In the Bible even menstruation is considered unclean because Goddess-worshipping people believed that blood was sacred. In prehistory monthly periods were called the "wound that heals itself" and the menstrual cycle was thought to deeply link body, soul, and mind, making this a time that a woman was at the peak of both her sexual and spiritual power. Again, the routine strategy of reversal was used to turn menstruation into "the curse," ensuring that it became hidden, secret, and filled with shame.[29]

But, probably the most significant biblical sop of all is the view that women were created from a man. In our particular branch of humanity, women are believed to have been giving birth to both boys and girls for some 150,000 years, so convincing people of the "sparerib of Adam" notion must have taken a great deal of persuasive salesmanship.[30] The fact that some 3,500 years later, people still have blind faith in this odd view of procreation shows that the only miracle at work was perhaps one of mass hypnotism.

## BEARING THE PAIN OF GENERATIONS

Even women's power as givers of birth was portrayed as a curse, as evidenced by the "punishment" of labor pains. But unlike Satan, whose evilness caused him to be cast out of the heavenly orbit, women were not quite so wicked that men didn't still wish to rule over them. "I will multiply your pains in childbearing; you shall give birth to your children in pain. Your yearning shall be for your husband, yet he will lord it over you" (Gen. 3:16).

Adam's only punishment for disobeying God was to suffer while toiling the fields for his daily meal, something he would likely have had to do anyway.

According to Annie Laurie Gaylor, author of *Woe to the Women: The Bible Tells Me So* and cofounder of Freedom from Religion Foundation, only one-tenth of biblical passages refer to women, and within these there are in excess of 200 verses that specifically belittle and demean females.[31] Stories of rape, pillage, and sacrificial death are among these passages, but the following focus upon female sexuality—and therefore have implications for paternity.

- In Numbers (5:16–31), jealous husbands could have a priest test their wife for adultery by forcing her to drink water fouled with dirt from the temple floor. If the woman became ill (wouldn't anyone?), her sickness was proof of her infidelity and she would be punished. In the same book, virgin girls are listed as war booty, but Moses ordered all the women who had slept with men to be killed (Num. 31:18–19).
- Deuteronomy contains many brutish rules controlling sexuality. Yahweh instructs men on the correct procedure for raping women that have been taken from an enemy (21:11–14). He also prescribes a peculiarly barbaric test for a young bride's virginity (22:13–21), insists on a woman marrying her rapist (22:28–29), and allows a man to divorce a woman he has defiled just because he may no longer like her. But if the same woman remarries and her second husband also dislikes her, the original spouse may not take her in, "for that is detestable in the eyes of Yahweh" (24:1). But my personal favorite from this book is the fact that if a woman touches the penis of her husband's foe, either in error or in defense of her husband, her hand shall be cut off without pity (25:11–12).

- In Genesis (19:1–8) Lot offers his virgin daughters to the marauding men of Sodom "to treat as it pleases you," instead of giving up the male angels he was protecting.
- A similar event is found in Judges (19:22–30), in which a man offers his virgin daughter to a local male mob to "do what you please with her" in order to safeguard a traveling Levite and his concubine—complete strangers he was hosting. When the "scoundrels" turn down the virgin, the Levite gives them his concubine. "They had intercourse with her and outraged her all night," and she died the following morning. The Levite takes her body home, cuts it up into twelve pieces, and distributes the chunks of cadaver to the tribes of Israel.
- As women are the root of all evil, problems existed for the birth of boy children. In Job (14:4), one of his speeches asks the question, "Who can bring the clean out of the unclean?" And in Leviticus (12:1–8) a woman who has a son is unclean for seven days (and she must wait for another thirty-three days for a priest to purify her), but those who have daughters are unclean for double that period. Even in the New Testament Jesus was presented for purification as laid down by the Law of Moses.
- In Proverbs men are told to keep away from alien women, "from the stranger with her wheedling words . . . toward death her house is declining, down to the Shades her paths go" (2:16–19). They are warned that "a harlot is a deep pit, a narrow well, the woman who is a stranger. Yes, like a robber she is on watch and many are the men she dupes" (23:27–28). Men are also instructed not to "spend all your energy on women, nor your loins on these destroyers of kings" (31:3).
- The text in Ecclesiasticus (Apocrypha) provides cautions about "giving your soul to a woman for her to trample on your strength." Men are warned about keeping the company of all manner of females, ranging from virgins, whores, married women, harlots, and even singing girls. This is "in case you succumb to her charms and in your ardor you slide down to your ruin" (9:2–13).

- Ecclesiastes says, "I find woman more bitter than death, she is a snare, her heart a net, her arms are chains. He who is pleasing to God eludes her, but the sinner is her captive" (7:27).

One wonders why the omniscient God created women if he knew that he would hold such repugnant views about them.

But Hebrew men claimed that God had preached these and many more edicts clamping down on females, which is how they vindicated unjust behavioral prescriptions for women.

Now that these ideas have been around for a good few thousand years, time alone is enough to convince most people that men like Abraham and Moses did have an open line to God. Although many religious people today claim the same privilege, somehow they aren't taken quite as seriously—unless of course they're in a position of power and their message happens to suit political purposes.

## DIVINE INSPIRATION?

Elizabeth Cady Stanton, a pioneering force in the early suffrage movement, gathered together writings of the foremost female biblical scholars of the late 1800s. When reading her work, *The Woman's Bible*,[32] I had to keep reminding myself that this enlightened sister wrote more than 100 years ago.

Claiming that our political and social degradation is merely an outgrowth of the state of women in the Bible, she believed that nothing would change unless the holy books dictating female roles were altered. Even within the suffrage movement her views were snubbed, and many of her contemporaries got past this hot button by tiptoeing around contentious religious issues. With 150 years of women's liberation under our belt, we need to ask, Has this pussyfooting helped further the women's cause?

One of the main themes of Cady Stanton's work is her adamant belief that the utterances of men were not divinely inspired—they were simply utterances of men. Commenting on the Pentateuch/Torah (the first five chapters of the Old Testament) she summed up Abraham and Moses's extraordinary claims about God communicating behavioral codes as follows:

"It was a very cunning way for the patriarchs to enforce their own authority, to do whatever they desired, and [to] say the Lord commanded them to do and say thus and so."

Cady Stanton's summary of her own views on the scriptures goes like this: "The Bible teaches that woman brought sin and death into the world, that she precipitated the fall of the race, that she was arraigned before the judgment seat of Heaven, tried, condemned, and sentenced. Marriage for her was to be a condition of bondage, maternity a period of suffering and anguish, and in silence and subjection, she was to play the role of a dependent upon a man's bounty for all her material wants, and for all the information she may desire . . . she was commanded to ask her husband at home."[33] In other words the false identity imposed on women originated from men using God much as a ventriloquist uses a puppet.

However, when it comes to the portrayal of God as a woman's cruel, harsh, unforgiving ruler, Ruth Hurmence Green, writer of *The Born Again Skeptic's Guide to the Bible,* has the final word: "Poor God! We can't always choose our biographers."[34]

## STRICTLY FOR THE BOYS

Because women in the scriptures are seldom referred to as individuals but merely as property, Cady Stanton avers that the Bible holds women in the lowest esteem. By portraying women as liars and seducers, men could justify the shoddy treatment of women with the conviction that females had no soul.

Although the Bible doesn't say this in so many words, the "fact" that Adam was created by God (soul) and Eve came from Adam's rib (flesh) has been used to imply that women have no soul. Voltairine de Cleyre (1866–1912), a contemporary of Cady Stanton's, said that in the sixth century the fathers of the Church met and proposed the question "Has woman a soul?"[35] It was only by a small majority that the question was decided in favor of women possessing souls.

Even so, at the time of Cady Stanton's writing, scientists were so influenced by such Judeo-Christian ideas that they claimed men provided their offspring with life, the spirit and the soul, and women offered only the covering of flesh.[36] When seen in the light of defending paternity rights, this was a particularly handy belief to uphold.

Cady Stanton was of the utmost conviction that this view of women was not of God's doing but simply a means of legitimately subjecting women to oppression. Because many of the passages prescribed self-sacrifice for women, men were guaranteed ready-made, willing slaves tied to the home, where their relationships could be supervised.

Work outside the home was not considered for married women, and education was strictly reserved for boys. Men also had final authority over a woman's spiritual life; her only source of information was secondhand from her husband, and her vows to God (prayers) required prior approval from a man, either her husband or father (Num. 30:4–17). This control of both incoming and outgoing communications with God was an ingenious way for men to censor the spiritual views of wives and daughters, thereby forcing them to follow the male religion.

Similar ideas can be found in the Hindu code of Manu where a woman is considered a nonperson and is passed from the guardianship of her father to that of her husband and finally to her oldest son. As said by Sjöö and Mor, she is controlled in both life and death, and "within the male-dominated family, she is never allowed freedom of movement, of thought, of desire—where her body, her mind, her labor, and her children are seen as property, wealth belonging to a man."[37]

So, no matter the religion, these artificially created rules afforded men complete control over a woman's physical, emotional, mental, and spiritual life. However, this oppression had nothing to do with good and evil—it was simply the only means men had of metaphorically imprisoning the force that threatened them most: the once all-powerful Goddess.

With males fully aware of the degree to which their man-made religions subjugate women, it's no wonder that the Orthodox Jewish religion contains a prayer said exclusively by men: "Blessed art Thou O Lord our God, who has not made me a woman."

Don't be mistaken though, Judaism is not by any means the only religion to radically pursue paternity, regard women as lesser beings, or view them as the source of all evil. The effect of the Christian view on institutions like marriage will be viewed in Chapter 9, while Islam too has its own prescriptions.

Having said this, patriarchal control and corruption in pre-Islamic

Arabia were precisely the ideas Muhammad intended to oppose with his religious message of "revolutionary social egalitarianism." This specifically deals with the equality of women. Muhammad's first wife, Khadija, was older and more successful than he, and many of the Prophet's early followers were women. After Khadija's death Muhammad married Aisha (among others) and nearly one-sixth of all "reliable" hadith (a collection of customs determining a Muslim way of life) can be traced back to her.[38]

Given the stereotypes about Islam, it often comes as a surprise to many Westerners that the Muslim religion is more egalitarian about male and female roles than other patriarchal religions. Within Islam, women have the right to own property, to negotiate or refuse marriage, to obtain divorce, and be granted custody of and child support for children; they also have the right to be educated, to work with equal reward, to have their voice heard, and to command respect.

But like other patriarchal religions, Islam too has been influenced by the power struggles and conflicting interests of its people over the centuries. In his book *No God But God,* Reza Aslan writes, "For hundreds of years, anyone who had the power and wealth necessary to influence public opinion—and who wanted to justify his own ideas about, say, the role of women in society—had only to refer to a hadith which he had heard from someone, who had heard it from someone else, who had heard it from a Companion, who had heard it from the Prophet."[39] This is why there are many contradictions about women in Islam. For instance, in the Qur'an (2:227), Muhammad is advised that "women ought to behave in like manner to their husbands as their husbands should behave toward them, according to what is just; but the men ought to have a superiority over them." Muhammad is also purported to have stated, "When Eve was created, Satan rejoiced."[40]

Today, Muslim feminists assert that the oppression of Islamic women is not about what is stipulated in the Qur'an but rather the adoption of ancient Arabic gender practices. Many claim that if men simply followed the teachings of Islam, Muslim women would get a far better deal.

But with a gradual social movement back to matriarchal power, it's not surprising that most religious groups are becoming more fundamental in their beliefs and are retaliating with promises of restoring men to the head of the household. For only with men installed as leader of the family unit are they able to assert their power in the world. With nothing less than world domination at stake, it's no wonder that men cling to the unyielding notion of male superiority.

## LOST IN TRANSLATION

More than a century ago, pioneers like Cady Stanton saw through the male political agenda and repeatedly cautioned women that men are unreliable interpreters of the holy books because of their unflinching belief in their own superiority.

Not only are the views of male preachers unreliable, but in the Bible many problems also existed in translation. Cady Stanton quotes the Church Union (a body founded in the 1850s to create visible unity in Christ's Church) as saying that between the translations from both Greek and Hebrew there are 163,000 errors in modern English versions. Cady Stanton therefore insisted that it was not possible to wrench, either from the Old or the New Testament, a God-given message of justice, liberty, or equality to the women of the 19th century.[41]

At the first Women's Rights Convention in 1848, Cady Stanton said that breaking the hold that institutionalized religion maintained over women was an integral part of the agenda calling for female enfranchisement. She could equally well have been writing about religious dogma in the 21st century.

Cady Stanton saw woman as "womb-man," believing that a woman with a womb is more than a man. "As long as religion teaches the combination of women's subjugation and male domination, we will have chaos in the world of morals," she said. Wisely suggesting that a woman's false subservience causes a man's unnatural arrogance, she encouraged women to follow self-development as a higher duty than self-sacrifice.[42]

In addition to the problems of diverse interpretations and different translations, over the centuries bishops and rulers also made purposeful changes, and the Roman Emperor Constantine (Council of Nicaea, 325 CE) is considered to be the most notable culprit in suppressing the truth about the origins of Christianity.[43] Similarly, many forgeries occurred to bring biblical writings in line with the politics of the time.

In *The Jesus Mysteries,* authors Timothy Freke and Peter Gandy writes, "Letters were forged in the name of various apostles. . . . Even Eusebius, the mouthpiece of Catholic propaganda, regarded the authenticity of the letters in James, Jude, 2 Peter and 3 John as dubious." The authors confirm that at the end of the 2nd century, Paul's original letters were interpolated and new ones forged.[44] This is relevant to the debate about women's roles because Paul's writings are particular about demanding female subjugation. For instance: "A husband is head of the wife" (Eph. 5:21–23); "wives give way to your husbands" (Col. 3:18–19); "women must be respectable, not gossips but sober and reliable" (1 Tim. 3:12); "women are not permitted to speak in the Churches, if they have questions they must ask their husbands at home" (1 Cor. 14:34–35).

Some of these passages also instruct husbands to love their wives, but this is not the major theological bone of contention for feminists; rather it is the numerous contradictions in Paul's writing in the New Testament that are questionable. In his letter to the Galatians, Paul writes about the equality of males and females, yet in examples like those listed above, he subjugates women. Forgeries or writing under the name of a respected scholar were commonplace at the time, which offers one plausible explanation for the contradictions, but despite the dubiousness of their origins, Paul's prescriptive rules about the sexual hierarchy are still enforceable gospel.

Freke and Gandy claim that the Gospel of John (known as the Gospel of the Beloved Disciple) was likely to have been written by Mary Magdalen. "As scholars have noted, the Gospel of the Beloved Disciple has been modified, creating obvious structural flaws, in order to turn the 'Beloved Disciple' Mary into the more 'palatable' male figure of John."[45]

Although conservative Christians believe that the Bible, as the word of God, contains no errors, we should not forget that men have been the Bible's superintendents.

## A GNOSTIC REVIVAL

Timothy Freke and Peter Gandy have also resuscitated the long-buried female deity in their book *Jesus and the Goddess.*[46] They advocate that all religions have two different levels: the literal schools for the plebeians, and the mystery, or Gnostic, schools for the enlightened, and scholars can "read" the scriptures at either of these levels. It goes without saying that the mystical meanings of holy works have been hidden from women for centuries. This has been done simply by reserving the texts as a male-only domain—in some religions the privilege is reserved for men over forty.

Freke and Gandy have plumbed the mystical depths of Christian literature and found that Goddess themes still remain. These mystery or Gnostic ideas (people who do not believe in taking the Bible literally) were obliterated from the literalist versions of religions, supposedly because the general populace is too simple to understand them. Yet with paternity rights as the central theme, it's more likely that the obliteration was self-protective.

Literalists spread guilt and fear in their religious versions, but Gnostic schools seek self-discovery and spiritual creativity. As such, the Gnostic schools view the scriptures from an allegorical point of view, something that offends literal Fundamentalists today. Literalists disallow questioning and instruct their flock to take the scriptures at face value, even though within their own ranks, a strange contradiction exists—Christians can't agree on whose interpretation is the most literal. (Go figure!)

Unlike the literalists, the mystery schools or Gnostics are not too concerned with the lives of biblical characters. Freke and Gandy show that Jesus is most likely to have been a composite figure inspired by the ancient philosophies of the many Greek and Roman pagan religions at the time. The mystery schools are more concerned with the lessons that offer a deeper and more profound spirituality than with having to prove the existence of biblical characters. In the same way as ancient Egyptian or Greek Gods and Goddesses are accepted as mythological, so too the mystery schools accept the allegorical lessons of the scriptures.

Within this Gnostic view, the original Christians believed that the Divine had both a female and male face. Freke and Gandy provide compelling evidence to show that Jewish Gnostics adopted the pagan Goddess Sophia into their religion. Within the mystery tradition, Sophia survived into the Christian Trinity where she had a spiritual partnership with the "Godman" Jesus.[47] In much the same way as the ancient Goddess embodied wisdom, Sophia represented all that was wise. Although Freke and Gandy quote Paul's letters in 1 Corinthians (2:7) as saying, "Among the initiates we speak of Sophia . . . " for it is "the secret of Sophia" that is "taught in our Mysteries," in more recent translations, such as *The Jerusalem Bible,* any mention of the name Sophia is replaced by the word "wisdom." It's also of interest to note that the Apocrypha includes the Old Testament chapter The Book of Wisdom, where wisdom is personified as female. Our word "philosopher" is a term coined by Pythagoras meaning those who love Sophia or those with a love of wisdom.[48]

Although the concept of the Trinity is not original to Christianity, Gnostics believe the figure now commonly considered as "the Father" to be "the mystery," with no gender attributed to this creative power. The Son was "consciousness" or "spirit," and the Holy Spirit was originally the female figure Sophia—"psyche" or "soul," the place where wisdom was thought to originate.

Alexander Waugh asks the question "Did God create her, then, or did she come into being *with* [his italics] God at the same time?" He claims that there appear to be 100 answers to this in the Bible—mostly conflicting—but one such can be found in the chapter The Book of Wisdom (7:25–6): "For she is the breath of the power of God, and a pure influence flowing from the glory of the Almighty. . . . For she is the brightness of the everlasting light, the unspotted mirror of the power of God, and the image of his goodness."[49]

The New Testament also makes reference to two female Christian leaders, the disciple Tabitha (Acts 9:36) and the apostle Junias (Romans 16:7). But, according to Riane Eisler—author of *The Chalice & the Blade*—the idea of female religious leaders outraged male Christian scholars because it threatened the power of men who were setting themselves up as the new "princes of the church." Men, like the Christian writer Tertullian (circa 190 CE), ensured that by the year 200 virtually all female imagery for God had disappeared from orthodox tradition. Today Christian historians rarely refer to the two female apostles.[50]

Denying the power of female influence in religion solved some of the big Christian quandaries like: If the Holy Spirit was originally female, how was this female spirit able to impregnate the innocent

Mary? Early Christian literalists, such as the Roman Catholic Church, which originally dominated Christianity, managed this feat of logic by neutralizing the gender of the Holy Spirit and reluctantly replaced the idea of a Goddess with the less-influential figure Mary. However, Mary, the mother, was not a Christian creation. According to the feminist theologian Mary Daly, the figurehead of Mary was "borrowed" from the pagan great moon Goddess Myrine (known also as Marian, Mariamne, and Marienna).[51] In her heyday Myrine was mother of all of the Gods. But while Myrine was most powerful, the patriarchs demoted mortal Mary's status to that of the domesticated mother of the Son of God who, apart from having Jesus' ear, had no spiritual rank herself. The real reason for reinstating a female figure, however, was to make Christianity more tolerable to the Goddess-worshipping people.[52]

For the clergy, who believed that sex soiled everything, the myth of Mary giving birth to a child presented another interesting problem. The only way she could be said to have produced a "pure" son was if she was deemed to be a virgin.

If the story of the Immaculate Conception happened, can you imagine the conversation between Joseph and Mary:

"Joseph, there's something I need to tell you."
"Hmmmm?" while he reads his Moses tabloid.
"I'm pregnant."
"What!" yells Joseph. "Well! Whose is it?"
"Wind pollination, I expect."
"Oh, come on, Mary!" he says angrily. "Give me a break!" And with that Joseph storms out of the room, never to be seen again.

Given men's behavior this is a likely scenario, but according to Jean Markale (author of *The Great Goddess*) the problem again lies in translation. He states that the origin of the word "virgin" referred to a woman of high social standing who was unattached and didn't have to answer to a man.[53]

But with the sales job that convinced the masses of Mary's literal virginity, the Goddess (and her potent sexuality) tumbled further from our consciousness. In the process, Freke and Gandy believe that religion left us all as motherless children.

## WOMEN'S WISDOM

As the Goddess embodies wisdom, it's interesting that many men today still put women down for their lack of reasoned or logical thinking. It's yet another example of the mechanism of reversal, but the original view of women embodying wisdom throws some light on the creation story of Adam and Eve.

Although the various translations are debated, some saying God created man in his own image and others stating the more equal position of male and female, Eve's actions are easy to explain when considered in the presence of a Goddess. Firstly, Eve was enticed by a serpent, a widely acceptable symbol of the female deity in ancient times, and secondly, she ate from the tree of knowledge (of good and evil), her natural inclination. Additionally, it was Adam who received God's instruction not to eat from this tree, not Eve, and although men (as the original creation) were considered superior, he didn't question Eve's actions but simply gave in to her enticement.

When children blame others for their own misdemeanors, we ask them: If you were told to put your hand in the fire would you do so?

With Adam claiming, "It was the woman you put with me; she gave me the fruit and I ate it" (Gen. 3:13), surely this story of Adam's figuratively burned hand speaks more about male weakness than his authority? Had something other than the enforcement of male power driven this interpretation, the beginnings of scripture would have strengthened women's position as knowledge seekers and highlighted male impotence.

But without the interpretation of Eve causing humanity's fall, what possible justification could men have had for demonizing female sexuality? And what's more, the reminder that part of Eve's punishment was to desire "only the husband that ruled over her" provides a very blatant justification for enforcing patriarchal rules of paternity.

## GAGGING THE GODDESS

Today the systematic removal of the power of the feminine is as relevant for men as it is for women.

If anything, the destruction of the Goddess was the most significant turning point in a man's relationship with the humane aspect of his nature. Instead of relying upon the wisdom of the feminine social conscience, which men also have within them, men attained and retained superiority by destructive forces. Starting with biblical stories, under the command of the male God Yahweh, hundreds of thousands of people were killed, and, as we've seen in Chapter 1, male power has since been symbolized by death and destruction. Within the context of a commandment stating, "Thou shalt not kill," societies are still being torn apart by warfare, and in His name, fear has been the weapon used to deprive millions of people of their lives. But as this is how male-dominant religions began, it appears that this is how they plan to continue. Apart from the atrocities male aggression has inflicted upon women, the biggest emotional problem facing any man is having to live up to the idea of being superior—by definition he can only do so by being destructive.

Gagging the Goddess was one such destructive measure, which kept knowledge away from the simple people, both men and women. This was necessary for those in power, as enlightenment would have made it virtually impossible to control masses of people. Within this context, the invention of dual afterlife options—heaven or hell—that no one could disprove was a particularly smart move.

So for thousands of years, people have lived according to these man-made rules because they fear God's wrath on the Day of Judgment. The final curtailment upon knowledge began with the systematic destruction of the literature and spiritual beliefs of paganism and culminated in the Dark Ages—the only time religion has completely ruled the world, controlling and oppressing all people.

## THE FORBIDDEN CRAFT OF THE WISE

With the tenacity shown by Goddess-worshipping people, the censorship of knowledge didn't entirely eradicate the Goddess's wisdom. So when gagging the Goddess failed, men throughout the Middle Ages used the phrase in Exodus (22:17), "Thou shalt not suffer a witch to live," as the big stick that could be wielded to rid the earth of "evil" women; in other words those who refused to be dominated by Father God religion. According to Daly, it is well-known that witches were charged with sexual impurity, and generally those who were accused were widows and spinsters, women outside of the direct control of men. However, the heat was turned up after the completion of the 1486 document *Malleus Maleficarum*—the ultimate catechism of demonology—and of course it was women who sported the horns. This tome informed its readers that females are naturally more impressionable than males, have slippery tongues, are feebler both in mind and body, and are more carnal than men. "All witchcraft comes from carnal lust, which is in women insatiable."[54]

As all women were evil anyway, and so many openly continued to flaunt their Goddess-worshipping rituals, men could simply deem a female to be a witch and she was extinguished.

Aside from sexual misdemeanors, women were also accused of witchcraft for the smallest of offenses . . . for example if their neighbors didn't like them, or sometimes if they owned a cat (another Goddess symbol).

But the height of the witch hunt was reached during the early beginnings of the closed male medical profession, which barred women from herbal medicine and midwifery. "Only God has the power to heal," so not only did the Church view female healers as economic rivals, but it also finally gave men total control of a woman's reproductive cycle from conception to birth. Even in the 19th century, when forms of anesthesia became available, the clerical and medical professions opposed its usage for childbirth based on Eve's original punishment.[55]

During the European Inquisition if a woman was murdered as a witch, her property and wealth would transfer to the church, and, in some instances, whole towns were ravaged, making the Catholic Church a wealthy institution.[56]

Daly quotes sources claiming that since the publication of the *Malleus Maleficarum,* the numbers of women put to death range from 300,000 to several million, although some modern skeptics claim it to be closer to the 50,000 mark. The last woman to be convicted and imprisoned under the U.K. Witchcraft Act was Helen Duncan in 1944, and only after Winston Churchill referred to this act as "tomfoolery" was it repealed in 1951.[57]

Women accused of witchcraft were killed by being burned at the stake or drowned. With drowning, if the woman was guilty she went to the bottom; if innocent she floated on the surface and was left to sink, so either way her fate was the same.[58]

What's interesting is that the word "witchcraft" means craft of the wise. So was the witch hunt not an attempt to finally destroy the Goddess of Wisdom—Sophia?

## A NEW SPIRITUAL PATH

But where does this leave us as females searching for spiritual enlightenment? Do we throw the baby out with the bathwater, or does the fact that men took over all aspects of religion leave no room for women to worship their creator?

Many women find answers in their holy books, but those who question or reject the ideas of organized religion can only really begin their search by looking within themselves. As a novice on this spiritual path, I don't have too many answers, except to say that it won't hurt to ensure that we are well-informed. Understanding the origins of male-dominated politics can help us fathom our history, and then we can stop our socialized self-loathing, the very thing that makes us most vulnerable to manipulation. We can start by treating ourselves with greater respect, then learn to trust our own convictions and stop damaging our sacred female bodies.

We can also celebrate, rather than denigrate, our feminine functions. Attitudes toward both menopause and menstruation show how totally female sexuality is equated with reproduction—and when this cycle of our life is over, it's assumed that we become sad and powerless.[59]

Menstruation is not a shameful "curse"; it is the pinnacle of our female spirituality, and menopause is not the downward slope to death; it is the most powerful period in our life. In *Passage to Power,* Leslie Kenton says that discomforts like hot flashes rid us of past emotional residue and, as such, are an important part of the cleansing and spiritual healing process. Extrapolating from the views of natural medicine, Kenton says that night sweats deep cleanse a woman's body. Menopause is a time of reevaluation and inner reflection; "They [the sweats] demand that we pay attention to our bodies and our lives."[60]

Menopause is an ideal time to replace self-sacrifice with self-development. With children having fled the coop, and the benefit of maturity, many women find great fulfillment in nurturing and feeding the emotional, mental, and spiritual aspects of themselves. Of course, one needn't wait for menopause to do this. Simply starting on the path of one's lifework can equally well fulfill our spiritual desires.

Certainly we need to rewrite our own stories without the influence of cultural myths and religious stereotypes. Instead of playing victim to Adam's betraying authority, we Eves can learn many lessons from the hardships women have endured. This is the wisdom of the Goddess, who, despite the best efforts of brutal megalomaniacs, lives on in each one of us today. Consult her by listening to your own intuition—it's the most powerful voice of the feminine psyche, one that can never be silenced by men.

## GOD'S LAST LAUGH—A CONVERSATION WITH EVE

"God I have a problem."

"What's the problem, Eve?"

"I know that you created me and provided this beautiful garden, all these wonderful animals as well as that hilarious snake, but I'm just not happy."

"And why is that, Eve?"

"I am lonely and bored, and I'm sick to death of apples."

"Well, in that case, Eve, I have a solution. I shall create a man for you."

"A man? What is that, God?"

"A flawed, base creature with many bad traits. He'll lie, cheat, be vain and witless, and he'll revel in childish things. He'll be bigger than you and will like fighting, hunting, and killing. He won't be too smart, so he will need your advice to think properly. He will have limited emotional capacity so will need to be trained. He will look silly when aroused, but since you've been complaining, I'll create him in such a way that he will satisfy your physical needs. And you won't ever be bored again!"

"Sounds great," says Eve. "But what's the catch, God?"

"Well . . . you can have him on one condition. As I said, he'll be proud, arrogant, and self-admiring . . . so you'll have to let him believe that I made him first. And this will have to be our little secret . . . you know, woman to woman."[61]

## A Fairer Tale: Jane and the Brainstalk

+ + + + + + + + + + + + + + + + + + + + + + + + + + + + + + + + + + + + + + + + + + + + + + + + + + + +

Long ago in a land far away, a poor woman lived in a tumble-down house with her two children, Jane and Jack. The house had dormer windows and shutters with hinges so rusty they wouldn't shut. Jane would help her old mother to maintain the household and earn money for food. Jack, however, was otherwise occupied. He languished about, dreaming of the day when he'd be Mr. Universe, while his mother and sister saw to his every need. Somehow or another Jack had developed the notion that it was his God-given right to be waited upon by women.

Jack was keen to build his body, so he spent hours and hours playing with his equipment—like weights and dumbbells. In the meanwhile the heavy work, like drawing water, tilling the field, and carting in the harvest, was left to his sister. Jane tried everything in her power to get him to help. She nagged, manipulated, cajoled, offered incentives, whined, and even cried, but all to no avail, Jack simply wouldn't lift a finger, except on occasion to give a rude one-finger signal.

Then one day the old woman called her children in despair: "Jack and Jane," she cried, "the worst has come; we have no more food and not a cent to buy anything. The two of you must go to the marketplace and look for work." Turning to Jack she continued, "I'm tired of working my fingers to the bone while you fantasize about being Superman. I need at least five gold pieces a week so I can live in the style I'd like to be accustomed to. It's high time you stopped letting the grass grow under your feet, so be gone with you."

For a while Jane had known that their plight was getting worse, but Jack was caught totally off guard. As he shuffled down the path with his sister, Jack's vision of muscles bigger than dumb-bells bulging all over his torso was shriveling away. With his head hanging low, he didn't notice that Jane had marched on ahead.

So it was that, lost in his gloomy thoughts about the mundane work he'd now have to do, Jack walked slap into someone. Looking up he saw a grizzled old man with clothes so ragged and filthy that even the birds and insects scuttled away in disgust.

"Who do you think you're shoving about, young shaver?" said the old man fiercely. "Don't you bother to look where you're going?"

Mumbling an apology, Jack explained his plight. With a sleazy smirk developing across his face, the dirty old man inquired: "So . . . is that perhaps your sister walking on ahead?" Jack nodded. "Well she looks nubile and energetic; for her I'll give you five gold pieces a week." Aghast, Jack exclaimed, "Five gold pieces a week for that nagging cow? I'll take it any day."

So, jingling his first down payment in his pocket, Jack quickened his step as he hastened for home. "I'm super smart," he told himself. "Not only have I managed to get rid of my pest of a sister, but all by myself I've earned enough to shut my mother up. Now I can resume my career plans without disruption."

On arriving home, Jack excitedly told his old mother about the marvelous job he'd landed, which required only that he work his physique to perfection. Jane, he said, had not been quite so lucky; she'd had to settle for a washerwoman's job so far off that it was unlikely she'd be sending home much money. The old mother heaved a great sigh of relief at Jack's good news and, before breaking into a merry little dance, demanded to see the money.

Delving deep into his pocket, Jack felt around for the coins but, to his horror, found only some musty old beans. Dumbfounded, he fished around again and—in his panic—even took off his trousers to shake out the pockets, but only one more stringy old bean could be found sticking to his underpants. "Moldy beans!" wailed his mother when she saw what Jack's fantastic story really boiled down to.

But the silver-tongued Jack quickly retorted, "Yes! . . . Umm . . . they're magical beans!"

"Magic! My ass!" yelled his mother. "Eating the product of spells and charms will only get me burned at the stake." And with that she threw the beans out of the window, not giving Jack's incredible tale another thought. That night both mother and son went to bed hungry, and while Jack lay awake listening to his tummy rumbling, he planned his revenge on the dirty old man.

Next morning when Jack awoke, something seemed to be blocking the light of the window. When he jumped up to investigate, a peculiar sight met Jack's eyes. In the place where the beans had landed, there was the enormous missilelike shaft of some sort of plant reaching right into the clouds.

"Wow!" yelled Jack. "This is just so super cool it's cooler than cool; it could have been planted by George Bush himself." For Jack this magnificent symbol of planetary power was just the incentive he needed. "Now I'm totally convinced I'm on the right career path," he announced to the monumental overnight erection.

So inspired was Jack that for once he forgot about his dumbbell obsession and started clambering up the shaft of the enormous plant. He climbed right through the clouds to where the stalk swelled out into a bulb like the tip of a lighthouse. Looking around, he saw a path stretching into the far distance where there was an enormous castle, bigger than anything he could ever have imagined. Immediately he set off in the direction of the castle. Soon he noticed that the trees along the edge of road were withered and the fields burned. He thought he saw a few people staring out from the run-down houses along the way, but they turned out to be mere shadows or phantoms.

Feeling slightly disturbed by the deathly hush and the shadowy presences, Jack quickened his step and made sure he stuck close to the track.

Soon he found himself at the entrance of the castle. The vast door was ajar, so Jack crept in. "Everything around here is enormously big," he thought. Suddenly Jack heard the heavy tramp of footsteps. A bit shaken by the sheer volume of the thuds, he hid behind a big wooden door and watched to see who came in. A formidable giant stomped into the room, bellowing:

> "FEE, FI, FO, FUM,
> I smell the gullibility of the little man.
> Be he smart or be he dumb,
> I'll twist his mind to make my sum!"

The giant looked around, sniffed with his cavernous nostrils, and then seated himself at the huge table. Wide-eyed, Jack watched while the giant tore hunks off a roast hog with his plate-size hands and crammed them past his muttonchop whiskers. When the whole hog, from snout to tail, had disappeared down the giant's gaping gullet, he licked his greasy fingers and bellowed, "Bring me my goose!"

Out of nowhere a few shadowy beings arrived carrying a plump white goose, which they silently placed on the table. "Is it charged up?" the ogre demanded to know. The shadows nodded in unison. Then the giant shouted, "Lay!" and immediately the goose began laying. But these were no plain white goose eggs; they were shiny golden eggs.

Jack's eyes were bigger than ever. "How I could use a goose such as this," he thought to himself. As he looked on, the giant slumped back in his chair and was soon snoring his head off. "Now's my chance," thought Jack. Stealthily he crept past the giant, snatched up the goose, and ran for his life out of the castle, along the track, and down the shaft of the enormous plant.

His mother was delighted with the goose, and news of the miraculous goose that laid golden eggs spread rapidly around the town. All the townsfolk were soon singing the praises of Master Jack and his golden goose. Jack rippled his muscles like Superman whenever anyone came to admire his marvelous goose. And, with so many townspeople bowing and scraping all about him, Jack was soon convinced that he was well on his way to becoming Mr. Universe.

One day, however, Jack shook his head and said, "What's wrong with you, goose? Your eggs are getting smaller." And they were indeed: Day by day the eggs shrank, until eventually they were as small as sparrow eggs, then even smaller than peas. Greatly annoyed, Jack started poking at his goose, trying to uncover any blockages. Suddenly the goose clamped onto his finger, and in a split second Jack felt his vitality drain away. He too had become a phantom.

Immediately the goose started laying great big golden eggs once more. Horrified, Jack realized that the goose was now using his vital energy to carry on with her egg-laying business. He also understood that the goose's original energy charge had been drained from the shadow people. "That's how they got to be that way in the first place," he lamented. "And now I'm just the same." With the last flickers of his fading vitality, Jack desperately started to think up a plan. "I'll have to convince the townsfolk to touch the goose to keep it charged," he told himself.

So Jack began to spread the story of the frightening giant who lived above the clouds. When referring to the giant, Jack would speak in hushed tones about a truly formidable ogre called MP, which stood for male power. Anyone who dared disobey MP, said Jack, would be barbecued for breakfast. Once they were frozen with terror, Jack would say, "I am the one and only person who has managed to overcome MP, this golden goose is proof, so I can offer you protection. All you need do is touch the magic bird." Based on what Jack said the giant demanded, he made up all the rules.

*"FEE, FI, FO, FUM"* Jack would shout, and the townsfolk, covered in gooseflesh, would gratefully flock to lay hands on the golden goose. So it was that Jack soon became the richest man in the land, while the vital energies of all the people slowly seeped away.

But one day the golden goose, whom Jack had begun to call Goz for short, simply wore out in midlay. "No problem," muttered Jack to himself, "I'll build a shrine to the dead goose, which I'm sure will work just as well."

Jack erected a marvelous goose-shaped monument. "Don't worry," Jack told the shadow people, "all you need do is pay your respects to the Goz shrine, for which there is naturally an entrance fee, and you will remain amply protected from the marauding giant."

This plan worked very well, with people queuing up to pay their respects to the Goz shrine, until one day a bandwagon arrived in the town, and on it were some songsters and a bleating goat. The townspeople were startled to hear this band of songsters denouncing Goz and singing the praises of their goat. With someone at the ready to interpret its every bleat, this holy goat—said the songsters—would put an end to the giant once and for all.

Jack was enraged. He rushed about denouncing the infidel

followers of the goat. Street fights broke out between those loyal to the golden goose and followers of the goat. Hundreds of shadow people fell, but in the end Jack's side was victorious. To ensure that his authority was never again questioned, Jack installed a permanent military force. He disciplined these soldiers by making them walk in an odd kind of way and called it the goose step.

Meanwhile Jack's sister Jane had long since escaped from the giant's emissary, the dirty old man. In her years of wandering, she'd gathered together a large band of young women who'd all been in similar plights. They called themselves the Brains Trust: a dedication to the female brainstalk that allows women to perform the complex but highly productive business of multitasking. Jane's group believed that everyone, even shadow people, had the ability to think and decide for themselves.

So it was that one morning after a lengthy brainstorm, Jane had a brilliant idea. She and some of her sorority would go in search of Jack's stalklike monument and discover the truth behind the fear he was spreading among the shadow people. Excited by this challenge, the sisterhood set out for the place Jane had once called home. Jane hardly recognized her old mother, who was pretentiously presiding over a tea party like a grand Mother Goose. As soon as they could, Jane and the members of the Brains Trust slipped out and began climbing up the giant stalk.

Upon reaching the top, Jane led the group to the castle. Like Jack they entered through the big wooden door, but were most surprised to hear a beautiful melody—a tune Jane recognized immediately as the Songs of Souls, once sung by every human being. Looking closer she could just make out a harp, but the strange thing was that it was playing itself. As they crept further, their ears were assaulted by the snores of the giant. Indeed the big ugly man was fast asleep.

Enormous as he was, Jane knew that he'd been made sick with power and greed and that she could outsmart him. Jane also knew the singing harp was what the people needed to restore the music they once had inside of them. But the harp sat so close to the snoring giant that the girls knew they'd have to outwit him. Huddled together outside they came up with a very clever brain wave. Stealthily creeping back into the room, each one quietly climbed onto one of the outsize kitchen chairs. When all the girls were in place, Jane addressed the giant, using an irreverent form of his name, "Hey MCP!"

Immediately the giant awoke, and so shocked was he that he was unable to utter even his normal bellowing threat. Then Jane and her clan jumped down, and each one started busying herself with so many things at once that the giant became bewildered by all the talking and multitasking going on. The only thing he could do was violently shake his head—in the same way that one does if a swarm of bees has flown into one's ears.

While the giant was dealing with his confusion, Jane hastily grabbed the harp, and she and the clan ran faster than they'd ever run before. Slowly the bamboozled giant came around from his bafflement, and, realizing his harp was gone, took off in hot pursuit of the sisters, shouting his predictable *"FEE, FI, FO, FUM!"* Although this line had once terrified so many, it didn't frighten Jane and her sisters. They knew it was just one of Jack's overused clichés that he had commandeered to brainwash the masses.

Racing down the stalklike monument, Jane and her team reached the bottom and quickly grabbed the axes they'd left behind for this purpose. *Whack! Whack!* went the axes, cutting deeply into the structure. *"FEE, FI, FO! . . . "* yelled the giant, and this gave Jane the information she needed; the giant was climbing down the stalk. With just two more *Whack! Whack!* the axes cut right through the manhood token, and suddenly the whole thing began to fall, taking the giant with it. *Crash!* the stalklike structure landed, making a big gaping hole that swallowed the giant right up.

Now, with the source of fear removed from the people, Jane and her clan built a new monument on the triumphant site. It was shaped like a more feminine dome, and they called it the Verum Dincum—a reminder to speak only the truth. While both the bona fide gods and goddesses smiled upon Jane's Brains Trust, the members each took it in turn to play the harp's music to the people. As the melodies sounded, the Songs of Souls awakened the brainstalk in each one.

Magically the shadows were shaken off and—with each phantom developing a vital glow once more—all could explore the personal gifts their creator had given them; this ensured that peace and prosperity reigned over the land for many long years. Even Jane's brother realized what a jackass he'd been and, on the insistence of the sisterhood, he was last seen refunding all his ill-begotten gains to the people.

+ + + + + + + + + + + + + + + + + + + + + + + + + + + + + + + + + + + + + + + + + + + + + + + + + + + + + + + + +

CHAPTER 9.

# Happily Ever After?

**H**appily ever after" is a sick joke played on many young girls at their most impressionable age. It implies that, upon marrying, a girl's every dream will be fulfilled. End of story.

What it actually means is that a young girl is whisked away from everything she knows and made to live in the prince's castle under his control. Translated into reality, this fairytale view of marriage is more like the end of a girl's life. And incidentally, have you ever come across a fairy story that actually describes a married couple's happily-ever-after domestic bliss? The reality for today's princess is more likely to be an "ever after" of Prozac.

## THE KILLER INSTINCT

So, what has the princess got to look forward to? If you look at the history of marriage, there's little to recommend it for women. Although many men like to believe that women are the ones who need marriage, there's nothing about a monogamous union that is naturally suited to women. While today monogamy may offer some protection from diseases like HIV/AIDS, it is a way of life that directly contradicts a woman's genetic encoding.[1] Survival of the fittest means that women are programmed to procreate with the strongest genes. Men who earn a lot of money or who are the most charming do not necessarily provide the most potent genetic material!

Monogamy is actually more appropriate for men. Although the male species prides itself on sowing wild oats, when it comes to raising children, men are genetically programmed to revolt against investing time and energy in a rival's offspring.

As in the animal kingdom, men in ancient times would kill infants born to other males. These days men who hook up with divorced women with children often have difficulty investing their energy into raising the offspring of a competitor's genetic material.

When human beings roamed, the possibility of sex didn't boil down to what a man could pick up in a local bar. Populations were small, and females were few and far between. So for males, living in a group guaranteed them far greater sexual frequency than roaming on their own did.

### THE BENEFITS OF HUSBANDSHIP

In prehistoric times it was the women who had loose arrangements with a "harem" of men. If a woman had sex with multiple partners, only the strongest genes would survive, but because of the genetic wrath of men, women needed to protect their offspring from males who were not the biological fathers.

This is why Jared Diamond, author of *Why Is Sex Fun?*[2] reports that the human female's body evolved to hide her ovulation, even though most animals have obvious signs of being in heat. Not only did this make recreational sex possible, but it also allowed women to keep their multiple sexual partners guessing. As no man would chance murdering his own offspring, the risk posed to all of a woman's children was lessened.

In terms of species survival, at a time when overpopulation was unheard of, it made sense that a woman's "marital" arrangements were loose and flexible. As the creators of new life, females were revered, and the Goddess protected women in their unions with men and in motherhood. Having no direct link with the Goddess themselves, men accessed spiritual power through "husbandship." So, not only was bonding with a woman necessary to fulfill a man's sexual needs, but females were also the essential link to both his social acceptance and spiritual vitality.

With religion in the hands of women, they also controlled the land they lived on, giving mothers a secure environment in which to raise their children. Pagan marriages were informal, a matter of common law, and had nothing at all to do with the will of the Goddess, or God.

## WOMEN AS BOOTY

Pagan unions continued for centuries, existing well into the Christian era, but these relationships were unlike marriage in the form we know it today. Patriarchal marriage has its roots in slavery, and according to Gerda Lerner, author of *The Creation of Patriarchy,* the first slaves were female, appropriated as war booty. Women were "stolen" for the purpose of reproduction with the intention of increasing numbers in male-dominant tribes.[3]

Physical terror is the usual means of turning free people into slaves, and for women this took the form of rape. Raping women made them pregnant, and this benefited men because it guaranteed that females would be obedient. Women would curry favor with their "master" to ensure their children were well treated, making "wives" and concubines vulnerable to exploitation.

In early patriarchal systems, like those in Mesopotamia, men adopted the status previously afforded women, such as land owner-ship, wealth, and occupation, but women were (and in most cases still are) ranked by their sexual activity: Highest rank went to wives and virgin daughters, but slaves and whores didn't count. In the upper classes male family members would exchange females who had land as their dowry, and marriage was a means of keeping property in the hands of male nobility. Marriage by contract and by purchase coex-isted, and women were granted status only if they handed over their rights to their husbands, especially their sexual freedom. Daughters of the poor didn't matter, so they were either sold as slaves to swell the family coffers, or their survival depended upon them resorting to prostitution.

The familiar custom of covering a woman's head with a veil was first used as a visible means for men to identify different classes of women. Only wives, virgin daughters, or concubines (serving one man) were allowed to wear veils as a sign of being "respectable" (read: being owned). Slaves and prostitutes were forbidden to cover their head, making them easily identifiable as fair game sexually. Assyrian law shows how seriously this was taken: "He who has seen a harlot veiled must arrest her and take her to the palace tribunal . . . the one who arrested her may take her clothing; they shall flog her fifty [times] with staves and pour pitch on her head."[4] Practically, this kind of disfigurement would have made it impossible for these girls to earn a living, forcing them to starve to death.

So it became that the only "decent" way for a woman to express her sexuality was in motherhood, and, as said by Lerner, marriage meant that women were left with power over two things only; food and dirt.

According to *The Women's Encyclopedia of Myths and Secrets,* in ancient Greece—where Mesopotamian-style patriarchy was adopted—men gained control by laying down strict social customs for women. The rules included "She should not be older than her husband, or of higher social status, or better educated. Women should not be paid equally for the same work, or be in positions of authority over males."[5] These are still the informal social norms that govern heterosexual relationships today.

Mesopotamian and Greek societies were the forerunners of male-dominant religions like Judaism, Christianity, and Islam, and although the early Jews were patriarchal, they were not monogamous. It is only later in Christianity that we witness the first signs of monogamy as an overarching norm for society.

## A "POLLUTED AND FOUL WAY OF LIVING"

Although modern Christianity reveres the sanctity of marriage today, early Christians were adamantly opposed to any form of sexual union.

So extreme was this view that in some sects only the celibate could be baptized as Christians.[6]

According to Sjöö and Mor, Yahweh is the only male God in history who never made love to a female or to the earth. In Christianity, his son was born without sex, from a sexless virgin, and followers were counseled to steer clear of sex forever if they wanted their spirit to reach heaven.[7]

In Paul's letters to the Corinthians, he states his opinion on celibacy, saying that "it is a good thing for them [the unmarried and widowed] to stay as they are like me, but if they cannot control their sexual urges, they should get married" (1 Cor. 7:8–9). In the same chapter Paul gives instruction to men about their daughters: "A man who sees his daughter is married has done a good thing, but the man who keeps his daughter unmarried has done something even better" (1 Cor. 7:38).

Marriage was common among Jews and heathens only, and because sex was used by pagans to invoke the Goddess, Christian fathers were against any institution that sanctioned lovemaking. *The Women's Encyclopedia of Myths and Secrets* quotes the Catholic St. Ambrose (340–397) as saying, "Married people ought to blush at the state in which they were living." St. Augustine (354–430) flatly stated that marriage was a sin, but more adamant was the 2nd century Christian apologist Tatian, who stated that marriage is "a polluted and foul way of living."[8] The manner in which modern Christianity upholds marriage is probably enough to make these Christian fathers spin in their saintly sarcophagi.

With celibacy as first prize, living a good Christian life, for men and women, meant dying a virgin, the way God had made you. Hangovers from these early times can still be seen in the way Mary's virginity is emphasized (even though she had children other than Jesus), as well as in the vow of celibacy taken by Catholic priests and nuns. But for the early Christians, faith in celibacy presented an obvious dilemma: How can one build a religion of people without procreation?

The Christian church responded to this quandary by simply leaving marriage, as a matter of common law, in the hands of the Jews and pagans and ignoring its existence. Although both the Old and New Testament provide many rules governing the behaviors of women, there is no biblical reference to how a marriage ceremony should be conducted.

The first marriage ceremony entered the Christian religion as late as the 15th century. *The Women's Encyclopedia of Myths and Secrets* claims some churches insisted that, at her wedding, a bride must kneel and place the bridegroom's foot on her head as a token of obedience. Although Christian vows remain largely unchanged, early versions included a commitment to be "bonny and buxom in bed!"[9] While obedience was expected until very recently, it seems that references to bedroom behavior were removed quite quickly.

## PROPERTY—A HUMAN RIGHT?

But marriage was not a matter of God's will—it was primarily a means of continuing to wrest property rights from women. Early religious marriage services were based on the property deeds used to transfer a woman's land into her husband's name.

In India, customs such as dowry murders and the now illegal, but sometimes practiced, tradition of suttee (burning widows on their dead husband's funeral pyre) are still about keeping property in the hands of men. Any land or wealth accumulated by a woman during her lifetime transfers either to her eldest son or to her husband's family when she dies.[10]

Although today it is common for Jewish men to register homes in their wife's name, Jewish women tell me this is more about protecting the household from financial calamity than it is about female power.

So, until recently, marriage was not a matter of love—it was about "endowing all a woman's worldly goods" to her husband. But, by keeping property out of the hands of women, female independence was removed. As a result, unmarried females in the Middle Ages were unable to support themselves. They were driven into marriage by economic conditions, and spinsterhood became an untenable option. Still today the word "spinster" has a more odious connotation than "bachelor," but it has been cleaned up considerably since its first usage. The term originated from unmarried women working as slave labor in spin houses. Many resorted to prostitution.

So if you've ever wondered why women marry for money, it's because we come from a long history in which our very survival has been dependent on men's material (financial) support. Even today the rules remain largely unchanged. But as said on the show *Dr. Phil* by author Phil McGraw: "If you marry for money you'll pay for every cent you get." And if you've ever questioned why modern fairytale brides still dress in medieval regalia, perhaps it's because society wants to retain the symbols of male ownership of women.

## TO HAVE AND TO OWN

As marriage reduced females to nothing more than men's chattels, the stage was set for institutionalized violence against women. Theologians in the Middle Ages were categorical: Women had sinned more than men, which meant that women deserved to be punished, for their own good. If nothing else this was how men defended the destructive behavior necessary to maintain their position of superiority.

There may be nothing in Jewish, Christian, or Islamic teaching that can rightly be used to justify the abuse of women, but there are instructions that can be misused and distorted to suggest that domestic violence is acceptable—sometimes even the will of God. This is about how religion has been abused as a political tool—it has nothing to do with spirituality.

In Christianity the primary justification was the Church's interpretation of the words of Paul: "Wives, submit yourselves unto your own husbands, as unto the Lord. For the husband is the head of the wife, even as Christ is the head of the church. . . . Therefore as the church is subject unto Christ, so let the wives be to their husbands in everything" (Eph. 5:21–24). In St. Ambrose's letters he wrote, "It is right that he whom that woman [Eve] induced to sin should assume the role of guide lest he fall again through feminine instability."[11]

## NOTHING A GOOD SLAP WON'T FIX . . .

In *Herstory of Domestic Violence,* a fascinating chronology of institutionally sanctioned abuse against women, the Minnesota Center against Violence and Abuse quotes a 12th-century medieval theological manual stating that a man is given permission to "castigate his wife and beat her for correction."

It goes on to say that in the 1400s, a Christian scholar, Friar Cherubino of Siena, wrote the *Rules of Marriage* in support of wife beating, and Christine de Pizan in *The Book of the City of Ladies* accuses men of cruelty and of beating their wives. Some authors suggested that male parishioners should exercise a little restraint and treat their wife with as much mercy as they would their hens and pigs![12]

Although during the mid- to late 1700s laws were passed to discourage violence against women (in both the early British and American legal systems) ,there were some notable exceptions. In the United States and the U.K., men were legally responsible for the actions of their women, so a man was allowed to use whatever was reasonably necessary for the discipline and correction of his wife. With civil law giving the husband full authority over his wife, matrimonial privilege allowed him to beat his wife for disobedience.

The big question is, of course, who deemed the punishment fit for the crime? Mostly this was left in the hands of the husband, but, in some instances, the "rule of thumb" was employed as a gauge to determine whether the abuse was reasonable. Although the phrase originated to describe a rough measure, legal record has it that some American judges originally used the "rule" to allow the husband the right to whip his wife provided that he used a switch no thicker than his thumb!

While laws may have been in existence to prevent abuse, further laws protecting the sanctity of the home largely counteracted these. This meant that a man's home was his castle, and as women were officially classified along with minors and idiots, those who were abused at home had little recourse to the law. Behind closed doors men beat their spouse with impunity, and this was often sanctioned by the highest power at the time—the Church.

## MARRIAGE—A SANCTUARY FOR ABUSE

This protection of the home environment meant that the violent actions of a stranger could amount to assault, but when committed by a husband against his wife, these same acts were sanctioned. Physical abuse and sexual coercion were so prevalent that they became accepted as the lot of a Christian wife. As millions of women are well aware today, abuse is not behavior that ended with modern enlightenment.

The contemporary author Alison Webster writes in her book *Found Wanting* that wife beating is still considered to be part of the responsible exercise of a man's marital rights, sometimes even a compulsory part of it. She writes, "It is not uncommon for Christian women who are subjected to battering by their Christian husbands to be told by clergy that this is an inevitable part of their submissive role."[13] There are also some abused wives who ask their pastor for help and are told to go home and read their Bible. Webster comments that they are instructed to resort to prayer, even if this means that they lose their power to act, to cope, or to solve their problems.[14]

Religious institutions of today are particularly adept at hiding the many instances of cruelty in their dark past, so you won't hear this version of "herstory" from a religious man—nor can we expect much more from the legal system.

In the United Kingdom, laws giving immunity for wife beating in the home were only repealed toward the end of the 19th century. In 1837, women were first granted limited custody of their children in divorce (but an adulteress had to petition for same), and it was only in 1869 that the first college for women opened, influenced by John Stuart Mill. With the Married Women's Property Act of 1882, women were legally allowed to own property for the first time in written history.

What's more disturbing is that in the United States, the "sanctity of the home" (read: the means of legitimizing abuse) was protected until the 1960s. It was only as late as 1994 that organizations like NOW (National Organization for Women) secured passage for the Violence against Women Act.[15] According to NOW, four women currently die every day in the United States as a result of domestic violence.

So if you've ever wondered why the man in your life turns his aggression on you, the history of marriage shows that it comes from a long tradition, sanctioned for centuries by both cultural ideas and religious institutions.

The final document of the Fourth World Conference on Women— *The Beijing Declaration and Platform for Action*—states, "Violence against women is a manifestation of the historically unequal power relations between men and women. . . . [Violence] derives essentially from cultural patterns, in particular the harmful effects of certain traditional or customary practices and all acts of extremism linked to race, sex, language, or religion that perpetuate the lower status accorded to women. . . . Violence against women is exacerbated by social pressures, notably . . . women's lack of access to legal information, aid, or protection; the lack of laws that effectively prohibit violence against women; failure to reform existing laws; inadequate efforts on the part of public authorities to promote awareness of and enforce existing laws; and the absence of educational and other means to address the causes and consequences of violence" (paragraph 118).[16] Can we really say all that much has changed?

For a long time now feminists, such as many of those present in Beijing, have been accused of politicizing everything about female lives, especially marriage. But as marriage was employed as a means of seizing power from women, it was already a "political" institution regardless of whether women tried to make it more egalitarian. Politics aside though, perhaps today it's more important to consider why so many wives still sacrifice the most vital parts of themselves to keep making the marriage tradition work.

## TRADITION—NOT A SYNONYM FOR "MORAL"

Some people don't want to mess with tradition because it's seen to be sacrosanct, but all it really means is handing down patriarchal doctrines, practices, and customs from generation to generation.

Given that traditional marriage sanctions male control, it's no wonder that conservatives are hell-bent on maintaining it.

Considering that violence against women has been handed down through countless generations, it's not surprising that globally one in three women is abused today. In most societies a woman is safer walking through the streets than she is living in her own home. For many females the home is far from being a place of security and self-fulfillment—too often it is a place of isolation, pain, fear, and degradation.

But how can anyone continue to believe in the righteousness of traditions that harm women? Rape (including marital rape), battery, wife murder, sexual abuse, misogyny, violence, pornography, and sexual harassment are not just the acts of sick individuals. They are rooted in the history of sick societies, the appalling consequences of men exploiting the tradition of staking their claim over women. Even though religious institutions may no longer be advocating disciplinary abuse, all the major religions of today still extol the virtue of male ownership of women. No other belief has created more problems for women than this.

At the closing of an Eve Ensler performance of *The Vagina Monologues,* she asked women who had been abused to stand. Next she asked the people who knew abused women to join them. By the end of the second question, more than half the 3,000-strong audience was on its feet. So problematic is the global abuse of women that misogyny is still the norm, not the exception. Virtually every woman I know, including myself, has at some point in her life been emotionally, physically, or sexually abused. Usually, the perpetrator is someone who claims to love her.

## ANALYZING THE ABUSER

Men who become abusive very often start off as Prince Charming. Their behavior is impeccable. Even women who know what to look for may get taken in by their charm. They are unusually interested in all aspects of you. Many will call regularly, read books that appeal to you, show interest in the clubs you attend, find excuses to meet or join you at work, and make strong overtures about meeting your family and all of your friends. You simply won't believe your lucky stars when the man of your dreams seems to be materializing before your very eyes.

Beware! This charm is a well-orchestrated act with a twofold purpose: to hook you into the relationship, and to identify your Achilles' heel. This will later be used against you as a manipulative tool.

Their unbending charm will continue for as long as it takes to secure you in the lair of the relationship. Commitments can range from you consenting to sex, moving in, getting engaged, or marrying.

One of the most common ploys misogynists use to trap women emotionally is the sympathy card. They'll tell you they're under a great deal of stress, they've lost their job/business or have just emerged from the most dreadful relationship or divorce. They will portray themselves as the abused victim.

Such misogynists are often most attracted to women who exude confidence and are more intelligent than themselves. The abuser's aim is to undermine the woman's self-esteem so that he can feel powerful. Once you are ensnared, instead of the wooing praise you got earlier, there'll be a slow increase in the gibes, criticisms, and undermining behavior. If you question this behavior, he'll swear he was only joking— don't you have a sense of humor?

Embarrassing you in company is a common ploy, including revealing delicate confidences. Increasingly over time your efforts to please him, with things like food or your appearance, will be ignored or dismissed with insults. Nothing you do will be good enough, and just like Cinderella or Snow White, you'll keep on trying even harder to be better.

The truth is these men can't deal with a mature partner, so they will slowly hook you into a sick codependent relationship, where you will feel pathetically reliant, like a child. Meanwhile you will be feeding his needs; both allowing him to look like the dominant partner and nurturing him like a baby. Any of your actions that don't directly feed his needs will be interpreted as rejection, and you will be duly punished.

With an overriding strategy to make you dependent on him, this type of man will not only undermine you with emotional attacks, but he may also start suggesting all sorts of reasons to systematically remove your independence. Whether it's your car, your job, studies, or interests, the misogynist will find every good reason for you to give up the life you had. Moving you from your hometown is particularly common, and pregnancy also serves to tie you down. Most predictable is his need to control the purse strings.

A further part of this strategy is to isolate you from close ties. While he may remain charming to your friends and family, behind their backs he will unashamedly criticize the people you care about. Deep down misogynists are "negaholics," addicted to negativity and extremely critical of everyone but themselves.

## NO MORE MR. NICE GUY

Misogynists are usually incorrigible womanizers—many have a wife plus an affair or two on the side, and dabbling with prostitutes fits their profile too. When it comes to other women, they will often compare you to those who are your opposite. So if you're blond, four foot two inches, and flat chested, they will blatantly swoon over tall brunettes with big breasts.

It's not uncommon for misogynists to drink excessive amounts of alcohol and have furious temper tantrums. These will be verbal, accusatory, and insulting. Nouns like "bitch," "slut," and "whore" will be combined with adjectives like "fat," "stupid," or "ugly." They'll also make you believe that you're emotionally unstable, a bad mother, or whatever else it takes to undermine your confidence. After their vile outbursts they may make a big show of apologizing and often weep profusely, but it won't stop them from repeating the same behavior again, probably tomorrow.

Misogynists are also compulsive liars. If you call them out they simply lie again to cover their tracks. In arguments they typically twist your words, using them against you. Although womanizers themselves, they will frequently accuse you of being unfaithful. Their possessiveness is suffocating; when you're not at home, they'll call your cell phone regularly to check up on where you are and who you may be with.

For many women this eventually becomes so unbearable that they opt to stay isolated at home. This is exactly what the misogynist wants.

The ongoing emotional violation usually precedes a physical battering, sexual abuse, or both. Beatings are likely to occur when the woman has reached her lowest point emotionally, and the offenders will often beat a woman in places that won't be seen by other people. After the battery they feign remorse, even cry if necessary.

Once the beating is over, the insecure little boy emerges, and frequently gifts will start rolling in. I know of one woman who paid for all her jewelry in the currency of severe beatings from her husband. Whether it's jewelry, flowers, or chocolates, whatever you treasure will be "generously" provided, and for a short time Prince Charming will return.

Then of course the vile toad will reemerge and the whole old cycle will begin all over again, and once more whatever he does will be your fault: He'll claim that no one else has ever had such an effect on him, which is why you deserve to be criticized, insulted, imprisoned, and battered.

## IS YOUR PARTNER A MISOGYNIST?

Not all abusers display all of the characteristics listed above, but if you're involved with someone who is showing some of these patterns, you will probably recognize one or more of the following symptoms in yourself:

1. A sense of worthlessness: If you feel worthless and believe that no one else will want to be with you, this is a sure sign that you are involved with a misogynist. Good relationships are important to women because they are supposed to add value to our lives, not destroy our sense of who we are.
2. Invisibility: Feeling invisible in the relationship means that he has gained control over your life. You no longer matter except in relation to meeting his demands. This is what misogynists aim for—you are simply a vehicle through which they get their own needs met, selfishly.
3. Confusion: A misogynist's compulsive lying and twisting of your words can make you think you are going crazy. Many women report this as a sense of claustrophobia in the relationship. Abusers manipulate to get you into this state because confused people are easier to control. So feeling constantly baffled by their contradictory words and actions can alert you to the cruel nature of their exploitative game.

People not involved in abusive relationships are bewildered as to why women stay in the union. But recent research points to unexpected issues like the romantic element within these codependent relationships. Women stay with batterers because they believe that no one else has ever known them as intimately as their partner does and apart from the coercion, the relationship between batterer and partner typically has romantic moments. "Both are drawn by the fantasy and reality of having found acceptance for the first time in their lives and feel the relationship is 'special,' a unique haven from the outside world."[17] This romanticizing of the batterer makes it difficult for women to leave, and even if they do so, they are likely to return.

The difficulty in leaving an abuser is further exacerbated by the sense of worthlessness a woman feels because the battering drains her of the very strength she'll need to leave. Leaving is complicated; any threat to the relationship can provoke more violence, and, with the batterer often controlling the finances, most women simply don't have the funds to support themselves. Many women in abusive relationships have children and single-handedly supporting youngsters requires a lot of personal strength and money. So does separation or divorce.

## SQUASHING THE TOAD

If females do find a way to leave, the toad can suddenly transform back into the prince, and the wooing process starts again. Even though the woman knows whom she is dealing with, Mr. Nice Guy will do whatever is required to regain her affection. Couples therapy, which was formerly "out of the question," may suddenly be accepted as a way to woo her back. Abusers will then try to convince even the therapist that the woman is the one who's being unreasonable.

Women will often do everything in their power to make the relationship work. This is especially true if children are involved. But when it comes to reforming, there are some who believe that misogynists can change, but personally I don't hold much hope. Deep down most abusers don't see themselves as the problem, and without this level of accountability, what would motivate them to change? After all, you—and everyone else who gets in their way—created the problem, so what can they be expected to take responsibility for?

After many years of self-sacrifice, most women come to the realization that, no matter what they do, nothing is going to improve the situation. The dawning of this realization is what's necessary for women to secretly prepare their exit from the relationship.

To get out and stay out of such alliances, women need to accept the reality of the toad's behavior, stop blaming themselves, and start rebuilding their sense of who they were before the manipulative abuse started. Most important, they need to understand why they complied with abusive behavior in the first place. If this issue remains unresolved, abused women tend to attract one vituperative toad after another.

## SPOTTING THE FAKES

Abuse issues are complex and deep-seated, so abused women often benefit from therapy. Counseling can help an abused woman to put her life into a more realistic perspective. If private therapy is not affordable, many women's organizations offer "survivor" programs, and these group sessions can be extremely helpful.

Too often survivors find it difficult to seek help because of the shame and embarrassment they feel. When survivors of abuse present for therapy, most spend a lot of time chastising themselves. Yet, the reality is these women have shown a great deal of courage in a most fearful situation. Once they see how brave they've been, they can start rebuilding their life from a position of far greater strength.

It's also important to note that the stereotype of a battered woman as fragile, passive, placating, and self-deprecating is not always accurate. Research shows that women often prove to be the more functional members in these couples. They reciprocate anger and contempt and do not back down, nor do they act as if they fear being beaten, even though they may feel it. A fact proving politically troublesome for victims is that the women themselves may become violent in response to their partner's attacks.[18]

One of the biggest emotional difficulties that abused women face is dealing with the disappointment they feel. When the reality hits that the prince is a fake, not only does the relationship collapse, but so does the fantasy of the long-term romance. All women who believe in the self-sacrificing version of romantic love are vulnerable to involvement with abusers. Here I'm not referring to romantic acts such as red roses, candlelit dinners, and Valentine's Day, but rather to the process of falling in love, where a woman loses her sense of self.

## ROMANTIC LOVE OR LOSS?

In his book *We: Understanding the Psychology of Romantic Love,* Robert Johnson says that falling in love is just a head trip that fulfills our fantasy.[19] All that really happens is our love partner is like the screen upon which we play the movie of our ideal mate. As misogynists can initially fulfill this role so adequately, they make it easy for women to give up reality and live the fantasy in the early stages. This seems so much more exciting than accepting our intuitive warnings and seeing the "mantoad" for who he is.

What complicates this situation further is people-pleasing behavior. According to Kevin Leman, author of *Women Who Try Too Hard,* people-pleasing makes women comfortable to be with controllers, and it is this that makes involvement with abusers feel artificially safe and predictable.[20] Disillusionment with men doesn't only happen to women who survive abuse. It occurs for most women once they hitch up with a male partner. From an early age we are set up to believe that men are superior. Whether from fairytales, movies, or just from looking at the world around us, young girls learn that making the grade means cleaving to the princes or kings who control the system. However, it doesn't take long for many a new wife to feel let down when she discovers that her man is in no way superior.

This is what some feminists call the "wife's trauma." It happens when she realizes that instead of the strong, self-confident, rational, intelligent, all-knowing, and capable father figure she wished for, she has bagged a dependent.

Marc Feigen Fasteau, who is known as the "Betty Friedan" of the men's movement, wrote that the disillusionment women feel is about having "subordinated yourself to a person who ... is probably not much smarter than you are in most ways and in some very important ways is a lot less perceptive, more dependent, and more childlike."[21]

In reality, men are reliant upon women's emotional fortitude to support them, but neither the fairytales (with the exception of Snow White) nor a girl's father prepares her for male dependency. Psychologists Luise Eichenbaum and Susie Orbach refer to this as the "hidden dependency," and although the male stereotype may show men to be independent, the hidden truth is they are needy.[22]

As this form of dependency never entered a girl's dreams as a youngster, she had no way of knowing that she would be called upon emotionally to be the stronger partner in the relationship.

Bearing in mind that girls are taught to stand on their own two feet emotionally, the biggest disillusionment sets in when a woman realizes that the strength a man shows exists only because she is feeding her energy to him. Only once a man is committed to the relationship does he relax the facade of being in control and unconsciously expect his wife to give up her strength and energy.

But once the fairytale notion starts to crumble, a wife begins to question (mostly silently) whether he is in fact worth the sacrifice she is making.

Given the disappointment women feel, coupled with abuse and the roles expected of them, it's no wonder that women instigate 75 percent of divorces.[23]

## MARRIAGE—GET REAL

If we as women are to survive marriage, perhaps we need to carefully examine the expectations we've grown up with. Many women come to this conclusion after a number of failed long-term relationships. Mostly the school of hard knocks (this can be taken very literally) teaches them that the most satisfying relationship with a man can only emerge from a deep friendship. Sadly, unrealistic female expectations make women shun this form of union initially.

Too often single females believe that "nice men are boring" because the whirlwind excitement of romantic love is absent. But it is exactly these unrealistic illusions about men that get women into trouble in the first place.

For women, once the garbage of knights on white chargers becomes as transparent as a wedding veil, a far deeper union is possible. This is a partnership in which a woman can truly be herself. It is one where trust is earned—not expected—and neither mate needs the other's dependency to feel secure. Mutual respect forms the foundation of such relationships, and the division of labor is based on choice, not tradition. So instead of getting involved in the games of role-playing, a woman is free to make her own decisions—some of which he may like, some of which he won't.

Having a mate rather than a marriage also means that neither partner is fulfilling a fantasy. They are independent individuals rather than two halves trying to make up a whole. Each partner then accepts the other person for who he or she is. Within the partnership, both rely upon their own strength and energy to drive their life and can therefore be true to their own values. Personal responsibility for one's actions is a given. With trust as a basis, sharing is common in these unions, and both feel comfortable letting down their guard and being vulnerable when necessary. Whereas traditional marriage can become stagnant over time, individual development is the catalyst for growth in these alternative relationships. Conflict is healthy rather than manipulative, and the union is not threatened in order for one person to get his or her own way. In fact, couples in such a relationship tend to bring out the best in one another. Just the safety of experiencing oneself in such a union can smooth out rough edges and shift old habits, such as knee-jerk defensive reactions.

These relationships offer a soft and safe place for both parties to land after doing battle with the external world. People in friendship unions also prefer each other's company. They tend to be attentive to one another's needs, and their conversations are nourishing, stimulating, and challenging. A relationship in which a woman can be loved, understood, and accepted is the most beautiful union—one that is possible only if a man matures beyond his need to own the woman. Likewise this kind of union requires women to stop being complicit with a man's need for control and to relinquish the fragile princess notion.

While in this book I've referred often to favoring one's authentic self over the nice-princess persona, relinquishing the princess is one of the most difficult challenges facing women. This is because there's far more to the story of being "nice" than we see on the surface. Unlike men, who have power because they are men, females believe that they are only able to get their own way with those who like them. As we've seen previously, this is a socialized notion and not the true female power I discussed in Chapter 1.

So the "likability" factor is not just about being nice for the sake of it; more importantly it is the glue binding the relationships that give us our sense of power—albeit falsely. (This will be dealt with in more detail in Chapter 10.)

## WAKING UP TO OUR POWER

What shows the frailty of this pseudo power base is some kind of "dark night of the soul." This can be divorce, disease, or any of the wake-up calls referred to earlier. But whatever the precipitating event, it forces us to make some real choices. Having come through a few wake-up calls myself, I know experiences like these are enormously traumatic, but—from the other side—I can also see that they were never without purpose.

Wake-up calls strip away the illusion of the pseudopower we've garnered and temporarily leave us feeling frightened, unprotected, and vulnerable. They are painful in the extreme, but the agony exists to make us more conscious about how we've been living. Without the pain there'd be little real motivation to change, and we'd simply pick ourselves up and carry on as before.

With a big wake-up call this is seldom possible, because it causes the world as we know it to crumble. This is precisely what provides the opportunity to restructure our existence. When we rebuild on the more solid foundation of what we want, we emerge healthy. When we try to re-create a semblance of our old life, we stagnate in frustration.

Knowing that we are at the center of our own life makes wake-up calls less necessary—it also makes all of our relationships easier. Whether with our children, friends, husband, or father, when we live according to who we are, they know where they stand with us. It also means that we can earn our self-esteem from our achievements, instead of having our self-value waver according to the fickleness of others' opinions.

So unless you've lived alone in a cave in Outer Mongolia and escaped the social conditioning women are subjected to, these bleak nights of the soul are the initiation rites that springboard us to show up in the full splendor of our female power. This means replacing the "likability" factor with sufficient self-respect to ensure that no one can bully us, trample on what we want, or emotionally blackmail us.

No toad on a white charger can do this for us; it's something only we can do for ourselves.

# CHAPTER 10.

# Yakkety, Yak

**W**omen love company and talking—in fact, we love to talk a lot—far more than men do. Men do stuff with other men, but women seek each other out mostly to talk. We like to communicate, and I'm no exception. People who know me laugh at the problem I have with scuba diving: not being able to talk for the fifty-odd minutes' duration of the dive. There's only rudimentary sign language to resort to; this is the reason my husband enjoys the sport so much!

According to Allan and Barbara Pease in their book *Why Men Don't Listen & Women Can't Read Maps,*[1] women need to work their way through about 20,000 expressions in a day—these are both verbal and nonverbal communications. Men on the other hand only get through about 7,000. When men get home from a day at the office, they may be all used up in terms of their daily verbal allowance—but women can still have a large portion of their allocation to get through.

## ALL TALKED OUT?

Most women notice that when their man arrives home, he gets busy tinkering with boy things or puts his face behind a newspaper. This is to avoid the "word onslaught." Many women are capable of talking all day long—some like me are even paid to do so—but still there's no apparent word shortage when we get home. In some instances it would appear that the 20,000 allocation for women must be the absolute minimum!

The variation in women's and men's communication patterns is grounded in history. In hunter-gatherer societies women were the earliest botanists. Knowing the difference between edible and poisonous foods, intoxicating or medicinal plants came about through trial and error, and communities of females spent their time discussing and naming vegetation as well as passing the information on to their children. Women were also custodians of their cultures and, in the absence of TV, storytelling was an important form of entertainment and education. The job of hunting, on the other hand, mostly required men to be silent, and these ancient habits are thought to have slowly developed into modern gender differences.[2]

Not only do men and women communicate at a different rate but they also communicate for different reasons. Communication guru Deborah Tannen claims that women communicate to build relationships but men speak to gain acknowledgment.[3] So when a woman is chatting about problems she experiences, too often a man will jump in with solutions to fix the problems. This incenses the woman because her talking is designed to give him a better understanding of who she is—while his part of the conversation is focused on finding a solution so that she can acknowledge his brilliance.

## THOSE NONVERBAL SIGNS

Another major difference between men and women is our sensitivity to the nonverbal content of conversations, which communicates feelings and moods. Since women are conditioned to manage the emotional life of their family, girls are sensitized to nonverbal content from an early age. Men are able to read nonverbal signals, but—as they are encouraged to suppress their emotions—they become less and less aware of the undertones of nonspoken content.

From an emotional intelligence point of view, reading other people's signals gives females an advantage, but we can sometimes overestimate our abilities and think that we are mind readers. While nonverbal content does communicate people's feelings truthfully, it is wide open to misinterpretation by others, which is where many of us run into trouble.

## NONVERBAL MISCOMMUNICATION

Take the example of a husband and wife attending a friend's party. He's been experiencing problems and is a bit grumpy of late. On the way to the party he grumbles about having to attend, but once they get there he's cheerful and lighthearted.

On the way home she regales him with tales about other couples who aren't on speaking terms; she tells him all about which one is eyeing that one's wife or husband, and even who may be cheating with whom. Then suddenly, out of the blue, she demands to know whether he still loves her. He's busy concentrating on driving and, unable to do many things at once, brushes her question off with a fairly bland response. "He must be losing interest in me," she concludes. "Otherwise why would he be so evasive?" An argument ensues. He swears he's only been preoccupied lately because of work issues, but she has a difficult time believing him.

This example illustrates how we jump to conclusions based on little or no information. The wife was attuned to nonverbal cues, but the conclusions she drew were colored by her own viewpoint and therefore likely to be distorted. We have to accept that quite often we're not reading people's minds, but projecting our own interpretation onto their nonverbal behavior. To improve communication in our close relationships, it makes sense to check out our nonverbal reading of a situation and, if contradicted, to accept what the other person says about their own feelings. Many of the difficulties in our relationships arise from the fact that women and men have different modes of communication.

The way women communicate is heavily influenced by our internalized belief that being liked is the first step to getting what we want and having any power. A study of women's speech patterns shows this belief in action: We use far too many submissive, "nice," bend-over-backward elements.

## I'M PROBABLY BEING STUPID, BUT . . .

Our desire to please can override other considerations like cutting through the bullshit and getting down to business. In *More Power to You!* Connie Brown Glaser and Barbara Steinberg Smalley detail ways that women jeopardize their credibility and their chances of being taken seriously.[4] Here are some common examples:

1. Excessive apologies: Women apologize far more than men do. Too often we start our sentences with "I'm sorry, but . . . " and proceed to apologize for our thoughts, our feelings, for interrupting, for disagreeing, or even just for being there. This detracts from the credibility of what we're saying. We also apologize when things go wrong, even if the events were beyond our control. This puts us in the firing line to accept blame even if we had little to do with the situation.

2. Disclaimers: Too often one hears women starting their sentences with disclaimers like, "I'm probably being stupid, but . . . " or "Perhaps I'm wrong, but . . . " or "You may not like this, but . . . " or "I'm not 100 percent sure, but . . . " Disclaimers such as these invite others to subconsciously agree with your own assessment of yourself. So while you're speaking, listeners are thinking, *Yes you are stupid . . . or wrong . . .* and *No, I don't like your idea.* Disclaimers strip us of our power and decrease our influence over our audience.

3. Using qualifiers: When women speak we often use qualifiers like "perhaps," "maybe," "kind of," "sort of," "you know what I'm saying," "I think," "I guess . . . " Other people read this as your being timid, weak, vague, uncertain, and uncommitted to what you are saying. If you don't believe in your own opinion, why should they be convinced by it?

4. Excessive chitchat: As far as men are concerned, this is the biggest conversational showstopper. Males just can't understand why we would use thirty words when three will do. For example, when requesting time off, a woman is likely to say, "I really hate to bother you because I know you're busy, but since I've finished going through the pile of reports you left for me, would it be okay if I took tomorrow off, because I need time

to go to a specialist?" After the first few words, the recipient of this conversation is thinking, "If you know that I'm busy, why take up more of my time with so many words?" Instead we could just announce, "I'm taking tomorrow off."

5. Superpolite speech: Allied to excessive chitchat is the ineffective habit of being overly polite. This expresses the learned "niceness" we've spoken about. Instead of being direct, women will say things like, "I would certainly appreciate it if you could please tell John, whom I spoke to yesterday, that due to unforeseen circumstances, I cannot attend the ten o'clock meeting." Women also use politeness instead of punctuation. The classic example here is to thank people when no gratitude is intended. Women often end their conversations with "thank you," but this is a full stop to end the conversation. When men reply with "you're welcome," women get annoyed because they don't understand how men could read the situation so incorrectly!

6. Softening the blow: When women reprimand they soften the blow by adding niceties, such as compliments for work done previously, or by rescuing the person from the hurt the interaction may cause. This behavior is so ingrained that I've actually seen it recommended in seminars aimed at supervisors. "Cushioning the blow" is taught as a standard practice in skills for reprimanding. Yes, of course women designed these programs! But the problem is that those receiving a softened reprimand don't know whether you are complimenting them or chewing them out.

7. Tag questions: When making a point, females will often tag a question onto the end to gain agreement or avoid confrontation, for example: "This could really work, don't you agree?" Or, after a lengthy discourse, women say, "Am I right?" The nonverbal tone may imply "don't you dare to disagree," but when a question is tagged onto the end of a statement, the listener forms the impression that the speaker lacks the courage of her own convictions.

Another habit that lets women down is what psychology refers to as the "hangman's laugh"—a tendency to giggle or laugh at the end of each statement, when no humor is contained in the conversation.

Not only is this habit annoying, but it devalues the statement being made. It loudly indicates that you are nervous or uncomfortable and shouldn't be taken seriously.

Along with submissive language, patterns of hesitance, and indirectness, we take too much responsibility for keeping the conversation flowing with fillers like "you know." Some believe that these habits developed because of experiences like having to converse with unresponsive men.[5]

Too often we sound vague, timid, and unsure of ourselves, particularly so when it comes to issues relating to our own lives.

## SO, WHAT DO YOU THINK?

When men face a decision, they quickly gather any facts they need then take the necessary action. They don't go around discussing the ins and outs of the actual decision with all and sundry. Women on the other hand run up and down, seeking as many opinions as there are people available, even when these people are not involved in the issue. The reason for all this opinion seeking is not actually to get concrete information, it's more like a form of canvassing to check out if other people agree with our line of thinking: Is it fair to others, for example? But mostly we behave this way to test our bottom line: Will we still be liked after making this decision?

Seldom do women make a judgment call without having our ideas endorsed, and not necessarily by people whose opinions we trust, but by all and sundry. Once we have the basic facts about an issue, canvassing opinions just makes us vacillate and procrastinate, and we become indecisive. It's very difficult for women to accept that certain decisions are theirs alone, and that making a decision will not always make them popular with everyone. Trying to please everyone just forces us to settle for mediocrity, but pleasing ourselves makes us decisive about pursuing what we want.

A friend of mine who appears to be highly assertive on the surface is a typical example. On being required to make some tricky business decisions, instead of focusing on what was right for her, she ran around soliciting solutions that would "allow everyone to win"— everyone except herself, of course. What's interesting is that despite her highly consultative process, and her attempts to give everyone else what they wanted, the resentment toward her kept on growing. Others just couldn't understand why she seemed to be procrastinating.

So fascinated was I with this idea that it became the focus of my attention. Not surprisingly, I too found myself behaving like a typical woman—I talked to female friends and colleagues about our indecisiveness, not necessarily just to share the information, but more to test the concept for endorsement. Although I'm accused of holding strong opinions, what I learned was that I only became firm in my convictions if my opinions had been sanctioned, either by literature or other people. While this was a difficult confession to make, even to myself, it caused sufficient discomfort to force a change in my habitual thinking patterns.

## IN OURSELVES WE TRUST

It's both unnecessary and exhausting to question the validity of every thought we have. We only do it because we've got a deeply conditioned lack of faith in our own opinions.

Because women have the tendency to think aloud, males who get acquainted with their female colleagues are constantly exposed to their vacillation and questioning. While women colleagues may find this irritating habit normal, men don't understand it because their upbringing encouraged them to be not just decisive but also self-focused in their decision making. In a highly competitive environment, men will use women's hesitance and uncertainty to put them down. So we're not doing ourselves any favors by thinking aloud and unwittingly exposing them to our indecisiveness.

Our indecisiveness boils down to needing to be liked, but there's more to this story than the triviality of niceness. The truth behind the "likability" factor is that it determines how much other people will allow us to manipulate them. If we are liked we can get away with making demands; if not we are punished by being left to our own devices. It's why so many women sculpt themselves into perfect corporate spouses, and it's why some of the most unlikable women I know are the most reclusive. It's also interesting today that so much more has been piled onto being likable than the sweet smiles on our faces. In women thinness is likable, fatness is not; listening is likable, opinions are not; youth is likable, age is not; being agreeable is likable, being yourself is not.

## KNOCK THE NICENESS TRAP

We don't need rocket science to know that the only way society accepts females getting their needs met is if our demands are wrapped up in nice packaging. So being "nice" is not simply a facade that women adopt; it is something we have been led to believe is the source of our power. So unless we change the things that are valued in women, we may die with that sweet smile on our face, but like millions before us, we too will die powerless.

## WHO'S THE COOLEST OF THEM ALL?

This need to be liked even applies to our dealings with children, especially for Baby Boomer mothers. Since many Baby Boomers are in denial about their age, the likability factor extends to the need to be seen as "cool" even as a maternal figure. This provides children, particularly smart teenagers, with ample opportunity to manipulate because they know Mom would rather be one of them than the old dragon who dictates and disciplines them.

The need to be liked is so pronounced in us that a friend who goes into combat fighting court battles for abused children mentioned that she believed it was important for the judge to think that she wasn't too aggressive. In the middle of an angry exchange, she may flutter her eyelids or shoot a smile at him (usually it is a man) to deliver the message "Beneath all the aggression, I'm really nice." She said she was perfectly aware that male attorneys would never bother with behavior like this, because their power base and credibility is not dependent on whether they are likable.

This friend is quite consciously using her need to be liked. She believes her cause is strengthened if men in particular think that she's a nice and noble person. And so far it's worked well for her.

The problems arise when we are unconscious about sacrificing huge chunks of our authentic selves just so that we will be liked. If for some reason people still don't like us, then the flimsy pack of cards upon which we've based our personal power comes crashing down.

Sacrificing what we want is the price women pay for being liked, and it's this need that keeps us in line as wives, mothers, sisters, daughters, and friends. We've got two choices: Either we keep on maintaining a pseudo power base that ends up in our being controlled anyway, or we meet our own real needs—and risk being unacceptable or unpopular.

## THE GAMES WE PLAY

Of course this also affects our female-to-female friendships. We know from the difficulties in the mother-daughter relationship that women don't trust one another easily, but recall too how this is exacerbated when we fail to see the true face of our friends because, like us, they're hiding behind niceness. How can friends really know what we're feeling when we're suppressing so much of ourselves behind the facade of coping or of social politeness? Sure, we may moan about men, but how many of your friends know about what's hurting you deeply or causing your loneliness?

For women "being real" breaks the rules of social nicety, so instead we "legitimize" our real needs by couching them in communication games that are more socially acceptable. They are commonly known as emotional blackmail, and we use these games to make other people respond to what we want without risking the power base of our social graces. These games are learned as early as grade school. At school the most popular girls seemed to have magical powers over other people, and—if we weren't one of them—we'd align ourselves with the little Ms. Popularitys, hoping that some of their charm would rub off onto us. As adults, when we sacrifice our own needs in the pursuit of being liked, how different are we?

Along with indirect communication we make use of the following games, which are not exclusive to women, but our sense of being powerless makes us prone to them:

- Neurotic nattering: Although women naturally talk a lot, those who literally have verbal diarrhea are extreme in their nattering. Women who play this game will monopolize all conversations, and it doesn't really matter what topic they talk about because their nonstop monologue is used as a verbal wall to protect their vulnerability. While they're holding court they feel in control, as there's no likelihood of anyone probing their lives by asking any potentially difficult questions. Without feedback, such women can live the illusion of existing in the cocoon of their self-created perfection, which would be shattered by any form of real relationship.
- Verbal bullying: Like all bullies, women who use this tactic are covering for the insecurities they feel. When women have a history of not being heard by other people, they tend to become argumentative, and any discussion presents as a good opportunity. Women with underdeveloped negotiation skills and an overdeveloped need to be right rely on this game to appear powerful. Conversation stoppers like "What rubbish!" or "You don't know what the hell you're talking about" precede most of their statements. Bullies don't listen to counterarguments and over time have no problem contradicting a firm stance they previously may have taken. This happens because the details of the argument aren't important. What matters is that, at the end, the bully thinks she's come out most powerful.
- Envious sniping: Our conditioning leaves us feeling not good enough about ourselves, so women can suffer from envy when others start achieving. "Who the hell do you think you are?" is the sentiment underpinning envious sniping. Typically, the sniper will proceed to undermine another woman by fault finding. Anything can be used as fodder for the sniper to undermine the recipient's confidence. As we are taught to value cooperation instead of competition, women achievers show up the inadequacies of those around them. This creates discomfort for those women who are dissatisfied with their own lives. But instead of dealing with their own discomfort, snipers inflict their hostility upon those who head for the top of the pile. Snipers speak indirectly and couch their put-downs in (often

cynical) humor, rather than stating their opinion overtly. They can then easily deny that a slur was intended, or accuse others of being humorless or oversensitive. The aim of sniping is to destroy the other person's power base, and gossip is the main weapon used in any character assassination. This is one of the prime reasons that women are accused of bitchy behavior in business.

- One-up(wo)manship: Unlike men, women do not naturally hold power in society. Consequently, we tend to look for status in external factors like the men we're attached to, where we live, how wealthy we are, cars, clothing, or jewelry. Staying thin can also be thrown in with our need to "keep up with the Joneses." As we've seen previously, thinness in women is incorrectly associated with power, discipline, wealth, and status. Many women also use fame by association as part of this game. They will name-drop unashamedly about people they know in high places. Similarly, women who live vicariously through their children blatantly play this game when talking about their offspring. It's as a result of this game that the fashion houses began flashing their labels on women's clothing and accessories. Instead of our having to allude to our one-up(wo)manship, Gucci, Versace, and Moschino did it for us. Whether Versace or Billabong, it's absurd that we're paying handsomely for the "privilege" of these names, using our already-abused bodies as free advertising billboards.

- Nay-saying: Nay-saying is the primary game of negaholics. They find it difficult to make their own life work, so it is challenging for them to interact with positive people. Naysayers will always focus on the negative, and they get themselves so stuck in problems that it's virtually impossible to find a solution. Nay-saying is the game of women who have based their life on gaining power from their sexuality or maternal role. Age forces them to lose the command they once had, and—as a result—they resort to spoiling everyone else's achievements and/or fun. Naysayers are petty and highly critical about everything, especially about those who ignore their manipulative moaning and insist upon remaining upbeat and positive in their company.

- Playing the drama queen: Girls are often taught that it's impolite to be the center of attention, and many have become drama queens to get themselves under the spotlight. Women who play this game always have a pressing problem on hand and will bombard others with their dilemmas at every given opportunity. As a means of getting attention, drama queens will dominate conversations with problems—even if these need to be exaggerated to capture their audience's attention. Should others attempt to give advice, drama queens will shut them up quickly, because solving the problem would divert attention away from their drama. The drama queens themselves are not supposed to be the center of attention, of course, so rarely do they make themselves the main player in the problems they're presenting. Mostly a host of issues including bosses, children, jobs, husbands, finances, friends, parents, or siblings are the problems that drama queens use to fulfill their unconscious need for attention. Continuously having an issue on the go, drama queens tend to be heavy company and seldom, if ever, understand that others may prefer to be fun and lighthearted.

- Playing the queen bee: In *Woman's Inhumanity to Woman,* Phyllis Chesler used the term to describe the exploiter-as-wounded-victim. Here demanding and abusive behaviors are used to take advantage of everyone.[6] The queen bee believes she deserves to be waited upon for all manner of reasons; some play on illness, while others just fancy themselves to be famous or important. I knew a woman who claimed psychic powers who was like this. Her weight had virtually immobilized her, so she had other people waiting upon her hand and foot; they were running around paying her bills, lending her money, doing her shopping, buying her gifts, sending flowers, typing manuscripts, and even paying for overseas trips—all because she claimed to have been wronged by her family and ex-husband. She used her "psychic" powers to make people dependent upon her and played up the sympathy card to have power over those who then became protective of her. But what her behavior boiled down to was merely a handy ploy to continue exploiting a band of ever-willing service providers.

- Playing the victim: Eric Berne, in *Games People Play,* first wrote about victim, rescuer, and persecutor games.[7] He talked about the most powerful manipulator of all as the one playing the game of victim. Although victims always present with a sob story and a broken wing, they are anything but fragile. Victims are the most powerful manipulators because they can easily rope in the other two players into their game. As these games have to do with gaining power, women who so often feel powerless frequently resort to the role of victim. A victim is the "poor little me" of this world and always has to present as sick, miserable, or depressed to get other people's attention. Unlike the drama queen, who uses other people in her game, victims are always suffering themselves. The victim aims to get other people to take responsibility and carry their load. They are never accountable for their actions; someone else is always to blame. Victims want pity, not advice, so no matter how many options you may give them, there will always be good reason why they can't help themselves.

- Playing the rescuer: Rescuers are the "fix-it" people of this world, and women are prone to playing this game as a means of addressing their poor sense of self-value. Recall that our self-esteem is often based on what we give, so if we can just keep giving, we hope to feel better about ourselves. Uninvited, rescuers jump in to solve other people's problems, but in so doing, they rob the person of important learning experiences. Rescuers need victims to play their game, and victims have a nose for rescuers. So if you are one of the fix-it types, expect your life to be filled with victims. Rescuers have a deep need to make a difference, but when this energy is not channeled into a lifework activity, the manipulations of each victim present as an opportunity to feel better about oneself. When the rescuer is feeling down, she can console herself that so many people are depending on her. However, as victims don't want to solve their problems, the victim-rescuer trap is an exhausting and unceasing game instead of a fulfilling existence.

- Playing the persecutor: Female conditioning drives this game underground, and persecution is more likely to be covertly expressed by behaviors such as the silent treatment or the "tyranny of niceness." Chesler says that females disconnect to show disapproval, and that this excluding of other women is a crucial form of female aggression. Silence is also used when a woman's ideas, physical appearance, or sexuality threatens and challenges other females. "Sometimes women fall silent as a way of punishing any woman who expresses herself directly," because it goes against women's "enforced/preferred" style of communicating.[8] We've discussed the "tyranny of niceness" previously, but it can be summed up by one woman asking a seemingly innocent question, like: "Do you *really* like those shoes?" in a disapproving tone.

A further all-encompassing game is deceit. By deceit I don't mean those who consciously lie to squirm out of a situation, but rather the kind of lying considered normal in conversation. One of the foremost researchers on deception, Bella DePaulo, found that in conversations lasting ten minutes or longer, the odds of people telling some kind of lie were one in three.[9] Men tend to lie to impress others, and women lie to spare other people's feelings and make them feel better. DePaulo believes that we tend to lie less to those who are closest to us, except when it comes to issues of fidelity and sexual history. Men are known to exaggerate their conquests while women underplay their experience.[10]

While manners and tact are important in relationships, when the white lies women tell become an unconscious part of their conversational routine, it makes them difficult to trust.

### GAME OVER

Games block intimacy, so if we want genuine and emotionally efficient communication, we need to stop them. This can be tricky, especially when a game has endured for the length of a relationship. In most games our silence is interpreted as compliance, so we have to be more assertive and actually name the game.

When games are named, the player feels caught out and that their power is being undermined, so don't expect a positive reaction. If you expose a person's game, they may respond with anger and resort to more-extreme forms of the game.

Verbal bullies may launch an even more powerful volley of put-downs, while victims or drama queens will stage a spectacular catastrophe. Rescuers may decide there's more mileage in the victim role and vacillate between both games, while naysayers and victims are not beyond a massive episode of sulking. Often the envious involve other people by making their gossip and sniping more public, and queen bees can become aggressive about their "victimization."

Game players do this to test your conviction. A key strategy of theirs is to wait for a lapse on your behalf, which is an indication that you're back in the game. Keeping your new behavior consistent is the best way to avoid getting roped in again. This means reminding the game player every time you detect their game, but be warned that game players are tenacious and predictable.

When it comes to your own communication, become a keen observer of your own behavior. Listen to your own decision-making routine; be aware of games you may be playing or the female speech patterns you fall back onto. The more conscious you are of your own ingrained communication habits, the better you will become at defining and getting what you need from others.

## ASSERTIVE OR SELFISH?

If we want to relate to others whom we respect for being themselves, then we too must learn to be more authentic. With women, being authentic usually boils down to overcoming our difficulties in asserting our own needs. Assertiveness—like personal power—comes from being decisive and having the courage of our convictions. It requires knowing what we want in the first place and sticking to our guns in any disagreement.

It's sad but true that we women are particularly good at manipulating, bullying, and outmaneuvering an opponent as long as we are fighting for the causes of other people. But how many times do we use the same strategies and tactics to fight for what we ourselves want? How many important decisions can you recall making that placed what was right for you as the central priority? This is also the reason that women often hesitate to put themselves forward in business—whether it is for a promotion or a new project or to justify a salary increase.

Until we accept that the rules in commerce differ from the rules we were taught for managing home and family, we will remain disempowered in the working environment.

Too often we forego asserting our own needs by masking these needs in the guise of fighting for our children, our staff, the poor or downtrodden—anyone rather than spotlighting ourselves. For example, when women aren't getting enough attention from men, they often plead with them to give more time to the family and children. If at work we are being overlooked, we may steam at bosses for ignoring the efforts of team members in our department.

Although our rearing makes behavior like this understandable, our indirect communication doesn't ultimately help get our own needs met. It is one of the reasons we so often feel unrecognized and unappreciated.

The emphasis on cooperation for girls means women are very often totally conflict avoidant. Instead of upsetting others with our views, we absorb and carry the pain or discomfort of the situation. Rather than being direct in our communication and ridding ourselves of the aggravation, we make ourselves the breeding ground for resentment. This inability to put our foot down allows other people to continue taking advantage of us, and predictably, our resentment grows. When our conflict-avoidant behavior is combined with our indecisiveness, we can be easily swayed by the arguments of others—especially those who appear more powerful.

Typical female upbringing discourages us from being self-directed or meeting our own needs. Therefore, deciding what would be "the right outcome for me" is akin to being tagged with the label women dread the most—selfish. This affects our ability to fight for ourselves and, ultimately, to win.

On top of this we are programmed to allow ourselves to be driven by an external locus of control. This means we place great value on other people's opinions, and we tend to take their judgments much too personally. But taking so many opinions personally just wastes the fuel we need—our personal power or energy. This is the "oomph" that makes fulfilling our lifework possible.

## PRIORITIES AND PASSIONS

Working on our sense of self-value can help us escape these communication traps. Unless we understand the concept of being appropriately selfish, we are unlikely to find the personal power necessary to make a stand on issues we deem important. This means being sufficiently self-aware to find out what our priority issues are. It could mean working through exercises like those in Chapter 7 to help discover our lifework or entering into therapy. We need to make decisions that direct our energy into the areas that stir our individual passions.

Women tend to talk excitedly about ideas, but sometimes this is not followed through with sustained action. A friend of mine often comes up with great ideas, which she then sets in motion with gusto, but invariably she fails to finish what she began. When I suggested that maybe she was "talking out" the energy of her enthusiasm, the realization dawned.

## ACTING OUT YOUR DREAMS

Don't burn your idea out with too much talk and too much looking for endorsement. When we hold on to our ideas, the energy buildup we feel triggers us into action. So instead of all the talk, talk, talk we're so addicted to, we find the discipline to direct this energy into forging an internal plan of action. We can stay focused on our direction and seek only those opinions that give us concrete, action-directed information. We can risk making mistakes, because the worst thing that can happen is that we'll learn something new that will help us move ahead with our project.

When negotiating, guard against the common female pitfalls of underselling yourself and covering up insecurity by too much talking. The most important thing I've learned about negotiation is that the person doing the most talking inevitably ends up on the losing end.

Men know they can sit back and watch while we talk ourselves out of a good deal or into being reasonable (read: doing it their way). It's so habitual for us to fill spaces with yakking that we'll behave in the same way whether we're having drinks with a friend or haggling over a big contract. In negotiation, while we're doing the "talk performance," our opponents have ample time and opportunity not only to size us up but also to clarify the key issues from their perspective. Often they are not even listening, but simply working out how they can rebut our argument or how far they can push us. So if we want to start thinking on our feet, we have to discipline ourselves to stop talking.

## EXPOSING OURSELVES IN THE BOARDROOM

Women tend to overlay their negotiations with words that are emotionally loaded. When dealing with other women this is not so big an issue, but men will often use a woman's emotional exposure of herself to control or stonewall further discussion. All they need do is accuse us of being emotional, and the rage we feel at being dismissed or humiliated diverts our attention from the prevailing issues. Instead of falling for this, it's more functional to simply say something like, "You're accusing me of being emotional to divert attention away from the real issue," then go straight back to the discussion.

It's also worth noting that men only understand direct communication. Allan and Barbara Pease say that men's sentences are short, direct, solution oriented, and to the point.[11] They communicate in this fashion to assert authority over others, so when dealing with them, we'll get further if we speak in terms that they understand. While men won't necessarily like you for putting your foot down or being demanding, they will respect you far more than they will women who resort to sweet, polite little-girl tactics. We can still be charming, but there's a big difference between being childishly helpless and consciously assertive.

## "LET ME GIVE YOU MY CARD . . . "

When it comes to networking, women are naturally more social, so a more social way of doing business is more appropriate for us. But the social mode can only work if we consciously overcome some of the problems it can create within our business networks. We have a tendency to build personal relationships within our business network, and, over time, many of us become bosom buddies with our suppliers, clients, and associates. When these relationship are going smoothly, this works brilliantly for us.

But what happens when conflict creeps into our negotiations? In business, disagreements are inevitable, and this is when the emotions of our personal relationships interfere with the process. Doing business with friends makes both parties self-conscious, particularly about issues like pricing. Many think that because we're buddies, we can expect things to get done cheaply, but in the process we're as guilty of devaluing women's work as the chauvinists in corporate business are.

As if these issues are not difficult enough, our relationships get even more complicated when discussions are necessary to troubleshoot problems. When friendships are at stake, it becomes more difficult for the parties to be honest about their issues. If the relationships are purely about business, the problems can be solved and the relationships salvaged. But when friendships are involved, we risk losing in both quarters.

Men are more likely to entertain pure business associations. Most have no qualms about using other people for their own gain and will remain impersonal with their network whether they interact in the boardroom or do business on the golf course. Sure they may seem all "buddy-buddy," but neither party is naive about the nature of the relationship. Both expect profit to be made and will negotiate without hesitation to get the best deal for themselves. Women need to learn to separate business from friendship by divorcing our personal power from how much other people like us.

## CHANGING TACK

Behavioral change occurs when we realize that our old ways are working against us. Often it helps if we rehearse the new behavior in our mind before acting. Visualization gives birth to more-appropriate actions and with repeated practice is forceful in creating change. But changing old habits takes time, so don't berate yourself if you slide back sometimes; the more aware you become, the less frequently such lapses will occur.

It's not easy to let go. Our compliant female behavior guarantees us a type of shallow acceptance, and we may not yet be convinced that positive self-assertion will indeed give us true respect.

But we can start by respecting ourselves enough to take this risk.

Conditioned female behavior is not part of our true female psyche, so let's throw out any socialized baggage that's weighing us down. This doesn't mean discarding our social skills and sensitivity; it just means that we don't automatically fall back on knee-jerk "female" habits that undermine us. For example, we're not obliged especially in a business context to make the person we are negotiating with feel "at home" with womanly nattering. If we can just endure a moment's silent discomfort, maybe our negotiation will be far more powerful and authentic. As women, we do love talking, and sometimes that's just fine, but at other times it's a less-than-effective way to communicate. The Roman playwright Seneca once remarked, "When I think over what I've said, I envy mute people."

# A Fairer Tale: Steeped in Duty

+ + + + + + + + + + + + + + + + + + + + + + + + + + + + + + + + + + + + + + + + + + + + + + +

O nce upon a time there lived a king and queen in a large and glorious palace next to a lake. As they were very old-fashioned (and needless to say very boring), they were unhappy because they couldn't reproduce. It wasn't for want of try-ing either. But although the king controlled everyone in his realm, he just no longer seemed able to rule over his own member. No matter what he did, little Prince William—as he so fondly called it —would only hang his small, sad head.

Then one day when the king and queen were walking along-side the lake, a magical fish swam very close to them, and—to their surprise—the fish spoke to the queen. It said, "Take the little prince in hand, blow him a few kisses, and he'll grow into a big proud fellow." Although shocked, the queen did as the fish recom-mended. Soon she produced not a hearty prince as everyone had hoped, but a healthy baby girl. The baby was no beauty, so it was decided that she'd follow the path of all plain women, resignation to a life of being dutiful.

Since Princess Duty was only a girl, the christening was a low-key affair. At the time it was custom to appoint godmothers, and the five available fairies were called upon to magically bestow the tiny tot with the talents she'd need to fulfill her fate as a girl. To begin the formalities, the first fairy—Cyril—limply waved his wand and wished "obedience" upon the little princess. Next Cedric, who impertinently had dressed like the queen, bade the princess "naivete." Thereafter, Howie, in a high-pitched flurry, con-ferred "passivity" upon her. Then Alaine in tutu and tiara gently granted Princess Duty the virtue of "self-sacrifice," and finally the more butch Algernon presented her with a lifelong obligation to serve others.

After the ceremony the whole company returned to the pal-ace, upon which the king and his fairies retired to the dungeons to have a gay cavort.

The romp was just reaching a crescendo when an ugly old

crone, dressed in black and leaning on a wooden crutch, materi-alized among them. Through the small gap between her hooked nose and chin she growled, "I am the Enchantress Yonita, protec-tor of the fairer sex. I have come to bestow my blessing on the princess, but I see that neither she nor the queen, nor any other member of the fairer sex, is here to partake in the celebrations."

"She's been christened; isn't that enough?" retorted the king. "After all she's only a female."

Waving her stick in the air, the old crone coldly asked the king, "Did you really think you could get away with this phallocentric ceremony to celebrate the dismissal of baby girls?"

Although the king prided himself on being a cunning linguist, he was at a loss for words. Terrified of Yonita's power, he quickly pulled rank, saying, "Under my sovereignty every man has a legiti-mate claim to show his superiority over the women in his life. So you can wave your crotch all you like, but in my kingdom no man shall be denied the right to have a dutiful wife." Then he quickly added, "of any gender he may desire!"

He had scarcely finished his orations when the queen, having heard the commotion, entered the dungeon with little Princess Duty in her arms. "Aha!" exulted Yonita as she admired the prin-cess. "One of my most wonderful creations." And before anyone could utter the word *spell*, Yonita swooped her staff over the baby and intoned: "I bestow upon this female child a sensuality so potent that all men will succumb to it." Alarmed at these words, the fairies fainted en masse, and the queen, covering little Prin-cess Duty's ears, rushed her away in horror.

A trembling seized the whole court, and as soon as the fair-ies could be revived, the king drew them into a huddle to devise a plan. They knew all too well that the return of female sexual power meant that Princess Duty would end up ruling the land.

Back and forth they debated: What about barbecuing the wicked old enchantress? But would this undo the spell? No one could be sure. Should they perhaps eliminate all the females in the land? But who then would be available for them to dominate? So they disregarded this suggestion too.

Finally inspired by Alaine's tutu, Howie came up with an idea:

YAKKETY, YAK + **261**

He would command the crafty elves to sew a garment that would constrain the young princess's sensual excesses. "Marvelous," proclaimed the king. "Set the elves to their needles this instant."

And so it was that very soon Howie triumphantly delivered a tightly stitched, sausage-narrow garment dangling with strings and fastenings. "Perfect," announced the king, and he and the fairies dashed off to Princess Duty's nursery.

Once the garment was safely secured on the little girl, Howie waved his wand and commanded the cradled babe, "On hearing the utterance of any words sexual you will immediately fall into a deep unconscious sleep." Across the land, censoring knights put a ban on the word "sex," and all smutty books and magazines and adult toys were removed and locked into the northern tower. Literature and dictionaries were scoured for offensive words, which were scratched out in the blackest of inks.

A great carnal hush fell over the kingdom. Parts of the body that people were wont to speak freely about were now referred to somewhat euphemistically as "privates" or the "bits downstairs." People talked about "it" instead of the "S" word, and even parlay about the "birds and bees" became discussions about nature instead.

Little Princess Duty grew up knowing only that her privates were for elimination. Corseted day and night, she accepted the fact that aches and pains were her daily companion. And as for the other strange tinglings she felt as she got bigger, she did her best to turn her mind from them, as her nursemaid advised. Soon, however, these tinglings, almost of themselves, transmuted into bizarre and distressingly unsettling desires.

The more the princess tried to turn her mind to virtuous things, the more unseemly her thoughts became. "It must be my body's appetite that is so wicked," she decided. "I will teach it a lesson by depriving it of all treats; then it will surely become more virtuous." So it was that Princess Duty refrained from eating her most favorite delights. But still the wicked thoughts persisted, so little by little she eliminated more and more of her daily nourishment in a desperate effort to starve her "disobedient" body into submission. Thinner and thinner she grew.

The nursemaid, deciding that things had gone too far, pleaded with the king and queen: "The princess is wasting away, and I'm sorry to say this, but I think it is because she is trying so desperately to fit herself into that constraining corset." "Bunkum," snapped the king. "If you had your way my princess would be gallivanting around like a lady of the night. Girdled she must remain."

And so it was, until one day, while the king and queen were off on a state visit to another kingdom, the princess simply ripped off her girdle and went cavorting through the palace. The nursemaid ran after her in hot pursuit, but the girl managed to elude her, skipping from one chamber to another and prancing up and down passageways, shrieking and bellowing with delight.

Having foiled her nursemaid, Princess Duty ascended a winding stairway that led to the northern turret. She was drawn higher and higher by an intriguing whirring sound, but then she found her way barred by an ancient wooden door. She turned the door handle but found it firmly locked. Normally the princess would have given up in the face of such an obstacle, but in her present feisty mood she was not to be stopped. She simply flung her body against the somewhat rickety door with all her pent-up might and found herself pirouetting into the room.

Inside the chamber there were strange toys aplenty. The one that jumped to her attention was in fact the source of the whirring noise. Shaped like a small turret, it vibrated gently, causing such a peculiar sensation in the palm of the princess's hand that she giggled with delight. "What a neat contraption," she thought. "It would be perfect for stirring the king's cocktails." She made a mental note to deliver it to him ASAP. But then, tragedy struck. . . . The princess's eyes alighted on a dusty tome, which hadn't been touched in sixteen years, and the first word that leaped out at her was "SEX!" She fell down in an instant swoon, which soon became a deep unconscious slumber.

Eventually, after frantic searching, the nursemaid found the princess in the turret. But alas, it was too late; no amount of shaking and pleading helped; the princess could not be awoken. Quickly the nursemaid dragged the sleeping princess down the stairs and back to her chamber. There she strapped on her corset, put on her finest dress, and then tucked her under the bed covers. In the meanwhile a messenger had been dispatched to recall the king and queen.

The princess fell into a monumental dream where she found herself plunged into a dark orgiastic world teeming with men and women doing all manner of bizarre things, things her sheltered upbringing prevented her from even recognizing. The first chamber she arrived in was seething with naked women wildly cavorting with not a thought for which part of their anatomy was laid open. To make matters worse there were men present. They appeared to be examining the few women who were keeping still, much in the way that doctors probe and prod.

In the next chamber were men who seemed to be depressing the women by lying on top of them and bouncing up and down until the women let out moans and wild screams. No matter how outrageous the men's requests, like automatons the women would simply nod, smile, and oblige.

Then a group of female skeletons appeared, all sporting enormous pairs of conelike protuberances on their clearly visible ribs. Delicately the princess pointed at one of these skeletal women's chests and asked, "What are those?"

"Silly-cones" answered the woman matter-of-factly as she began squirting the princess with a gooey liquid from one of her leaky balloonlike breasts. Terrified, Princess Duty thought that this nightmare was never going to end; already it seemed to have gone on for at least a hundred years.

Back in the palace the king summoned his fairies and broke the news that the princess had stumbled upon the turret. Howie began pacing up and down in deep contemplation, then suddenly announced, "Milord, I have a cunning plan . . . even if I say so myself."

The king should send for Prince Deflorimond, said Howie, who went on to explain, "The only means of breaking the enchantress's spell is to find a man who can completely possess Princess Duty." The king knew Deflorimond had taken many a flower from a young maiden, but as the last unattached royal bachelor left in the land, this cad was the only one who could save the princess now. Without delay the king's knights were dispatched to fetch the prince.

However, instead of welcoming the idea of marrying the princess, Prince Deflorimond muttered, "Bloody women . . . always in need of rescuing. . . . How many more dragons do I have to slay?" Only after the knights had explained that the princess was in a comalike slumber did Prince Deflorimond's ears prick up: "Unconscious . . . did you say?" The knights nodded. "Well that's a different story." Then he added, almost as if speaking to himself, "All my life I've been looking for an unconscious woman to wed; perhaps this rescue won't be a waste of time after all."

So, taking up his dragon-slaying kit, Deflorimond mounted his trusty steed and set off at a gallop. Having slayed a dragon en route, the prince appeared at the palace to receive his prize. After a few cursory exchanges with the king and queen, Deflorimond gathered Princess Duty in his arms and sped off into the sunset, faintly aware that the king was still muttering, "Oh Deflorimond, there's just one thing . . . "

He took the sleeping princess to a tacky little chapel that advertised instant weddings in bright neon lights. It was a very brief ceremony, and once the marriage had been pronounced the priest instructed Prince Deflorimond to kiss his sleeping bride. That's when things took a nasty turn: Instantly Princess Duty awoke.

The king hadn't had time to finish his story about how one kiss would arouse the sleeping princess. When they arrived at the prince's castle, Princess Duty, who was now fully awake, began describing all the terrible things she had witnessed in her dream. "The king has tricked me," thought Deflorimond, and "horror upon horror, instead of an unconscious princess, I'm now landed with one of those loudmouthed, whining feminist/lesbian types." Quickly he checked under her arms and—because she'd been asleep for so long—sure enough there were the telltale signs, hairy armpits.

Before Princess Duty could say another word, the prince bellowed, "I am your husband now! Take the saddle off my steed; unpack my dragon-slaying kit; polish it all up; put my equipment in the shed; wash, feed, and brush my horse; and when you're done, make my supper and bring me some wine . . . right away, I said, go, Go, GO! GO NOW!"

On the surface Princess Duty wasn't really one of those weird unruly females, as Deflorimond had concluded, so he was pleasantly surprised when she compliantly set to work washing, polishing, cooking, and cleaning up. On the rare occasion when she did try to strike up a conversation, he'd shout, "Don't you know a woman's place is to serve her husband dutifully? So shut up and get on with it." And like the women in her ghoulish dream, she would just nod, smile, and oblige.

Night after night the princess's nightmare visions would become a reality as her husband did the most unspeakable things to her delicate body. Despite the horror and pain she felt every day, Princess Duty strove to cast all troublesome and rebellious thoughts from her mind by keeping herself as busy as could be. Soon all thoughts of a happier life were deeply buried, and Princess Duty had fallen in wholly with the prince's expectations.

Then one day Princess Duty had a dream so different from all the others that it startled her awake. A strange old woman called Yonita appeared to her and said, "I imbue you with self-respect, intuition, wisdom, insight, and all the ancient knowledge of the world." Then the old woman explained to the princess that all these qualities had always been present within her, and that it had only been a matter of turning the right key. "Ha," thought Princess Duty. "Obviously this old woman doesn't have a husband like Deflorimond." Brushing off the dream, she went back to sleep.

Next morning, to Princess Duty's great surprise, there was a large shiny golden key next to her bed. Picking it up, she saw the word "Recall" written in bold letters upon it. While she was pondering what this could possibly mean, she felt a great surge of energy snake through her body. Suddenly she was charged with potent thoughts and ideas. "I feel even more alive than I did that day when I threw off my corset," she remarked to herself in wonder. But fearing Deflorimond's reaction, she decided to keep her feelings and thoughts to herself.

At midday the prince emerged from the misty haze of the night before. Instead of showing the grouchiness Princess Duty had become accustomed to, he took one look at her and dropped to his knees. Thinking Deflorimond must be ill, she rushed to his aid, but all he could say was, "I bow down before your superior wisdom, my goddess of a wife." This served as confirmation for Princess Duty: The prince was delirious. She hurried him onto his steed and posthaste they sped to the royal medical chambers.

En route, despite their haste, Princess Duty began to notice that many of the townsfolk seemed altered in humor toward their wives. They came upon a husband manhandling his wife, but as soon as the man set eyes on the princess, he fell to his knees and humbly begged his wife's forgiveness. After numerous similar incidents Princess Duty stopped dead in her tracks. She then kicked Deflorimond off the steed and galloped to the nearest town square, where she gathered as many women as she could find.

Sharing the wisdom of the key, the princess inspired the masses with her newfound wisdom and power, which she called "Flower Power." Her main manifesto was: Never again will men rip out the magical blossoms of a woman's talents by treating her like a deflowered sex object. Princess Duty went on to write the *Vagina Vade Mecum*—a now well-known mystical text that inspired both men and women to achieve higher levels of consciousness through the all-powerful creative feminine energy.

When she died, the princess was immortalized as the Goddess Cunti—Yoni of the universe. If you listen carefully you can still hear angry men yell out to her using a slightly shorter four-letter version of her name. As for the transformed Deflorimond, he is lobbying tirelessly to make sure that in the future the letter Dubya stands only for profound ideas, like "Wisdom," for instance.

+ + + + + + + + + + + + + + + + + + + + + + + + + + + + + + + + + + + + + + + + + + + + + + + + + +

CONCLUSION:

# Future Forward?

**W**here are the female visionaries or the powerful wise women who can guide us toward better ways of living? Where are the Amazons who will fight the injustices inflicted upon our gender? Where are the stoic leaders who will take on the responsibility of mentoring generations to come? Where have all the real women gone?

Many of the second-wave feminists who jolted millions into action with their righteous anger have faded from the political canvas, and why is it that some of the women who are still prominent seem to fritter away their own power by raging against one another?

Many females now hold positions that count, but how different are they from a Margaret Thatcher who failed to use her power to benefit more than 50 percent of her constituency? We know that women are not above misusing their positions in precisely the way that men may do. Like the Condoleezza Rices of this world, many choose to follow man-made economic and political solutions that exacerbate women's problems and, when taken to task, turn their back upon the concerns of their gender.

But more importantly, where are the rest of us when these men or women make decisions that harm us? Are we at the fitness center or cosmetics counter? Or maybe our "low-cal" diets are simply making us too weak to speak out.

While we stare into the mirror bemoaning our fat thighs and cellulite, warmongering politicians are making nonsensical decisions that kill, maim, and rape millions. Where is the power of our collective social conscience when we allow decisions to be made that favor economics over the planet's long-term sustainability? What are we doing as armaments spending rockets out of sight while budgets for basic healthcare and homes are being slashed?

What are we thinking when we allow unscrupulous companies to get harmful products passed by agencies that are funded with tax money to protect us? And what are we doing to protect our daughters from becoming the mannequins of consumerism?

## FEMINIZING OUR CULTURE

The stage is set for the 21st century to be a woman's world, but the feminization of our culture is by no means a certainty; presently it's delicately hanging in the balance, and right now the scales could tip either way. By remaining passive all we're doing is allowing men to reclaim their macho power. However, if each of us takes a stand and starts doing things differently, our determination can bring about changes that can truly benefit our gender, and the world.

So, what are the risks and opportunities we are facing? Three possible scenarios follow:

## 1. STEPFORD WIFE REGRESSION

So far the postfeminist revolution has been a silent one, but if we fail to find our collective voice soon, we may find ourselves back home behind the Hoover and the picket fence.

If you think this is unrealistic, look at the conditions that led to social reversals for women. During the Second World War millions of women left home and went to work, maintaining both the war machine and the world economy. Epitomized by a character called "Rosie the Riveter," these women of the 1930s and '40s produced and maintained airplanes, warships, heavy equipment, bombs, food, and clothing. They worked equally well in factories, fields, and offices—wherever their services were needed.

But after the war, by male decree, all jobs were reserved for the returning soldiers, and the women who had left their hearth to fill the breach were forced to swap their pop-riveters for frying pans. Even the thousands of war widows who found themselves to be the sole bread-winner were no longer allowed to work. For their war effort they were rewarded with breadline starvation.[1]

It wasn't long after the war that lobotomy became a popular form of treatment for women. In the 1960s, a psychosurgeon revealed the medical profession's agenda: "Lobotomized women make good house-keepers. . . . It is more socially acceptable to lobotomize women [than men] because creativity, which the operation completely destroys, is . . . an expendable nullity in women."[2]

It's true that in the last sixty years, progress in legislation has occurred beyond these real-life Stepford wives' wildest dreams. But what of it? Do you see evidence of this progress being taken into account in the sentiments of the growing body of conservative think-ers? Although organizations like Promise Keepers reached a peak in the late 1990s, the three million or so men they claim to have hosted have been tantalized by the carrot of regaining the absolute power men once held.

At a Promise Keepers conference in the mid-1990s, Ami Nei-berger, a journalist for the *Freedom Writer,* a publication monitoring the Religious Right, reported on the evangelical-paternal sentiments that these exclusively male groups are expressing.[3] For example, a Promise Keepers speaker exhorted men to take back the leadership of their home from their wife: "I am not suggesting that you ask for your role back," he said. "I am urging you to take it back. There can be no compromise here."

According to Neiberger, Promise Keepers downplays the histori-cal contributions made by women in society and encourages them to stay home. She goes on to report that speakers refer to women as "weaker vessels" and teach that women should submit to their husband, yield to their final word in decision making, and remember to look good for their man.

Neiberger comments that the only women you'll see at a Promise Keepers event are those hawking hot dogs or selling T-shirts. With male ownership of women taken for granted, it's not surprising that incidents of sexual harassment by one of the organization's more-lecherous members were reported.[4] It's also a no-brainer that groups such as these are violently opposed to feminism. Promise Keepers speakers like Tony Evans, author of *No More Excuses,* describes feminists of the more aggressive persuasion as "frustrated women unable to find proper leadership in men."[5] In keeping with the male penchant for violence and destruction as a means of gaining and maintaining control, their language is also splattered with war terminology.

So whether it's the Promise Keepers or any of the other organizations that are mushrooming worldwide, it's clear that conservative men are mobilizing to halt the process they fear most: feminization.

Now, is there any part of this commentary that sounds like these men have heard or understood one word of the feminine dialogue discussed over the last few decades? Instead of hearing women, these conservative men have colonized the minds of their wives and now use them to front as female spokespeople. As obedient Stepford wives, these women too turn a deaf ear to the "devilish" notion of women's freedom.

As examples, women like Connie Marshner (director of the conservative Free Congress Foundation's Center for Governance and an ardent profamily activist) and Beverly LaHaye (founder of the ultra-right Concerned Women for America) have regularly admonished women for not staying at home.

But as was made plain by the author Susan Faludi, when these conservative women were on their soapbox, they themselves happened to have put their own children in care and left their husband to fend for himself.[6] Faludi quotes Marshner as saying, "I'm no good with little kids and I'm a terrible housekeeper. To me it's very unrewarding and unfulfilling work. By contrast what I'm doing in Washington has real tangible rewards and accomplishments." Did I hear anyone utter the word "hypocritical"?

If media programming has successfully convinced us that flesh-covered skeletons are desirable, it's not that far-fetched to think that conservatives could brainwash us en masse into being housewives once more. Already they are busy doing so. Have you noticed how the phrase "family values" is becoming more and more audible in popular language? Does this mean that men are being encouraged to call strikes for increased paternity leave? Or could it be that the biggest protagonists of "family values," such as conservative presidents, will be closing international summits early to attend their children's soccer games? Somehow I doubt it. More likely the thumbscrews are being sized for women.

### Who's Afraid of "Family Values"?

Organizations like Focus on the Family and the Christian Coalition of America are the largest Religious Right entities in the United States, and it is not without purpose that they use the term "profamily" as a euphemism for the Religious Right. "Profamily" is antiabortion, despises homosexuality, and fights separation of church and state; it also argues against gun control, state-controlled education . . . and of course feminism. In the abortion debate, profamily supporters are pro-choice, but the irony is that they're not antiviolence or antiwar. So, is "morality" only an issue when women are making decisions about their own body and their own life?

When it comes to feminism, Pat Robertson, founder of the Christian Coalition of America, wrote, "The feminist agenda is not about equal rights for women. It is about a socialist, antifamily political movement that encourages women to leave their husbands, kill their children, practice witchcraft, destroy capitalism, and become lesbians."[7] This view of "equal rights" affords ample opportunity for conservatives to legitimize the guilt factory for working mothers and promotes the nuclear family model, which is the very structure that impedes women's progress. Without natural links to the community collective, women's isolation makes their passivity inevitable. After all, who's got time to be concerned about the global subjugation of women when the washing's piling up and little Johnny hasn't done his homework? No other structure in history has been more powerful at promoting the kind of self-centered behavior that destroys our natural compassion for other people.

Combine this with high levels of consumerism, and it's inevitable that droves of women will be concerning themselves primarily with the state of their own patch (no pun intended).

Not only does female-to-female mistrust guarantee that we'll have trouble lobbying together, but male power continues to prevail because the nuclear family makes us so self-protective that there's not much room to respond to anything broader. Conservatives aren't suggesting that the nuclear family structure is the primary disaster area, and because of this, appropriate support systems to remedy family problems are not being constructed. Instead, the blame for the dysfunctional model is dumped in the usual place, on women.

### Adding Up Our "Worth"

Did you know that it's built into our global economic system that women's needs and concerns be ignored? Marilyn Waring, author of *Counting for Nothing,* researched the United Nations' system of national accounts and concluded that in the economic system that governs the world, only money-generating endeavors count for something.[8] Anything that generates a demand for more goods is good, whether it is war, pornography, child prostitution, or trading in prescription drugs, street drugs, or deathly diet products. The aim is always to expand the market, regardless of whether the product is destroying people's humanity or their lives. Self-supporting ventures that would make people's lives more sustainable are not encouraged by a consumerist economy. Feeding one's family from subsistence farming, raising well-balanced children, avoiding planetary disaster, or maintaining world peace don't generate much money and therefore have little value. This is the accounting system that sets global priorities and allocates huge amounts of resources such as World Bank funding.

The fact that an economic system such as this continues to govern global decision making shows that behind the scenes men have successfully been disregarding women's needs for decades.

Marilyn Waring makes the pertinent point that men aren't going to give up a system in which half the world's population works for a pittance and has no energy left to fight. Perhaps the decades of dialogue have only resulted in men appeasing us with the veneer of a more feminine look rather than any genuine attempt at power sharing.

We know that America has refused to ratify the Convention on the Elimination of All Forms of Discrimination against Women (CEDAW), but globally it matters not whether George W. Bush, Bill or Hillary Clinton, Tony Blair, or Maggie Thatcher is the figurehead of world power, because it's the people who put up the money to get them into power who call the shots. These are the business leaders controlling the giant corporations, and they are seldom anything but conservative when it comes to their deeper vested interests. Author and journalist Greg Palast aptly described the United States as "the best democracy money can buy."[9]

Powerful political leaders have garnered the support of mass groupings such as religious Fundamentalists, and Christian zealots openly state that they plan to take over the country. A March 2003 issue of *Newsweek* reported that, at age thirty-nine, George W. Bush joined the evangelist Billy Graham's flock,[10] and Pat Robertson of the Christian Coalition claims that his organization is dominant in the Republican Party of eighteen states and has substantial influence in thirteen more.[11]

Although there is some dispute about Robertson's claim, at election time religious groups issue some forty-three million voter guidelines influencing who their flock should vote for and—should the Fundamentalists team up with the Catholics (something already happening)—the Religious Right could have the demographic majority.

### Going Back Home

With voters increasingly sanctioning conservative thinkers, in both government and the media, conservative male leaders are influencing policy, not within the open forum of government but behind the closed doors of the Church.

So it's not crazy to imagine that traditional men could once more pass laws to pull in the reins of female power. But writers such as Tom Peters[12] and Faith Popcorn[13] remind us that female economic power is growing, and in the system of national accounting, women who earn and spend money are the only ones who count. Women in commerce with their direct link to both money and power are the biggest threat to the patriarchal system, so banning females from business would make sense as a first line of attack on female power.

Conditioned passivity, which encourages women to fall in with men's conservative ideas, could well play into the hands of the forces that want to see women sent back to their "rightful place" at home.

If through self-sacrifice we're already sitting back and allowing those whom we've placed in authority to control us—such as husbands who provide, doctors, pastors, the diet industry, cosmetic surgeons, the media, and even our children's schoolteachers—then how are we going to stop world leaders from bullying us?

Furthermore, there are a lot of women who prefer to be financially dependent on men, who will cooperate with the existing system.

Religious systems have hoodwinked these women into supporting the righteousness of male power, and, as witnessed by the support that got George Junior a second term, they aren't in the least bit taken aback by regressive legislation. Just look at how easily he got away with signing the "partial-birth abortion" law in 2003, which means that every abortion can now be questioned, and in 2006 South Dakota was the first state to reverse *Roe v. Wade*. . . . The big question now is, How many more states are likely to follow? The countless females who support the return of these antiabortion laws don't seem able to accept that female independence may be the right choice for other, more-liberated women. No prizes for guessing who gets the vote of this growing number of traditional women.

According to Gerda Lerner, author of *The Creation of Patriarchy*, male dominance only functions because of the cooperation of women. "This cooperation is secured by: gender indoctrination; educational deprivation; the denial to women of knowledge of their history; the dividing of women from one another by defining 'respectability' and 'deviance' according to women's sexual activities; by restraints and outright coercion; by discrimination in access to economic resources and political power; and by awarding class privileges to conforming women."[14]

### Cheated by Political Games

When George W. Bush declared war on the conservative Taliban regime in Afghanistan, he and his cronies played heavily on the card they needed most—the women's issue. He needed female voters to support the atrocities he was about to commit—and did you notice how quickly the word spread? All over the Western world the plight of Afghani women was suddenly on everyone's lips. Duped by Bush's political game, men and women bayed for blood. But could someone please explain how pitching pound after pound of explosives at these women helped to free them? Surely bombing these desperate women for the sake of their freedom is just as preposterous as "fighting for peace" or "fucking for virginity." And talking of hypocrisy, what of the preceding decades of abuse these women had endured, abuse under U.S.-supported governments, what's more?

Already in this so-called age of enlightenment, abuse is the lot of one-third of women. And with women making up two-thirds of illiterate people, what are the hopes of emphasizing female education as a priority in the future? The more uneducated we are and the less we're able to fend for ourselves financially, the faster we'd regress back to nothing more than domestic slave labor. As such we could end up being deprived of our "voice," and, along with censorship of feminist sentiments, women could well end up being disenfranchised too.

But the male backlash is likely to be subtler than this. Gender oppression is more likely to come under the guise of a holy war. Even before 9/11, the Western media consistently damned Islam, and now the so-called fight against terrorism is fast escalating into a full-scale religious war. And we all know that there's no better way to unite stubbornly independent sects than to find a common enemy.

Annie Laurie Gaylor said, "There is nothing new in this religious war against women. . . . Every freedom won for women in this country, small or large—from wearing bloomers to riding bicycles, to not wearing bonnets in church, to being permitted to speak in public, to attending universities, to entering professions, to voting and owning property—was opposed by the churches."[15]

So it's certainly not too much of a stretch to believe that anything standing against the dictates of the Bible, including feminism, would be condemned as the Antichrist. It's not at all unthinkable that gender issues could be used alongside oppressive laws to once again silence the female voice, much as was done in the wake of World War II. Potentially all major freedoms, such as our right to economic liberation, information, expression, contraception, and abortion, are being threatened.

At this stage we can thank the goddess that different religious cults have had a devil of a job agreeing on most things. But with religious coalitions forming, NOW reports the following examples of how administrations—like that of George W. Bush—trash women's rights: In 2003, welfare subsidies to single mothers were cut, but the "marriage-promotion agenda" was well funded.[16] If these moms are unable to find work and they are not funded, could this be the conservatives' underhanded way of imitating Middle Age rulers who forced women into marriage for economic reasons? Additionally, funding for family planning has been cut and papers were placed on the agenda in 2002 to designate fetuses as persons. This gives unborn babies full human rights, and if such legislation is passed, the fetus will have more rights than the pregnant woman. Proposing legislation such as this takes us right back to early Catholic beliefs where the fetus was considered more sacred than the "vessel" carrying it, the human mother.[17]

In addition to these archaic notions, the administration also restricted Medicaid funding for mifepristone (the abortion pill) to cases of rape, incest, and where abortion is necessary to save the pregnant women's life.

In the 2002 budget, Bush proposed eliminating contraceptive coverage for female federal employees (and their dependents), and military women serving abroad have been prohibited from obtaining abortions at military hospitals.

The motive behind this barefaced assault on women's reproductive freedom is conspicuous: Nonstop pregnancy is the surest means of sending women back home. It's also why daycare for children regularly comes under fire.

In education, George W. proposed gender segregation in schools when he mounted an assault on Title IX, the clause in the education act that provides women with equal opportunities to participate in all educational activities, including sports.

According to Michael Moore in his book *Stupid White Men,* many of the issues raised by George Dubya had their origins in the Clinton administration.[18] While we know that the person in power is no more than a puppet, of greater concern is the stacking of the Supreme Court with conservative judges. Although we may only have to endure politicians for a term (or two), judges are appointed for a lifetime. This means that decisions made by George W.'s legal buddies could last for a number of decades, potentially setting the States back some twenty years when it comes to women's rights.

Although organizations like NOW are urging women to actively make a stand by signing petitions, writing to senators, and supporting liberal candidates, the fact that the conservatives are getting away with reversing women's progress (no matter who is in power) shows the extent of our passivity.

But why are actions that violate our rights still not a potent enough catalyst to blow the rage simmering inside of us as women? Are we waiting for even greater oppression to kick-start another round of raging feminism in years to come? At best this would inflame the existing battle of the sexes; at worst it could spark a full-scale gender war.

Unlike the males of the 1950s, traditional men today realize the gains females have made and are unlikely to continue laughing off women activists.

### Fighting Oppression without the Weapons

When it comes to war, well, men ultimately control the guns, tanks, and ammunition, and while many women are in the military, they are fighting for male-dominant agendas. But if you think women are too passive to stage a rebellion, think again. Push them far enough and they will actively join revolutions, just as women have in China, Nicaragua, and South Africa, and as many are now doing in Palestine.

Whether this results in out-and-out warfare or an underground revolution, like any other war in history it would only lead to a massive waste of lives and resources without resolving anything.

But with so many signs pointing to the possible increase in the oppression of women, it appears that, regardless of consequences, the only thing conservatives are hell-bent on conserving is the privilege that goes with the territory of absolute power. Family values, my ass! Male domination is the more likely agenda.

## 2) THE QUIET REVOLUTION

Alongside the growing group of conservatives, there is a less-vocal movement of men who are agreeing with feminists such as Betty Friedan, who said, "Man is not the enemy, but the fellow victim."

These males are acutely aware that gender roles have a significant impact upon their lives and are relinquishing the traditional scorecard. They no longer feel the need to notch up machismo points by swilling down lots of beer and demeaning women. Their attitude is a far cry from that of traditionalists, who cannot see beyond the controlling domains of pregnancy and kitchens for the fairer sex. One of the most probable reasons for the change in these men is that they are the first generation who grew up with working mothers as the norm rather than the exception.

These are not men who are buckling under the pressure of feminism. Instead they are examining their role as men and are questioning how their behavior continues to contribute to the existential distress of women. By reading modern men's literature and attending group sessions, these men are getting more acquainted with the humane side of their masculinity. Drumming to a different tune, they're renouncing traditional stereotypes and finding more depth to themselves. In areas of spirituality and emotion they have developed their capacity when it comes to communication, particularly in discussions with women.

Although men such as these may be the miracle many women have been waiting for, not enough of them yet exist to make a meaningful impact on the world—and there are good reasons for this.

Unlike the Promise Keeper–type promises, the motivational carrot for reworking gender roles is not absolute power over other people, it is power over oneself. As such the journey to becoming more conscious requires far greater courage than rallying in an existing structure of rules like those imposed by religion.

As both structure and the promise of overt power are compelling to men, it's unlikely that these new men's organizations will become popular as quickly as their ultraright counterparts. So these individuals may be able to support our growth, but they won't be the messiahs who transform the world for us.

### Do We Need New Messiahs?

What drives men into personal exploration is the sense of their own spiritual impoverishment. Books about the current masculine crisis, like *Iron John*,[19] *Fire in the Belly*,[20] and *At My Father's Wedding*,[21] show that men are becoming fed up with the hollow promises of the old macho scorecard. Now they are recognizing that the biggest price they're paying for consumerism is being all consumed by it. Those who have achieved some measure of success and have money, a trophy wife, a big house, fancy cars, and all the toys are not feeling fulfilled; in fact they are feeling cheated and let down. Most have growing children they don't even know, and many are reaching the same conclusion as the actress Lily Tomlin, who said, "The trouble with being in the rat race is that even if you win you're still a rat."

For them, playing a more significant role at home is the driving force to living a more meaningful existence. The idea of "making money at all costs" is being shifted to second place in the search for quality of life.[22] This growing trend away from status-based consumerism and toward a sense of greater humanity is particularly helpful to the cause of women.

But as with women who are working to reprogram their socialized ideas, men are working against the odds. Traditionally, greater emphasis is placed on intellect in boys than it is in girls, and many males are struggling to get past their rational views to explore themselves differently. So while the motivation may exist for some men to change, socialized habits are not easy to dismantle.

Male facilitators believe that the search for spiritual enrichment in men usually begins as an intellectually driven exercise, and if it fails to move beyond this it can simply become a substitute for weekend golf.[23] But with more and more men becoming disillusioned with the provider-protector role, male facilitators predict that growing male awareness has the potential to reach critical mass and, over time, to make a difference.

Awareness among men about the importance of things beyond the material can be witnessed in businesses that are having success with programs to balance work and family. *BusinessWeek* completed a survey of American companies that employed work-family strategies (like DuPont, Hewlett-Packard, Johnson & Johnson, and Motorola) and found that these programs increased productivity and considerably reduced both absenteeism and staff turnover.[24]

Even so, macho males are revolting against the sissification of their brothers. They believe that the feminization of our culture is making men more passive, and in some instances this could be true. Previously we've looked at collapsed men who become immobilized by their wife's achievements. But, these are not men who are exploring their masculinity, they are males whose machismo has failed them, and the old scorecard has not been replaced with anything of substance. Although collapsed men are held up as warnings to others, the last laugh is on the John Waynes of this world when one looks at the billionaire nerds who have far more influence today than does the "jock" brotherhood.

### Avoiding a "Comfort Zone"

So social transformation is indeed afoot, but women will not make much headway if their eagerness to celebrate progress obscures their capacity to see just how much things have really stayed the same.

Crawling into the comfort zone of the independence we've gained will just keep us grateful for the crumbs men leave at their tables. While many women are tired of fighting, standing still and clinging to the gains already made can only be a form of prolonged suicide. We have to live in the present, and this means we can't simply rest on the laurels of women who've struggled to bring us this far.

The good news is that it looks as if the quiet female revolution has already begun. As an example, we've seen how women are leaving male-dominant corporate structures in droves. Instead of bashing their heads against the glass ceiling, hundreds of businesswomen are choosing to build their own successful corporation.

Additionally, with scientific advances such as stem cell research, it is now possible for women to procreate without the necessity of sperm. So if females become really fed up, they could choose to live without men altogether. Signs of this can already be seen in the marked increase in women opting to have children outside of marriage.

The U.S. Census Bureau (2000) shows how single parent demographics have changed over the years. Among children who live with a single mother, only 2 percent in 1950 had a "never married" mother (as opposed to a divorced or widowed mom). In 1980, that figure rose to 15 percent and in 1998, to 40 percent.[25]

When it comes to opting for single parenthood, Susan Maushart says that "to have babies, without strings attached is not simply a new lifestyle option. It is an unimaginably radical act of cultural subversion."[26]

Another sign of rebellion is the high level of divorce that females are instigating.[27] Clearly wives are realizing that if men aren't contributing anything of value, the undue level of maintenance a husband requires simply adds to a woman's emotional burden—so what's the point? According to Maushart divorced women are generally financially poorer, but they are twice as likely as divorced men to describe themselves as being happy.[28] It's no wonder that after a couple of divorces, many women are content to remain single. Evidently, having been twice bitten by marriage, they are three times more likely to shy away from it in the future.

With more and more women shunning bad relationships with men, perhaps the groundswell of the next round of angry feminism has already begun.

When women reject male participation, this is no longer about who washes the dishes but more an assertion repudiating the constraints men place on women's lives. In itself it is a statement about removing the emotional corsets that prevent women from living authentically, and, taken to its obvious conclusion, this could well lead to a stronger focus upon the broader injustices committed against our gender. After all, so many women are realizing, if we don't take a stand against atrocities like rape, domestic violence, wife murder, and the poverty that drives so many into prostitution, who will address these issues? Somehow I doubt it will be orthodox men.

It may be only a minority of women who are taking the higher moral ground by liberating themselves from male control, but with more and more women becoming increasingly frustrated by the paternalistic systems that control us, female leaders will be able to round up more troops to support them in the future. Having learned from the experience of second-wave feminists in the 1960s and 1970s, the next round of libbers will be more likely to avoid the pitfall of using their anger to alienate women. Many signs now point to the fact that female activists will use the energy of their rage to inspire others instead.

### The Next Revolution?

The ever-progressing sophistication of communication tools makes the next revolution easier to mobilize. Although men never expected women to embrace technology, they overlooked the fact that it was the fairer sex that first used office equipment in business. Now women connect globally via the Internet, and, even if they're simply circulating thousands of fun friendship messages, women are fulfilling their need for connection.

Even grandmothers who may confess to being technophobes are comfortably emailing their family or friends, and, for those interested in motivating change, the Internet is a gift from the Goddess.

Although American and British futurists, like John Naisbitt *(Global Paradox)*[29] and Patrick Dixon *(Futurewise),*[30] predicted that increasing globalization will lead to more tribalization, neither of them saw the extent to which a tribe of women would be connecting. Along with the Internet, another good example is the recent explosion of all-female book clubs.

Replacing the Tupperware party, these clubs show that women are bored of swapping recipes and kitchen hints; now they're seeking stimulation from their connections. These forums also present great opportunities for female leaders to motivate and inspire women.

With independent vehicles now available to circulate more-substantial information, we can expect that the quiet revolution will sound the death knell for women's magazines as we know them. Women of all ages are seeing these shallow wads of pulp for what they are: the primary propaganda tool for our own brainwashing.

After reading exposés like Cyndi Tebbel's *Body Snatchers*,[31] many women are no longer willing to have these publications assault their self-esteem and insult their intelligence. The demise of these sorry excuses for advertising is also being accelerated by the fact that women are no longer slavishly following the magazines apparent raison d'être, fashion. Many women are finding haute couture nothing more than laughable, and instead are sticking to their classic suits for business and their comfy T-shirts to loll around in.

Although the diet industry was formerly viewed as nothing more than women's frivolity, the spreading awareness that women are perishing in droves is making this a deadly serious part of the new agenda.

Fat acceptance movements like NAAFA, which originated in 1969 to counteract the "thin-ideal" image of women, are starting to attract a growing number of ears. Terry Poulton reports on a number of victories for the size-acceptance movement, the most significant of which was the investigation of the Federal Trade Commission in the 1990s.[32] It resulted in five of the nation's largest commercial diet programs being charged with deceptive advertising practices, and there were some casualties. In 1994 when the stock of Jenny Craig—one of the largest weight-loss companies—thinned to an all-time low, the company was forced to close thirty branches. Weight Watchers also took a 15–25 percent plunge in membership, and NutriSystem declared bankruptcy (although it has since reemerged under a new name).

Among others, manufacturers—like that of the Enforma System (Fat Trapper and Exercise in a Bottle)—were taken to task for unsubstantiated advertising claims. Ads were banned that did not include vital points like having to eat less and exercise more to lose weight.[33]

New attitudes are developing too—many women are now discouraging their children from making nasty judgments about fat, and mothers (such as my sister-in-law) tell their daughters that Barbie is overly thin because of her terminal anorexia. The more women educate themselves about the reality of their own bodies, the more organizations trying to maintain the unrealistic marketing standards of "bodyism" will be put under pressure. When the telephone lines of companies regulating advertising practices are jammed daily by women lodging their grievances, we'll know that the revolution is working.

We can also expect that the cosmetics industry will be unable to escape the onslaught.

When women themselves stop overidentifying with their physical aspect and start exploring a broader and deeper version of themselves, all we'll need to do is stand on the bridge and watch the bodies of cosmetics moguls float down the river of nonsense they've created.

### Advertising—Profits to the Girls

Already we're approaching a time when women are getting fed up with products that can't live up to the lies. So the more discerning we become, the more the advertisers and manufacturers will let themselves down by the ridiculous claims they make. Perhaps when we get systems going like the one to force the cosmetics industry to contribute a substantial portion of its profit to women's causes, we'll feel more in control of our destiny.

Marilyn Waring has some good ideas about having fun with the system. As most systems are protected from intelligent enquiry by a blanket of jargon, she suggests mastering the art of the dumb question.[34] She found that continued questioning forced those in authority to see the idiocy of the glib statements they were making.

In census forms, Waring recommends that women avoid using labels like housewife or anything to do with the family or homemaking. Being creative about your title and number of working hours isn't illegal, and it means that in the economic system your voice will count for something. Additionally she suggests that women join political parties and relentlessly demand that half the candidates should be women. When you're done with one, join another, and continue until the number of women in Congress represents the proportion of females in the population.

Along with the dumb question, a further great tactic to unveil another's hidden agenda is the strategy of Harriet Rubin, author of *The Princessa*.[35] She suggests asking an opponent five relevant "why" questions consecutively. Each of the following could lead to another four questions depending upon the inanity of the answers one receives:

"Why are women underrepresented in management?"

"Why aren't women given the same educational opportunities as men?"

"Why does the company not have a family-friendly strategy?"

"Why is there no company daycare facility for children?"

"Why are salaries not comparable for men and women?"

By the time you've asked your opponent five direct "why" questions about their strategy (or lack thereof), Rubin says those opposing you will be forced to see the inanity of their own argument.

So although the quiet revolution may be in full swing, progress is somewhat dependent upon a few courageous female leaders taking a stand. As we've seen, vociferous conservative men are plentiful in influential places and—even if we're successful at teaming up with the growing number of new, more humane, men—both the swords and lawmaking pens of traditionalists could easily override us if we resort to our fallback position of passive acceptance.

It's well known that fear is the easiest means for the powers that be to control the masses. The tragic events of September 11 provided many opportunities to spawn high levels of fear, and the "war on terror" is resulting in many more of our freedoms being curbed. As our upbringing has already engendered high levels of fear in women, we are even more vulnerable to manipulation. To comprehend the extent of this, we need look no further than how the emphasis on body image has distracted us from our real purpose.

If freedom is what we want, the first line of attack must be for women to heal themselves—particularly in areas where we are fearful.

## 3) SOCIAL EVE-OLUTION

Harriet Rubin says, "Learn the art of war and as a woman you will balance the terror of your sex with the wonder of it. The terror lies in constantly being seen as a threat and being diminished because of it. The wonder is that the more womanly a fighter becomes the more she wins."[36] She goes on to say that this is not a fight against men, it's a strategy to fight for ourselves. This is not a strategy about performing to standard, it's about setting those standards. This is not a strategy to change the system, it's a strategy about rewriting the rules.

The starting point for rewriting the rules is to get to know our authentic selves. As a means of addressing hardcore social issues, this may seem oversimplified, but as you will see, much hangs on it.

Releasing our innermost being means little more than uncovering the crap that female conditioning lays upon us, and we can do this by continuously questioning our motives. Practically, it means listening to our inner voices. One voice will speak to us about what we want and the second will coerce us to act against our own wishes. The first is the voice of our authentic womanhood and the second is that of our super-ego—the place in our minds where the beliefs of parents and authority figures are held.

The real voice will speak through positive emotions delivering energizing messages about what we want, while the second will hammer us with bad feelings like fear, worry, and guilt.

### Proof of the Pudding

From the recent history of feminism we know that the majority of women are unwilling to join mass rallies to demand change, but the one area where all of us are powerful is on a personal level. Although social transformation may seem like an overwhelming task, it's really quite simple: As women, we need to keep reinventing ourselves, and the benefits will be considerable. If the behavior of half the world's population changes, what do you think will happen to the remaining 50 percent?

In his book with the diagnostic title *Affluenza,* psychologist Oliver James identifies a social "virus" that infects well-off people. He claims that moneyed-malaise is a contagious disease that causes depression, anxiety, addiction, and ennui. It contaminates people striving to appear successful because they confuse their wants with their needs. Affluenza is reaching pandemic proportions in the English-speaking world, with the United States at the top of the heap.

In his studies, James compared a progressive country like Denmark with other developed nations and found Danish people to be relatively virus free. In his example he writes about the male editor of one of Denmark's most popular newspaper, who comments that this is because Danes have "very strong, real life gender equality." James finds that "Danish men actually want to make a huge commitment to their domestic lives and if they did not put in the hours, their wives would leave them. An alpha workaholic in the classic American Donald Trump mold would be very hard-pressed to find any Danish woman prepared to serve as his trophy, Barbie doll housewife."[37]

James concludes that when men are valued for pulling their weight at home, their "provider-caveman" position shifts from activities that reinforce status and power to behaviors more in line with being an equally accountable partner. Danish women are also free from the neurosis of "bodyism." They attract their men with their intelligence and far greater emphasis is placed on communication than on superficial issues like being overtly sexy.[38]

### Lasting Peace

Most people's behavior is reinforced by what they get acknowledged for. As long as women value men for the bling they provide, men's ego-based drive for superiority will continue to be strengthened. But if we shift our perception from seeing men as providers of trendy trash to acknowledging them for their real involvement at home, then we will make far more progress with equality issues.

Men who make family their primary concern are also far less likely to want to go to war. Why would any man who is truly dedicated to his children desert them for many months to fight for some arbitrary political agenda aimed at destroying the lives of other families in another country? The Baha'i Universal House of Justice (an organization aimed at uniting humanity through common faith) presented a paper to world heads of state recognizing that "the achievement of full equality between the sexes is a prerequisite for world peace."[39]

### Tree Huggers Rule

Riane Eisler, author of *The Chalice & the Blade*, shows us that historically, during times when male domination declined, creativity increased and there was less warfare, fundamentalism, and violence.[40] So dancing to our own female tune is not an act of narcissism. Rather, it is essential to our individual and collective survival.

The idea of world peace is being helped along by the greater emphasis on values important to women. Not so long ago, if men staged peace protests or fought environmental issues they were ridiculed as wussy hippies or tree-huggers, but today, more and more traditional types of men are starting to respond. Although accused of political grandstanding, Al Gore has made thousands of people pay attention to environmental concerns with his documentary, *An Inconvenient Truth*.

If we fight ignorance, the last barricade protecting traditional systems, this groundswell of people valuing ideas more noble than overt power has the potential to escalate. In particular, it means scrutinizing the shenanigans going on in world affairs.

Today there is more information available than ever before. We no longer need rely on the propaganda-spewing media-machine to inform us. Trendsetter Michael Moore has turned documentaries into a popular form of infotainment, and, whether you support his views or not, the consequent flood of political and social-cause documentaries coming into the market is a good starting point for developing alternative opinions.

War is always about economics, but the idea of conflict must be "sold" to the public, and it is always based in moral righteousness, which is why so many conservative women support it. It's clear that the war in Iraq was about oil, but it was couched in moralistic terminology that allowed the public to swallow it hook, bait, and sinker. Finally, now, it's becoming increasingly transparent just how much politicians are still using religion to justify their own economic crusades.

With tell-all books like *Confessions of an Economic Hit Man,* by John Perkins, and *Lords of Poverty,* by Graham Hancock, the unethical hidden agendas dominating world politics are making even the wildest conspiracy theories look tame. The more books that emerge onto the market revealing what really goes on behind the scenes, the less likely that the voting public will be taken in by future weapons of mass deception.

With antiwar protests raging around the world, the failure of the twin politicians—Blair and Bush—will force political newcomers to see things differently, purely because their popularity will depend upon it. If we demand that future leaders learn from the success of compassionate statesmen like Nelson Mandela, more feminine forms of dealing with conflict, such as negotiation, will become the only acceptable option in the future.

The biggest contribution women can make is drawing upon the powers assigned to us—things like ethics, morals, and wisdom. Imagine how different the state of affairs would be if wisdom, morals, and ethics replaced power and control as the most important values driving vital decisions. By way of example, Marilyn Waring says that the amount of money spent by the U.S. military in just two weeks is enough to provide good quality drinking water for every human being on the planet.[41] If these "feminine principles" were also applied to stop the injustice of the wealthiest nations plundering the resources of the poorest countries, then all people worldwide would have a better shot at living happy, prosperous lives. This can become a reality if half the population demands a complete switch in the modus operandi that governs world affairs.

### Undoing Unholy Alliances

If gender politics is the biggest obstacle to world peace and these role "rules" were established by patriarchal religions—the same religions still used to justify warfare and destruction—then Richard Dawkins's book, *The God Delusion,* will provide huge relief to those striving for a better world.

Dawkins provides a compelling argument for seeing religion as no more than a collection of myths and superstitions passed down from one generation to the next. While most self-respecting modern individuals wouldn't balk at walking under a ladder, many follow religious practices that, in Dawkins's opinion, are equally nonsensical. And when they're used to justify warfare and oppression, they're downright harmful.[42] The fact that a book advocating freedom from religion has hit bestseller lists provides a glimmer of hope that these rigid dogmas may be changing.

How women are inspired by or benefit from patriarchal religions baffles me, but more important is the relationship in many countries between religious institutions and the state.

Realistically, there is nothing to justify the legitimacy of any national border, especially those created by religion. Free-thinking women and men are proposing alternatives as a form of social organization. Antiauthoritarian writers, such as Carol Moore, are calling for the dissolution of the nation state because, she believes, this will increase choice for families, equalize political power, end oppression and exploitation, minimize violence and crime, and improve social welfare. Thinkers such as Moore are not advocating socialism as we have known it. Instead, she is calling for the creation of confederated communities where all people have far greater say over their own lives.[43]

With religion in its various forms having formed the very foundations of our civilization, it's difficult to imagine a world not dominated by myths and superstitions. But, if we start questioning what value there is in raising children to be scared stiff of an all-knowing mythical Superman in the sky, then we can raise our kids to love life rather than fear it. Fear breeds a "scarcity mentality" that feeds into the existing power and control model.

### Abundant Living

The modern movement toward an abundant view of the world started in the 1930s with Napoleon Hill's book *Think and Grow Rich*. With a plethora of mind-power books on the market, as well as movies like *What the Bleep Do We Know!?* and *The Secret*, ancient knowledge has entered mainstream life, showing how simple it is to use the strength of our mind to manifest the life we want. This releases both men and women from the oppression of artificially created structures that resigned people to the scarcity of poverty, including status, class, and access to education. This ultimate form of freedom is a boon for thinking women, but it won't alter business practices as we know them.

### The Cost of Control

No matter how much big business claims to have changed, the fact remains that large corporate institutions are still run by men who use male strategies to control thousands of people's existence. The writing's on the wall, though, for "business as usual."

Lynn Brewer, whistleblower and author of *Confessions of an Enron Executive*, said there were three shortcomings in Enron's leadership that brought the company to its knees: arrogance, short-term exploitation, and denial. These are typical tactics of patriarchal systems and the risk grows proportionately as the need to prop up the illusion of control becomes more important than reality. In an interview, Brewer said that the U.S. Securities and Exchange Commission (the governing body for publicly traded companies) is currently receiving 20,000 whistle-blowing reports a month.[44] It's clear that corporate monkey business on a grand scale could cause capital markets to crash, but what's not so obvious is just how the same arrogance that brought down Enron could be the demise of organizations configured according to the old command-and-control military model.

Hope can be gleaned from the fact that many women are structuring their businesses differently these days. In countries like Norway, Sweden, and Belgium, laws dictate that 40 percent of board members of listed companies be female. Legislation such as this subverts the male strategy of having token women at high levels. This stifling approach has virtually guaranteed that these women would battle to garner support and finally give up after years of frustration and resign, allowing men to erroneously conclude that women can't hack it at the top.

Today there is also much talk about "compassionate capitalism." Danish author Tanya Ellis has compiled information about the growing impact of social entrepreneurs who form part of a new economic subdivision known as the Fourth Sector.[45] The first three sectors include: 1) businesses for profit; 2) the public sector; and 3) NGOs (that do good work but often struggle to make money). The Fourth Sector incorporates businesses that make real social contributions and which are profitable. We know women work to make a difference, and when the notion of self-sacrifice is replaced with the idea of being appropriately selfish, women can put their minds to creating a better world, and make money in the process.

Social conscience is what drives most women, so fear not that we may fall into the kind of lawlessness that angrily destroys other people's lives. This is the domain of the power-hungry; it is not what the majority of women want.

According to Martin Seligman, founder of the movement Positive Psychology, making other lives breathe easier is important for our well-being. In his book *Authentic Happiness,* he compares the effect of making a difference to that of being wealthy, good-looking, getting promoted, or even having good health. He found that the only way for human beings to experience lasting happiness is by making a contribution to others.[46] This is not about altruism; when we add value to other people, we get worthwhile feedback telling us that our own lives matter. Thus, Fourth Sector businesses are not only good for our pockets, but they also contribute to our well-being and that of others.

### Schools of Control

Fundamental changes to the business model will require a radical reworking of the educational institutions that feed adults into the economic system. For too long now schools have been structured with the primary intent of teaching young people to succumb to rigid controls. With greater opportunities for personal freedom, schools will only benefit children when they return to Aristotle's philosophy that "the teacher is only a midwife at the birth of an idea." Parrot-style book learning only produces educated morons; instead of spoon-feeding young people, learning institutions need to inspire students to think, explore, and gather as much knowledge as possible from life experience.

With psychology and the self-help movement teaching principles that affirm children's self-esteem and support their dreams, we have the opportunity to encourage the growth of more balanced citizens. Some institutions are taking the lead in this area, particularly those that are emphasizing emotional intelligence over academic results.

### Sister Support

One of the biggest breakthroughs for women is just how much support those who have matured beyond their stereotypical conditioning are able to provide to each other. Greater self-confidence makes this possible. Instead of grappling with the usual female insecurities, self-assured women are able to form strong friendships in which they can be vulnerable with one another. Women who do are already creating lucrative partnerships, forming investment clubs, or simply having a lot of fun together.

With the lack of trust between women often serving as the greatest obstacle to creating a female collective, what we need is a critical mass of women egging each other on to create change. This brings to mind the concepts in Michael Gladwell's *Tipping Point,* in which he asserts that with critical mass, there comes a boiling point where the unexpected becomes expected, where radical change is suddenly seen as more than hypothetical.[47]

This "tipping" toward being more authentic and supportive of each other has huge implications on the way we raise our children, bringing them up to believe, truly, that they live in a world of gender equality. We are at the edge of this tipping point, waiting for the right set of factors to come into play to witness the change that needs to happen to undo the old style of business as usual.

### The Third Wave

With women having made so much progress, the impact of the feminine influence in every aspect of life can no longer be ignored. First-wave feminism addressed basic rights, the second triumphed over personal freedom, and the third is about dismantling political, economic, and social systems that maintain the imbalance of male dominance globally.

Our greater collective clout means that women have the power to find wiser solutions to poverty alleviation, land usage, childcare, how people invest their time, planetary conservation, global peace, or even our own personal spiritual pursuits. Of course, as individuals we can't respond to all of these issues, but if each of us picks the problem that concerns us most and channels our energy into addressing that issue, many more of our social and environmental concerns will be dealt with. No matter what areas women tackle, no system is sufficiently powerful to block those who take a stand collectively.

### More Technology, More Time

Advances in technology are also giving us the benefit of more time. With the increasing number of gizmos to assist us in our daily pursuits, we have more freedom to explore what we want. As soon as women start rejecting the insatiable time-devouring demands of consumerism, the hours gained can be used to examine the state of our physical, emotional, mental, and spiritual lives and maintain a healthy balance.

Balance is the stasis the human system demands. This is not something we need to learn; it is a condition that comes naturally. As such it is something that a subsistence farmer in India is equally likely to strive for as an executive in New York.

Technology is also proving to be a big asset for some of the most oppressed women in the world. In a recent conversation I had with a representative from a market research company, it appears that some interesting developments are happening in countries like Saudi Arabia. During focus groups conducted by his group, they discovered that Saudi women toe the line about male dominance in certain public spheres, but behind the scenes they are using technology to get all manner of university degrees, many even doing it secretively. In time it will be interesting to observe how these empowered women weigh up their sophisticated education against the terms of their oppression.

### The Long Road

Feminism has encouraged women to walk the lengthy, painful road back to our freedom—the freedom women originally had. While it may have seemed as though women's actions were initially shifting toward more masculine behavior, extreme swings are normal in the process of a system regaining its balance.

Now that so many are on the path to enlightenment, the compassion and collective responsibility that forms part of our social conscience can start to again take its rightful place in the world.

While there's no question that society needs the energy of the masculine drive for mastery, the removal of the feminine counterbalance means that unchecked egos plunge us into the negative qualities of male power. These destructive forces include unhealthy competition, dictatorship, harshness, violence, cynicism, self-interest, glorified ego-power, control, and domination.

With the increasing number of women determined to show up in all their power, and with the growing volume of men taking steps to cultivate humanity in business and personal pursuits, radical social restructuring is feasible.

By being authentic we release both ourselves and men from the straightjacket of predefined roles, which in turn frees us to start working toward more meaningful goals. Only then will the natural flow between masculine and feminine energies result in a social transformation that may take us into a greater evolution than we've previously imagined.

We already have a glimpse of an extraordinary future, and to materialize these changes on a global scale little else need change except for each of us to make a conscious decision to kill the princess of self-sacrifice and nurture the healthier, more deliberate process of self-development.

So it would appear that the leaders of the future who will mentor us, the wise women who will guide us, the Amazons who will fight for us, and the spiritual gurus who will inspire us, are no more than the ancient wild females internalized in each of us as our womanhood. And the success of a more egalitarian and peaceful world will rest or fall by whatever you and I do about it right now.

# NOTES

## INTRODUCTION: TO SLEEPING BEAUTY: A WAKE-UP CALL

1. Tom Peters, *Re-imagine!* (London: Dorling Kindersley Limited, 2003).
2. Patrick Dixon, *Futurewise* (London: HarperCollins, 2002).
3. Elizabeth Cady Stanton, *The Woman's Bible* (Boston: Northeastern University Press, 1993).
4. M. Centron, "Trends Shaping the Future: Economic, Societal and Environmental Trends," *The Futurist* 37, no. 1 (2003): 27–42.
5. Mary Daly, *Gyn/Ecology: The Metaethics of Radical Feminism* (London: The Women's Press, 1979).
6. "Letter to the Bishops of the Catholic Church on the Collaboration of Men and Women in the Church and the World," quoted in *The Sunday Times*, South Africa, August 1, 2004.
7. The Feminist Majority Foundation, March 9, 1999, www.feminist.org/news.
8. National Organization for Women, newsletter, spring 2002, www.now.org/nnt/spring-2002.
9. United Nations Report, www.un.org/womenwatch/daw/beijing/platform/poverty.htm.
10. World Health Organization, World Health Report, 1998, www.who.int/whr/1998.
11. World Health Organization, World Health Report, 2001, www.who.int/whr/2001.
12. V. Beral and the Million Study Collaborators, "Breast Cancer and Hormone Replacement Therapy in the Million Women Study," *Lancet* 362 (2003): 419–427.
13. UNICEF, Beijing + 5 Report, 2000, www.unicef.org/vaw.
14. National Organization for Women, 2003, www.thetruthaboutgeorge.com.
15. Stephen R. Covey, *The Seven Habits of Highly Effective People* (London: Simon & Schuster, 1989).
16. Peter Senge, *The Fifth Discipline: The Art & Practice of the Learning Organization* (New York: Currency/Doubleday, 1990).
17. Daniel Goleman, *Emotional Intelligence* (London: Bloomsbury Publishing, 1995).
18. Mary Daly, *Beyond God the Father: Toward a Philosophy of Women's Liberation* (Boston: Beacon Press, 1973).
19. CIA: World Fact Book, 2002, www.cia.gov/cia/publications/factbook.
20. Martha Burk, *Cult of Power: Sex Discrimination in Corporate America and What Can Be Done about It* (New York: Lisa Drew/Scribner, 2005).

## CHAPTER 1. THE KISS OF LIFE

1. Patrick Dixon, *Futurewise* (London: HarperCollins, 2002).
2. *New Webster's Dictionary of the English Language* (New York: Delair Publishing Company, 1981).
3. Susan Maushart, *Wifework: What Marriage Really Means for Women* (London: Bloomsbury Publishing, 2001).
4. Tom Peters, *Re-imagine!* (London: Dorling Kindersley Limited, 2003).
5. Faith Popcorn and Lys Marigold, *EVEolution: The Eight Truths of Marketing to Women* (London: HarperCollins Business, 2001).
6. Leslie Kenton, *Passage to Power: Natural Menopause Revolution* (London: Ebury Press, 1995).
7. Sherrill Sellman, *Hormone Heresy: What Women Must Know about Their Hormones* (Honolulu, HI: GetWell International, 2001).
8. R. M. Sharpe and N. E. Skakkebaek, "Are Oestrogens Involved in Falling Sperm Counts and Disorders of the Male Reproductive Tract?" *Lancet* 341 (1993): 1,392–1,395.
9. Linda Babcock and Sara Laschever, *Women Don't Ask: Negotiation and the Gender Divide* (Princeton, NJ: Princeton University Press, 2003).
10. Ira Levin, *The Stepford Wives* (New York: Random House, 1972).
11. *The Shorter Oxford English Dictionary,* 3rd ed. (Oxford: Clarendon Press, 1973).
12. Andrea Dworkin, *Pornography: Men Possessing Women,* reprint ed. (New York: E. P. Dutton Inc., New York, 1991).
13. Mary Daly, *Beyond God the Father: Toward a Philosophy of Women's Liberation* (Boston: Beacon Press, 1973).
14. Susan Faludi, *Backlash: The Undeclared War against Women* (London: Chatto & Windus Ltd., 1992).
15. Alexandra Middendorf, executive producer. *Science of Beauty* (Wall to Wall, Discovery Communications, 2001).
16. A. T. Langford, *Why Men Marry* (Holbrook, MA: Adams Media Corporation, 1999).
17. David Smiedt, *Delivering the Male* (Victoria: Penguin Books, 1999).
18. Clarissa Pinkola Estés, *Women Who Run with the Wolves* (London: Rider, 1998).
19. Stephanie Vermeulen, *EQ: Emotional Intelligence for Everyone* (Cape Town: Zebra Press, 1999).
20. Anthony Robbins, *Unlimited Power* (London: Simon & Schuster, 1988).

## CHAPTER 2. POOR LITTLE ME

1. Luise Eichenbaum and Susie Orbach, *Understanding Women* (New York: Penguin, 1982).
2. Luise Eichenbaum and Susie Orbach, *What Do Women Want?* (Glasgow: Fontana Paperbacks, William Collins Sons & Co. Ltd., 1984).
3. William Pollack, *Real Boys* (New York: Henry Holt and Co., 1998).
4. C. Malatesta and J. Haviland, "Learning Display Rules: The Socialization of Emotion Expression in Infancy," *Child Development* 53 (1982): 991–1,003.
5. Luise Eichenbaum and Susie Orbach, *What Do Women Want?*
6. Susie Orbach, *Fat Is a Feminist Issue and Its Sequel* (London: Arrow Books, 1988).
7. Luise Eichenbaum and Susie Orbach, *What Do Women Want?*
8. Mary Pipher, *Reviving Ophelia* (New York: Ballantine Books, 1995).
9. Naomi Wolf, *Fire with Fire* (London: Random House, 1993).
10. Suze Orman, *The Courage to Be Rich* (London: Vermilion, 1999).
11. Colette Dowling, *The Cinderella Complex* (Glasgow: Fontana Paperbacks, William Collins Sons & Co. Ltd., 1982).
12. Nathaniel Branden, *How to Raise Your Self-Esteem* (New York: Bantam Books, 1987).
13. Daniel Goleman, *Emotional Intelligence* (London: Bloomsbury Publishing, 1995).
14. Harriet Rubin, *The Princessa: Machiavelli for Women* (London: Bloomsbury Publishing, 1998).
15. B. Risman, "Can Men Mother? Life as a Single Father," *Family Relations* 35 (January 1986): 95–102.
16. P. R. Clance and S. A. Imes, "The Imposter Phenomenon in Hi-achieving Women. Dynamics and Therapeutic Intervention," *Psychotherapy Theory, Research & Practice* 15 (1978): 241–247.
17. Barbara A. Kerr, *Smart Girls, Gifted Women* (Columbus, OH: Ohio Psychology Press, 1992).
18. M. Sadker and D. Sadker, *Failing at Fairness: How America's Schools Cheat Girls* (New York: Charles Scribner, 1994).
19. Susie Orbach and Luise Eichenbaum, *Between Women* (London: Arrow Books, 1988).
20. Ibid.
21. Ibid.
22. Phyllis Chesler, *Woman's Inhumanity to Woman* (New York: Plume Books, 2001).
23. Ibid.
24. Susie Orbach and Luise Eichenbaum, *Between Women.*

25. Phyllis Chesler, *Woman's Inhumanity to Woman*.

26. Luise Eichenbaum and Susie Orbach, *Understanding Women*.

27. Harriet B. Braiker, *The Disease to Please: Curing the People-Pleasing Syndrome* (New York: McGraw Hill Contemporary Books, 2002).

28. Adapted by Justine Korman, *Disney's Beauty and the Beast* (New York: Golden Books, 1993).

29. Mary Pipher, *Reviving Ophelia*.

30. Betty Friedan, *The Fountain of Age* (New York: Touchstone Books, 1994).

31. Naomi Wolf, *Fire with Fire*.

32. Ibid.

33. Barbara A. Kerr, *Smart Girls, Gifted Women*.

34. B. C. Rollins and H. Feldman, "Marital Satisfaction over the Family Life Cycle," *Journal of Marriage & Family* 32 (1970): 20–28.

35. The National Center for Health Statistics, www.cdc.gov/nchs/.

36. Sylvia Ann Hewlett, *Creating a Life: Professional Women and the Quest for Children* (New York: Miramax Books, 2002).

37. Rosalind Barnett and Caryl Rivers, *She Works/He Works: How Two-Income Families Are Happy, Healthy, and Thriving,* reprint ed. (Harvard University Press, 1998).

38. J. B. Rotter, "Generalized Expectancies for Internal versus External Control of Reinforcement," *Psychological Monographs* 80 (1966): 1, whole no. 609.

## CHAPTER 3. HELL HATH NO FURY

1. Daniel Goleman, *Emotional Intelligence*.

2. Harriet Goldhor Lerner, *The Dance of Anger* (London: Pandora Press, 1990).

3. Ibid.

4. Murray A. Straus and Richard J. Gelles, "Societal Change and Change in Family Violence from 1975 to 1985, as Revealed by Two National Surveys," *Journal of Marriage and the Family* 48 (August 1986): 465–480.

5. Alix Kirsta, *Deadlier Than the Male: Violence and Aggression in Women* (London: HarperCollins, 1994).

6. Phyllis Chesler, *Woman's Inhumanity to Woman*.

7. Mary Valentis and Anne Devane, *Female Rage* (London: Piatkus Books, 1995).

8. Ibid.

9. Daniel Goleman, *Emotional Intelligence*.

10. C. M. Stoney and T. O. Engebretson, "Plasma Homocysteine Concentrations Are Positively Associated with Hostility and Anger," *Life Sciences* 66 (2000): 2,267–2,275.

11. Harriet Rubin, *The Princessa: Machiavelli for Women.*

12. Phyllis Chesler, *Woman's Inhumanity to Woman.*

13. Naomi Wolf, *The Beauty Myth* (London: Chatto & Windus Ltd., 1990).

14. Susie Orbach, *Fat Is a Feminist Issue and Its Sequel* (London: Arrow Books, 1988).

15. Naomi Wolf. *The Beauty Myth.*

16. Mary Valentis and Anne Devane, *Female Rage.*

17. Ibid.

18. Laura Schlessinger, *Ten Stupid Things Women Do to Mess Up Their Lives* (London: Headline Book Publishing, 1995).

19. Wayne Dyer, *Pulling Your Own Strings,* reprint ed. (London: Arrow Books, 1992).

20. Susan Jeffers, *Feel the Fear and Do It Anyway* (London: Arrow Books, 1987).

21. Caryl Rivers, Rosalind Barnett, and Grace Baruch, *Beyond Sugar and Spice* (New York: Ballantine Books, 1981).

22. Lance Morrow, "Through the Eyes of Children," *Time Magazine,* August 8, 1988; Jessica Reaves, "Do Preschools and Nannies Turn Kids into Bullies?" *Time Magazine,* April 19, 2001.

23. E. Harvey, "Short-Term and Long-Term Effects of Early Parental Employment on Children of the National Longitudinal Survey of Youth," *Developmental Psychology* 35 (1999): 445–449.

24. Rosalind Barnett and Caryl Rivers, *She Works/He Works: How Two-Income Families Are Happy, Healthy, and Thriving.*

25. T. S. Zimmerman, S. W. Bowling, and R. M. McBride, "Strategies for Reducing Guilt among Working Mothers," *The Colorado Early Childhood Journal* summer 3, no. 1 (2001): 12–17.

26. Caryl Rivers, Rosalind Barnett, and Grace Baruch, *Beyond Sugar and Spice.*

27. T. S. Zimmerman, S. W. Bowling, and R. M. McBride, "Strategies for Reducing Guilt among Working Mothers."

28. Betty Holcomb, *Not Guilty! The Good News about Working Mothers* (New York: Scribner, 1998).

29. Wayne Dyer, *Pulling Your Own Strings.*

## CHAPTER 4. SURVIVAL OF THE PRETTIEST

1. H. Dugmore, "Body and Soul," *The Big Issue* 55, no. 6 (South Africa, February 2002).
2. Naomi Wolf, *The Beauty Myth.*
3. Cyndi Tebbel, *The Body Snatchers* (Sydney: Finch Publishing, 2000).
4. L. M. Irving, "Mirror Images: Effects of the Standard of Beauty on Women's Self- and Body Esteem," *Journal of Social and Clinical Psychology* 9 (1990): 230–242.
5. D. M. Garner and A. Kearney Cooke, "The 1997 Body Image Survey Results," *Psychology Today* 30 (1997): 30–41.
6. A. E. Field et al., "Exposure to Mass Media and Weight Concerns among Girls," *Pediatrics* 103, no. 3 (March 1999).
7. K. Harrison and J. Cantor, "The Relationship between Media Exposure and Eating Disorders," *Journal of Communication* 47 (1997): 40–67; E. Stice and H. E. Shaw, "Adverse Effects of the Media-Portrayed Thin-Ideal on Women and Linkages to Bulimic Symptomology," *Journal of Social and Clinical Psychology* 13 (1994): 288–30; E. Stice, D. Splangler, and W. S. Agras, "Exposure to Media-Portrayed Thin-Ideal Images Adversely Affects Vulnerable Girls: A Longitudinal Experiment," *Journal of Social and Clinical Psychology* 20, no. 3 (2001): 270–288.
8. P. N. Myers and F. A. Biocca, "The Elastic Body Image: The Effect of Television Advertising and Programming on Body Image Distortions in Young Women," *Journal of Communication* 42, no. 3 (1992): 108–133.
9. J. Demarest and R. Allen, "Body Image: Gender, Ethnic, and Age Differences," *The Journal of Social Psychology* 140, no. 4 (2000): 465–472.
10. Susan Faludi, *Backlash: The Undeclared War against Women.*
11. D. Singh, "Adaptive Significance of Female Physical Attractiveness: Role of Waist-to-Hip Ratio," *Journal of Personality and Social Psychology* 65, no. 2 (1993): 293–307.
12. Feminist Majority Leadership Alliance, "Who Contributes to and Profits from Women's Negative Body Image," http://orgs.unt.edu/fmla/information/bodyimage.html.
13. Naomi Wolf, *The Beauty Myth.*
14. C. M. Marlowe, S. L. Schneider, and C. E. Nelson, "Gender and Attractiveness Biases in Hiring Decisions: Are More Experienced Managers Less Biased?" *Journal of Applied Psychology* 81, no. 1 (1996): 11–21, www.feministcampus.org/fmla/printable-materials/BodyImageBrochure.pdf.
15. Jonathan Kingdon, *Self-Made Man and His Undoing* (New York: Simon & Schuster, 1993).

16. Cyndi Tebbel, *The Body Snatchers.*

17. Ibid.

18. Ibid.

19. "Feeling Flirty," *Shape,* South Africa, Weider Publications Inc., November 2002.

20. Naomi Wolf, *The Beauty Myth.*

21. Ibid.

22. Ibid.

23. National Center for Policy Research for Women and Families, quoted in www.breastimplantinfo.org/implantfacts.html.

24. National Cancer Institute: www.center4research.org/implantfacts.html.

25. Cyndi Tebbel, *The Body Snatchers.*

26. Ibid.

27. Feminist Majority Leadership Alliance, "Who Contributes to and Profits from Women's Negative Body Image."

28. V. Peter Misra, "The Changed Image of Botulinum Toxin," *British Medical Journal* 325 (November 2002): 1,188.

29. The International Association for Physicians in Aesthetic Medicine: www. theiapam.com.

30. W. Harth and R. Linse, "Botulinophilia: Contraindication for Therapy with Botulinum Toxin," *International Journal of Clinical Pharmacology and Therapeutics* 39, no. 7 (2001): 460–463.

31. Amnesty International, www.amnesty.org/ailib/intcam/femgen/fgml.htm.

32. Sam Keen, *Fire in the Belly: On Being a Man* (London: Piatkus Books, 1992).

33. A. T. Langford, *Why Men Marry* (Holbrook, MA: Adams Media Corporation, 1999).

34. Naomi Wolf, *The Beauty Myth.*

35. Letter of Elizabeth Barrett Browning, quoted in Mary Daly, *Gyn/Ecology: The Metaethics of Radical Feminism* (London: The Women's Press, 1979).

## CHAPTER 5. LOOKS THAT KILL

1. Terry Poulton, *No Fat Chicks: How Women Are Brainwashed to Hate Their Bodies and Spend Their Money* (Toronto: Key Porter Books, 1996).

2. Ibid.

3. Hillel Schwartz, *Never Satisfied: A Cultural History of Diets, Fantasies and Fat* (New York: Free Press, 1986).

4. Laura Fraser, *Losing It: False Hope and Fat Profits in the Diet Industry* (NewYork: Plume Books, 1997).

5. Ibid.

6. Robert Atkins, *Dr. Atkins' Diet Revolution* (New York: Bantam Books, 1981).

7. Judy Mazel, *The Beverly Hills Diet* (New York: Macmillan Publishing, 1981).

8. O. W. Wooley and S. Wooley, "The Beverly Hills Eating Disorder: The Mass Marketing of Anorexia Nervosa," *International Journal of Eating Disorders* 1, no. 3 (1982): 57–69.

9. Laura Fraser, *Losing It: False Hope and Fat Profits in the Diet Industry.*

10. L. Lissner et al., "Variability of Body Weight and Health Outcomes in the Framingham Population," *New England Journal of Medicine* 324 (1991): 1,839–1,844.

11. Ancel Keys et al., *The Biology of Human Starvation* (Minneapolis: University of Minnesota Press, 1950).

12. Naomi Wolf, *The Beauty Myth.*

13. Laura Fraser, *Losing It: False Hope and Fat Profits in the Diet Industry.*

14. Hillel Schwartz, *Never Satisfied: A Cultural History of Diets, Fantasies and Fat.*

15. Terry Poulton, *No Fat Chicks: How Women Are Brainwashed to Hate Their Bodies and Spend Their Money.*

16. Laura Fraser, *Losing It: False Hope and Fat Profits in the Diet Industry.*

17. Ibid.

18. Alicia Mundy, *Dispensing with the Truth: The Victims, the Drug Companies, and the Dramatic Story behind the Battle over Fen-Phen* (New York: St. Martin's Press, 2001).

19. Ibid.

20. Abbott Laboratories correspondence with the U.S. Department of Health & Human Services, www.fda.gov/ohrms/dockets/dailys/02/Jun02/060602/80047a94.pdf.

21. Public Citizen correspondence with the U.S. Department of Health & Human Services, www.fda.gov/ohrms/dockets/dailys/02/mar02/032202/02p-0120_cp00001_vol1.pdf.

22. Michael D. Lemonick, "Are We Ready for Fat-Free Fat?" *Time* 147, no. 2, January 8, 1996.

23. Roche Pharmaceuticals, www.rocheusa.com/products/xenical/pi.html.

24. K. M. Hvizdos and A. Markham, "Orlistat: A Review of Its Use in the Management of Obesity," *Drugs* 58 (1999): 743–760.

25. In interview with Nigel Crowther, obesity researcher, University of the Witwatersrand, Johannesburg, South Africa.

26. Nanci Hellmich, "Americans' New Craving: Diet Drugs" *USA Today,* April 29, 2002.

27. FDA News, HHS Acts to Reduce Potential Risks of Dietary Supplements Containing Ephedra, www.fda.gov/bbs/topics/NEWS/2003/NEW00875. html.

28. Laura Fraser, *Losing It: False Hope and Fat Profits in the Diet Industry.*

29. FDA News, HHS Acts to Reduce Potential Risks of Dietary Supplements Containing Ephedra.

30. Aspartame Information Center, www.aspartame.org.

31. Dr. Janet Starr Hull, *Sweet Poison: How the World's Most Popular Artificial Sweetener Is Killing Us* (Far Hills, NJ: New Horizon Press, 2001).

32. Dr. Joseph Mercola, www.mercola.com.

33. Dir. Cory Brackett, *Sweet Misery: A Poisoned World* (Sound and Fury Productions, 2005).

34. Dr. H. J. Roberts, *Aspartame Disease: An Ignored Epidemic* (West Palm Beach, FL: Sunshine Sentinel Press, 2001).

35. J. E. Manson et al., "Body Weight and Mortality among Women," *New England Journal of Medicine* 333 (1995): 677–682.

36. Laura Fraser, *Losing It: False Hope and Fat Profits in the Diet Industry.*

37. Paul Campos, "Diet Industry's Dangerous Lies," *Rocky Mountain News,* Denver, May 7, 2002.

38. Abbott Laboratories, www.abbott.com.

39. Thomas Moore, *Lifespan: New Perspectives on Extending Human Longevity* (New York: Touchstone Books, 1994).

40. The National Association to Advance Fat Acceptance, www.naafa.org.

41. Terry Poulton, *No Fat Chicks: How Women Are Brainwashed to Hate Their Bodies and Spend Their Money.*

42. Laura Fraser, *Losing It: False Hope and Fat Profits in the Diet Industry.*

43. Ibid.

44. The National Association to Advance Fat Acceptance.

45. Jack A. Yanovski and Susan Z. Yanovski, "Recent Advances in Basic Obesity Research," *Journal of the American Medical Association* 282 (1999): 1,504–1,506.

46. Beth A. Abramowitz and Leann L. Birch, "Five-Year-Old Girls' Ideas about Dieting Are Predicted by Their Mothers' Dieting," *Journal of the American Dietetic Association* 100, no. 10 (2000): 1,157–1,163.

47. K. M. Flegal et al., "Prevalence and Trends in Obesity among US Adults, 1999–2000," *Journal of the American Medical Association* 288 (2002): 1,723–1,727.

48. D. B. Allison et al., "Annual Deaths Attributable to Obesity in the U.S.," *Journal of the American Medical Association* 282 (1999): 1,530–1,538.

49. J. Stevens et al., "The Effect of Age on the Association between Body Mass Index and Mortality," *New England Journal of Medicine* 338 (1998): 1–7; K. R. Fontaine et al., "Years of Life Lost Due to Obesity," *Journal of the American Medical Association* 289 (2003): 187–193; A. Peeters et al., "Obesity in Adulthood and Its Consequences for Life Expectancy: A Life-Table Analysis," *Annals of Internal Medicine* 138, no. 1 (2003): 24–32.

50. Paul Campos, "Weighting Game: What the Diet Industry Won't Tell You," *The New Republic,* January 13, 2003.

51. Joanne P. Ikeda, "Health at Every Size: A Size-Acceptance Approach to Health Promotion," *Radiance,* Fall 1999.

52. National Institutes for Health, "Study of Health Outcomes of Weight-Loss (SHOW)," RFA-DK-98-020, November 18, 1998.

53. J. I. Robison et al., "Redefining Success in Obesity Intervention: The New Paradigm," *Journal of the American Dietetic Association* 95, no. 4 (1995): 422–423.

54. S. N. Blair and S. Brodney, "Effects of Physical Inactivity and Obesity on Morbidity and Mortality: Current Evidence and Research Issues," *Medicine and Science in Sports Exercise* 31 (1999): S646–S662; S. N. Blair et al., "Physical Fitness and All-Cause Mortality: A Prospective Study of Healthy Men and Women," *Journal of the American Medical Association* 262, no. 7 (1989): 2,395–2,401.

55. C. E. Barlow et al., "Physical Fitness, Mortality and Obesity," *International Journal of Obesity* 19, no. 4 (1995): S41–S44; C. D. Lee, A. S. Jackson, and S. N. Blair, "U.S. Weight Guidelines: Is It Also Important to Consider Cardiorespiratory Fitness?" *International Journal of Obesity* 22, no. 2 (1998): S2–S7.

56. Russell R. Pate et al., "Physical Activity and Public Health: A Recommendation from the CDC and ACSM," *Journal of the American Medical Association* 273 (1995): 402–407.

57. Federal Trade Commission, www.ftc.gov.

58. Naomi Wolf, *The Beauty Myth.*

59. Laura Fraser, *Losing It: False Hope and Fat Profits in the Diet Industry.*

60. Susan Faludi, *Backlash: The Undeclared War against Women.*

61. Terry Poulton, *No Fat Chicks: How Women Are Brainwashed to Hate Their Bodies and Spend Their Money.*

62. Ibid.

63. Geneen Roth, *Feeding the Hungry Heart* (New York: Plume Books, 1993).

64. Timothy Freke and Peter Gandy, *Jesus and the Goddess: The Secret Teachings of the Original Christians* (London: Thorsons, 2002).

65. Roberto Assagioli, *The Act of Will* (Northamptonshire, U.K.: Turnstone Press, 1974).

## CHAPTER 6. THE WICKED WITCH OF BUSINESS

1. Christian Coalition of America, www.cc.org; Focus on the Family, www.family.org; Family Research Council, www.frc.org; Concerned Women for America, www.cwfa.org; Eagle Forum, www.eagleforum.org; Promise Keepers, www.promisekeepers.org.

2. Bureau of Labor Statistics, www.bls.gov.

3. Family and Home Network, www.familyandhome.org.

4. National Institute of Mental Health, www.nimh.nih.gov.

5. Terry Arendell, "Co-parenting: A review of the Literature National Center on Fathers and Families" (1997), www.ncoff.gse.upenn.edu/litrev/cpbrief.htm.

6. Ibid.

7. Ralph LaRossa, "Fatherhood and Social Change," *Family Relations* 37, no. 4 (1988): 451–457.

8. Michael Lamb and David Oppenheim, "Fatherhood and Father-Child Relationships," in *Fathers and Their Families,* ed. Stanley Cath, Alan Gurwitt, and Linda Gunsberg, 11–26 (Hillsdale, NJ: Analytic Press, 1989).

9. Gayle Kimball, *50–50 Parenting* (Lexington, MA: Lexington Books, 1988).

10. Terry Arendell, *Fathers and Divorce* (Newbury Park, CA: Sage Publications, 1995).

11. Pepper Schwartz, *Peer Marriage: How Love Between Equals Really Works* (New York: Free Press, 1994).

12. Frank Furstenburg and Andrew Cherlin, *Divided Families: What Happens to Children When Parents Part?* (Cambridge, MA: Harvard University Press, 1991).

13. Kathleen Gerson, *No Man's Land: Men's Changing Commitments to Family and Work* (New York: Basic Books, 1993).

14. Phyllis Berman and Frank Pedersen, "Research on Men's Transition to Parenthood: An Integrative Discussion," in *Men's Transitions to Parenthood: Longitudinal Studies of Early Family Experiences,* ed. Phyllis Berman and Frank Pedersen, 217–242 (Mahwah, NJ, Lawrence Erlbaum Associates, Inc., 1987).

15. Christine Winquist Nord and Jerry West, "National Household Education Survey: Fathers' and Mothers' Involvement in Their Children's Schools by Family Type & Resident Status," *Statistical Analysis Report,* U.S. Department of Education, National Center for Education Statistics, 2001.

16. N. Radin, "Primary-Caregiving Fathers in Intact Families," in *Redefining Families: Implications for Children's Development,* ed. A. E. Gottfried and A. W. Gottfried, 11–51 (New York: Plenum Press, 1994).

17. M. A. Zimmerman, D. A. Salem, and P. C. Notaro, "Make Room for Daddy II: The Positive Effects of Fathers' Role in Adolescent Development," in *Resilience Across Contexts: Family, Work, Culture and Community,* ed. R. D. Taylor et al., 233–253 (Mahwah, NJ: Lawrence Erlbaum Associates, Inc., 2001).

18. T. S. Zimmerman, S. W. Bowling, and R. M. McBride, "Strategies for Reducing Guilt among Working Mothers," *The Colorado Early Childhood Journal* summer 3, no. 1 (2001): 12–17; Women's Bureau, U.S. Department of Labor.

19. Monica Sjöo and Barbara Mor, *The Great Cosmic Mother: Rediscovering the Religion of the Earth* (San Francisco: Harper & Row, 1987).

20. Linda Babcock and Sara Laschever, *Women Don't Ask: Negotiation and Gender* (Princeton, NJ: Princeton University Press, 2003).

21. Harriet B. Braiker, *The Disease to Please: Curing the People-Pleasing Syndrome* (New York: McGraw Hill Contemporary Books, 2002).

22. Susan Maushart, *Wifework: What Marriage Really Means for Women* (London: Bloomsbury Publishing, 2001).

23. Korn/Ferry Survey (University of Michigan) quoted by Feminist Majority Foundation, Research Center, www.feminist.org/research/business/ewb_toc.html.

24. Bureau of Labor Statistics, May 2003, www.bls.gov.

25. Stephanie Boraas and William M. Rodgers III, "How Does Gender Play a Role in the Earnings Gap? An Update," *Monthly Labor Review,* 126, no. 3 (March 2003).

26. Marilyn Waring, *Counting for Nothing: What Men Value and What Women Are Worth,* reprint ed. (Toronto: University of Toronto Press, 1999).

27. Naomi Wolf, *The Beauty Myth.*

28. American Psychological Association, www.apa.org.

29. Mary Daly, *Gyn/Ecology: The Metaethics of Radical Feminism* (London: The Women's Press, 1979).

30. Susan Maushart, *Wifework: What Marriage Really Means for Women.*

31. A. T. Langford, *Why Men Marry* (Holbrook, MA: Adams Media Corporation, 1999).

32. "Women Entrepreneurs: Why Companies Lose Female Talent and What They Can Do about it" (New York: Catalyst, 1998), www.catalystwomen.org.

33. National Association of Women Business Owners, www.nawbo.org.

34. The National Council for Research on Women, www.ncrw.org/research/iqm.htm.

35. Alysia Lebeau, "Are We There Yet?" The New Workplace Woman, 2001, www.bpwusa.org.

36. The National Council for Research on Women.

37. A. David Silver, *Enterprising Women: Lessons from 100 of the Greatest Entrepreneurs of Our Day* (New York: Amacon Books, 1994).

38. Center for Women's Business Research, founded as the National Foundation for Women Business Owners, www.nfwbo.org.

39. Faith Popcorn and Lys Marigold, *EVEolution: The Eight Truths of Marketing to Women*.

40. Tom Peters, *Re-imagine!*.

41. Center for Women's Business Research.

42. Dun and Bradstreet Small Business Survey, quoted in "Entrepreneurship. Business Women's Network WOW! Facts," www.ewowfacts.com.

## CHAPTER 7. PRINCESS WITHOUT A CAUSE

1. Gallup Poll, "Family, Health Most Important Aspects of Life," January 2003, www.gallup.com.

2. Ellen McGrath, *When Feeling Bad Is Good* (New York: Bantam Books, 1994).

3. *Summit on Women and Depression: Proceedings and Recommendations,* American Psychological Association, 2002, www.apa.org/pi/wpo/women&depression.pdf.

4. Ellen McGrath et al., *Women and Depression: Risk Factors and Treatment Issues* (Washington D.C.: American Psychological Association, 1990).

5. *Summit on Women and Depression: Proceedings and Recommendations.*

6. Dana Crowley Jack, *Silencing the Self: Women and Depression* (Cambridge, MA: Harvard University Press, 1991).

7. Ellen McGrath et al., *Women and Depression: Risk Factors and Treatment Issues.*

8. Ibid.

9. Ibid.

10. *Summit on Women and Depression: Proceedings and Recommendations.*

11. Christopher J. L. Murray and Alan D. Lopez (eds), "A Comprehensive Assessment of Mortality and Disability from Diseases, Injuries, and Risk Factors in 1990 and Projected to 2020," in *The Global Burden of Disease and Injury Series,* vol 1 (Cambridge MA: Harvard University Press, 1996).

12. Irving Kirsch and Guy Sapirstein, "Listening to Prozac but Hearing Placebo: A Meta-analysis of Antidepressant Medication," *Prevention & Treatment* 1 art. 0002a (June 1998), http://content.apa.org/journals/pre/1/1/2.

13. Irving Kirsch et al., "The Emperor's New Drugs: An Analysis of Antidepressant Medication Submitted to the U.S. Food and Drug Administration," *Prevention & Treatment* 5, art. 23 (July 2002), http://content.apa.org/journals/pre/5/1/23.

14. Joe Collier, *The Health Conspiracy: How Doctors, the Drug Industry and the Government Undermine Our Health* (London: Century Hutchinson Ltd., 1989).

15. Martin E. P. Seligman, *Authentic Happiness* (London: Nicholas Brealey Publishing Ltd., 2003).

16. Laura Schlessinger, *Ten Stupid Things Women Do to Mess Up Their Lives* (London: Headline Book Publishing, 1995).

## CHAPTER 8. DOES GOD REALLY HATE GIRLS?

1. *The Jerusalem Bible,* popular ed. (London: Darton, Longman and Todd Ltd., 1966).

2. Marija Gimbutas, *The Living Goddesses* (London: University of California Press Ltd., 2001).

3. G. Y. Craig and E. J. Jones, *A Geological Miscellany* (Princeton, NJ: Princeton University Press, 1982).

4. Marija Gimbutas, *The Living Goddesses.*

5. Marilyn French, *Beyond Power: On Women, Men and Morals* (New York: Ballantine Books, 1986).

6. Merlin Stone, *When God Was a Woman* (Orlando, FL: Harvest/Harcourt Brace, 1976).

7. Monica Sjöo and Barbara Mor, *The Great Cosmic Mother: Rediscovering the Religion of the Earth* (San Francisco: Harper & Row, 1987).

8. Ibid.

9. Ean Begg, *The Cult of the Black Virgin* (New York, Penguin Books, 1997).

10. Jean Markale, *The Great Goddess* (Rochester, VT: Inner Traditions International, 1999).

11. Marija Gimbutas, *The Living Goddesses.*

12. Barbara G. Walker, *The Women's Encyclopedia of Myths and Secrets* (Secaucus, NJ: Castle Books, 1996).

13. Monica Sjöo and Barbara Mor, *The Great Cosmic Mother: Rediscovering the Religion of the Earth.*

14. Jean Markale, *The Great Goddess.*

15. Elizabeth Gould Davis, quoted in Mary Daly, *Beyond God the Father: Toward a Philosophy of Women's Liberation* (Boston: Beacon Press, 1973).

16. Merlin Stone, *When God Was a Woman.*

17. Lotte Motz, *The Faces of the Goddess* (New York: Oxford University Press, 1997); Cynthia Eller, *The Myth of Matriarchal Prehistory: Why an Invented Past Won't Give Women a Future* (Boston: Beacon Press, 2000).

18. Sam Keen, *Fire in the Belly: On Being a Man* (London: Piatkus Books, 1992).

19. Merlin Stone, *When God Was a Woman*.

20. Riane Eisler, *The Chalice & the Blade* (San Francisco: HarperCollins, 1987).

21. Merlin Stone, *When God Was a Woman*.

22. Alexander Waugh, *God* (London: Headline Book Publishing, 2002).

23. Monica Sjöo and Barbara Mor, *The Great Cosmic Mother: Rediscovering the Religion of the Earth*.

24. Riane Eisler, *The Chalice & the Blade*.

25. Monica Sjöo and Barbara Mor, *The Great Cosmic Mother: Rediscovering the Religion of the Earth*.

26. Gerda Lerner, *The Creation of Patriarchy* (New York: Oxford University Press, 1986).

27. Barbara Kingsolver, *The Poisonwood Bible* (London: Faber & Faber, 1999).

28. Marija Gimbutas, *The Living Goddesses*.

29. Monica Sjöo and Barbara Mor, *The Great Cosmic Mother: Rediscovering the Religion of the Earth*.

30. Stephen Oppenheimer, *Out of Eden: The Peopling of the World* (London: Constable & Robinson, 2003).

31. Annie Laurie Gaylor, *Woe to the Women: The Bible Tells Me So* (Madison, WI: Freedom from Religion Foundation, Inc., 1981).

32. Elizabeth Cady Stanton, *The Woman's Bible* (Boston: Northeastern University Press, 1993).

33. Ibid.

34. Ruth Hurmence Green, *The Born Again Skeptic's Guide to the Bible* (Madison, WI: Freedom from Religion Foundation, Inc., 1999).

35. Voltairine de Cleyre, "Sex Slavery" (1890), in *Women without Superstition: "No Gods–No Masters,"* ed Annie Laurie Gaylor (Madison, WI: Freedom from Religion Foundation, Inc., 1997).

36. Elizabeth Cady Stanton, *The Woman's Bible*.

37. Monica Sjöo and Barbara Mor, *The Great Cosmic Mother: Rediscovering the Religion of the Earth*.

38. Reza Aslan, *No God But God: The Origins, Evolution, and Future of Islam* (New York: Random House, 2005).

39. Ibid.

40. Merlin Stone, *When God Was a Woman*.

41. Elizabeth Cady Stanton, "The Christian Church and Women" (1888), in *Women without Superstition: "No Gods–No Masters,"* ed Annie Laurie Gaylor (Madison, WI: Freedom from Religion Foundation, Inc., 1997).

42. Elizabeth Cady Stanton, *The Woman's Bible*.

43. Timothy Freke and Peter Gandy, *The Jesus Mysteries: Was the Original Jesus a Pagan God?* (London: Thorsons, 1999).

44. Ibid.

45. Timothy Freke and Peter Gandy, *Jesus and the Goddess: The Secret Teachings of the Original Christians* (London: Thorsons, 2001).

46. Ibid.

47. Ibid.

48. Ibid.

49. Alexander Waugh, *God*.

50. Riane Eisler, *The Chalice & the Blade*.

51. Mary Daly, *Gyn/Ecology: The Metaethics of Radical Feminism*.

52. Mary Daly, *Beyond God the Father: Toward a Philosophy of Women's Liberation*.

53. Jean Markale, *The Great Goddess* (Rochester, VT: Inner Traditions, 1999).

54. Mary Daly, *Gyn/Ecology: The Metaethics of Radical Feminism*.

55. Monica Sjöo and Barbara Mor, *The Great Cosmic Mother: Rediscovering the Religion of the Earth*.

56. Ibid.

57. Helen Duncan, the Official Pardon Site, www.helenduncan.org.

58. Elizabeth Cady Stanton, *The Woman's Bible*.

59. Monica Sjöo and Barbara Mor, *The Great Cosmic Mother: Rediscovering the Religion of the Earth*.

60. Leslie Kenton, *Passage to Power: Natural Menopause Revolution* (London: Ebury Press, 1995).

61. Posted on http://monster-island.org/tinashumor/humor/adameve3.html.

## CHAPTER 9. HAPPILY EVER AFTER?

1. David P. Barash and Judith Eve Lipton, *The Myth of Monogamy: Fidelity and Infidelity in Animals and People* (New York: Henry Holt and Co., 2002).

2. Jared Diamond, *Why Is Sex Fun? The Evolution of Human Sexuality* (London: Weidenfeld & Nicolson, 1997).

3. Gerda Lerner, *The Creation of Patriarchy* (New York: Oxford University Press, 1986).

4. Ibid.

5. Barbara G. Walker, *The Women's Encyclopedia of Myths and Secrets* (Secaucus, NJ: Castle Books, 1983), 585–597.
6. Ibid.
7. Monica Sjöo and Barbara Mor, *The Great Cosmic Mother: Rediscovering the Religion of the Earth.*
8. Barbara G. Walker, *The Women's Encyclopedia of Myths and Secrets*, 585–597.
9. Ibid.
10. Monica Sjöo and Barbara Mor, *The Great Cosmic Mother: Rediscovering the Religion of the Earth.*
11. St. Ambrose (340–397 CE), Letter 63 (396 CE).
12. Minnesota Center against Violence and Abuse, www.mincava.umn.edu/reports/herstory.asp.
13. Alison Webster, *Found Wanting: Women, Christianity and Sexuality* (New York: Cassell, 1995).
14. Ibid.
15. National Organization for Women, www.now.org.
16. *The Beijing Declaration and Platform for Action,* www.un.org/womenwatch/daw/beijing/platform.
17. Virginia Goldner and Gillian Walker, (New York's Ackerman Institute for Family Therapy) reported by Hara Estroff Marano, "Inside the Heart of Marital Violence," *Psychology Today* 26 (1993): 48–53.
18. Neil Jacobson, reported by Hara Estroff Marano, "Inside the Heart of Marital Violence," *Psychology Today* 26 (1993): 48–53.
19. Robert A. Johnson, *We: Understanding the Psychology of Romantic Love,* (San Francisco: HarperSanFrancisco, 1985).
20. Kevin Leman, *Women Who Try Too Hard: Breaking the Pleaser Habits* (Grand Rapids, MI: Revell Books, 1998).
21. Marc Feigen Fasteau, *The Male Machine* (New York: Dell Publishing Co, 1975).
22. Luise Eichenbaum and Susie Orbach, *What Do Women Want?*
23. Susan Maushart, *Wifework: What Marriage Really Means for Women* (London: Bloomsbury Publishing, 2001).

## CHAPTER 10. YAKKETY, YAK

1. Allan Pease and Barbara Pease, *Why Men Don't Listen & Women Can't Read Maps* (Mona Vale, Australia: Pease Training International, 1998).
2. Monica Sjöo and Barbara Mor, *The Great Cosmic Mother: Rediscovering the Religion of the Earth.*
3. Deborah Tannen, *That's Not What I Meant!* (London: Virago Press, 1992).

4. Connie Brown Glaser and Barbara Steinberg Smalley, *More Power to You!: How Women Can Communicate Their Way to Success* (New York:Warner Books, 1992).
5. Allan Pease and Barbara Pease, *Why Men Don't Listen & Women Can't Read Maps.*
6. Phyllis Chesler, *Woman's Inhumanity to Woman.*
7. Eric Berne, *Games People Play: The Basic Handbook of Transactional Analysis,* reissue ed. (New York: Ballantine Books, 1996).
8. Phyllis Chesler, *Woman's Inhumanity to Woman.*
9. Bella M. DePaulo and Deborah A. Kashy, "Everyday Lies in Close and Casual Relationships," *Journal of Personality and Social Psychology* 74 (1998): 63–79.
10. Bella M. DePaulo, Jennifer A. Epstein, and Melissa M. Wyer, "Sex Differences in Lying: How Men and Women Deal with the Dilemma of Deceit," in *Lying and Deception in Everyday Life,* ed. Michael Lewis and Carolyn Saarni (New York: Guildford Press, 1993): 126–147.
11. Allan Pease and Barbara Pease, *Why Men Don't Listen & Women Can't Read Maps.*

## CONCLUSION: FUTURE FORWARD?

1. Susan Faludi, *Backlash: The Undeclared War against Women.*
2. Monica Sjöo and Barbara Mor, *The Great Cosmic Mother: Rediscovering the Religion of the Earth.*
3. Ami Neiberger, "Promise Keepers: Seven Reasons to Watch Out," *Freedom Writer,* September 1996.
4. Ami Neiberger, "Women and Weirdos: My Adventures at Promise Keepers," *Freedom Writer,* September 1996.
5. Tony Evans, *No More Excuses: Be the Man God Made You to Be,* (Westchester, IL: Crossway Books, 1996).
6. Susan Faludi, *Backlash: The Undeclared War against Women.*
7. Robert Boston, *The Most Dangerous Man in America? Pat Robertson and the Rise of the Christian Coalition* (New York: Prometheus Books, 1996).
8. Marilyn Waring, *Counting for Nothing: What Men Value and What Women Are Worth,* reprint ed. (Toronto: University of Toronto Press, 1999).
9. Greg Palast, *The Best Democracy Money Can Buy* (New York: Plume Books, 2003).
10. Howard Fineman, "Bush and God," *Newsweek,* March 10, 2003.
11. Robert Boston, *Why the Religious Right Is Wrong* (New York: Prometheus Books, 1993).

12. Tom Peters, *Re-imagine!.*

13. Faith Popcorn and Lys Marigold, *EVEolution: The Eight Truths of Marketing to Women.*

14. Gerda Lerner, *The Creation of Patriarchy* (New York: Oxford University Press, 1986).

15. Annie Laurie Gaylor (ed.), *Women without Superstition: "No Gods–No Masters,"* (Madison, WI: Freedom from Religion Foundation, Inc., 1997).

16. The National Organization for Women, www.thetruthaboutgeorge.com/women/index.html.

17. Monica Sjöo and Barbara Mor, *The Great Cosmic Mother: Rediscovering the Religion of the Earth.*

18. Michael Moore, *Stupid White Men . . . and Other Sorry Excuses for the State of the Nation* (New York: HarperCollins, 2002).

19. Robert Bly, *Iron John: A Book about Men,* reprint ed. (New York: Vintage Books, 1992).

20. Sam Keen, *Fire in the Belly: On Being a Man* (London: Piatkus Books, 1992).

21. John Lee, *At My Father's Wedding: Reclaiming Our True Masculinity* (London: Piatkus Books, 1991).

22. Janice Castro, "The Simple Life," *Time Magazine,* April 8, 1991.

23. In conversation with Norman Roux, facilitator, "The Male Scorecard," South Africa.

24. Keith H. Hammonds, "Balancing Work and Family: Big Returns for Companies Willing to Give Family Strategies a Chance," *BusinessWeek,* September 16, 1996.

25. U.S. Census Bureau, www.census.gov.

26. Susan Maushart, *Wifework: What Marriage Really Means for Women.*

27. Ibid.

28. Ibid.

29. John Naisbitt, *Global Paradox* (London: Nicholas Brealey Publishing Ltd., 1994).

30. Patrick Dixon, *Futurewise* (London: HarperCollins, 2002).

31. Cyndi Tebbel, *The Body Snatchers* (Sydney: Finch Publishing, 2000).

32. Terry Poulton, *No Fat Chicks: How Women Are Brainwashed to Hate Their Bodies and Spend Their Money.*

33. Federal Trade Commission, www.ftc.gov

34. Marilyn Waring, *Counting for Nothing: What Men Value and What Women Are Worth,* reprint ed..

35. Harriet Rubin, *The Princessa: Machiavelli for Women.*

36. Ibid.

37. Oliver James. *Affluenza* (London: Vermillion, 2007).
38. Ibid.
39. Riane Eisler, *The Chalice & the Blade*.
40. Ibid.
41. Marilyn Waring, *Counting for Nothing: What Men Value and What Women Are Worth*.
42. Richard Dawkins. *The God Delusion* (Boston: Houghton Mifflin, 2006).
43. Carol Moore, "Woman vs. the Nation State," 2006, www.carolmoore.net.
44. Sharon Temkin, *Business Day,* South Africa, July 14, 2004.
45. Tanya Ellis, *De Nye Pionerer* (Copenhagen, Denmark: Jyllands-Postens Forlag, 2006).
46. Martin Seligman, *Authentic Happiness: Using the New Positive Psychology to Realize Your Potential for Lasting Fulfillment.*
47. Malcolm Gladwell, *The Tipping Point: How Little Things Can Make a Big Difference* (New York: Back Bay Books, 2002).

## ACKNOWLEDGMENTS

I have been enormously privileged in my life to have had the opportunity to work in areas that passionately engage me. This has put me in contact with some extraordinary people and exposed me to thinking that stretched my ideas way beyond my own expectations. At times it's been a bumpy ride, and it's especially during the difficult periods that I've been very grateful for the generous support I've had. Firstly to my husband and very best friend, Mark Porter, who courageously endured the writing of my second book, thanks for all the listening, the encouragement, the willing exploration of ideas, and for knowing when to drag me away from the PC and plant me in the countryside. I am also thankful to my mother, a far better writer than I, who worked tirelessly on the original drafts to knock them into shape. Thanks, Mum, for the care you have put into my work and my life.

I am deeply grateful to my treasured friends Liza Baggott, Gwynne Conlyn, Denise Ground, Liz Hazell, Michelle Kay, John and Sylvia Kehoe, Denise Momberg, Debbie Peckover, Colleen Renew, and Lynne Watney, some of whom waded through manuscripts but all of whom helped influence my thinking through much conversation, many arguments, and mostly through some really good laughs. Thanks too to Josh Freedman of 6 Seconds, Esther Orioli, and Laura Mari i Barrajón for being such generous supporters of my work in the fields of Emotional Intelligence and on the women's front. The numerous "red wine" discussions I had with my friend Norman Roux were invaluable in keeping me from idealizing the women's issue, as was the balance I learned from my wise and strong mentor, Marlyn Abrams. Meeting powerful women like Cheryl Carolus has enriched my life, and I am indebted to her for her meaningful contribution as well as the inspiration and many laughs we've had on a number of energizing walking expeditions. I am also grateful for the input offered by Dr. Leila Rajah, who worked through some of the medical issues, and other professionals who helped prop me up through the exhaustion: osteopath Dr. Leslie Pleass and massage therapist Lynn Hughes. To Brooke Warner and all at Seal Press, thanks for your enthusiasm about this book and for your efficiency, which is both impressive and inspiring. Publishers have a reputation for being unapproachable, and there is not one member of Seal's staff who has lived up to this reputation. Also to literary agent

Adam Marsh who very generously referred me to Seal Press, without which this project may not have happened. Much gratitude also goes too to the people who have used my work to change their life—this book is especially for you.

I am also enormously privileged to be inspired by the many children who've come into my life but particularly to Ben, Luke, Charles, and Joseph Baggott for so much joy over so many years. There is one special little girl who has been a constant source of delight to me, so a big thanks to Phila Baloyi for lighting up my life with her side-splitting humor and insightful wisdom. In her inimitable style, she also taught me just how much I must have been boring those around me when she said she didn't think she'd need to read my books because I've already told them to her! Thanks for being there to my mother-in-law, Jean Porter; my family, Dirk, Keith, Andrew, and Ian Vermeulen; and especially to my "sisters," Mimi and Ellie, and the beautiful Tim and Mia. Lastly, to fulfill a promise made in dedication more than a decade ago to the late Feroza Adam, although it saddens me that I didn't know her for long enough, her energy for women's issues was a major source of inspiration when it came to getting going with this book—Fee, you are sorely missed.

## ABOUT THE AUTHOR

Throughout her womanhood, Stephanie Vermeulen has been an ardent and outspoken supporter of women's issues. As a powerful speaker who has the ability to tackle tricky topics and taboos with large doses of humor, she has been delivering life-changing seminars for more than fifteen years. Known as one of the most controversial voices in her field, her boundless energy makes her a highly sought after speaker, and her meaningful work has been instrumental in positively  influencing thousands of people's lives. She lives in Johannesburg, South Africa, and is also the author of *EQ: Emotional Intelligence for Everyone.* Visit her online at www.stephanievermeulen.com.

# Selected Titles from Seal Press

**For more than thirty years, Seal Press has published ground-breaking books. By women. For women. Visit our website at www.sealpress.com.**

*Cunt: A Declaration of Independence* by Inga Muscio. $14.95, 1-58005-075-1. "An insightful, sisterly, and entertaining exploration of the word and the part of the body it so bluntly defines. Ms. Muscio muses, reminisces, pokes into history and emerges with suggestions for the understanding of—and reconciliation with—what it means to have a cunt." —Roberta Gregory, author of *Naughty Bitch*

*Body Outlaws: Rewriting the Rules of Beauty and Body Image* edited by Ophira Edut, foreword by Rebecca Walker. $15.95, 1-58005-108-1. Filled with honesty and humor, this groundbreaking anthology offers stories by women who have chosen to ignore, subvert, or redefine the dominate beauty standard in order to feel at home in their bodies.

*We Don't Need Another Wave: Dispatches from the Next Generation of Feminists* edited by Melody Berger. $15.95, 1-58005-182-0. In the tradition of *Listen Up*, the under-thirty generation of young feminists speaks out.

*The F-Word: Feminism in Jeopardy* by Kristin Rowe-Finkbeiner. $14.95, 1-58005-114-6. An astonishing look at the tenuous state of women's rights and issues in America, and a call to action for the young women who have the power to change their situation.

*Listen Up: Voices from the Next Feminist Generation* edited by Barbara Findlen. $16.95, 1-58005-054-9. A collection of essays featuring the voices of today's young feminists on racism, sexuality, identity, AIDS, revolution, abortion, and much more.

*Full Frontal Feminism* by Jessica Valenti. $14.95, 1-58005-201-0. A sassy and in-your-face look at contemporary feminism for women of all ages.

4/1/15